T0351928

Wine by Design

Wine by Design

Santa Barbara's Quest for Terroir

Victor W. Geraci

UNIVERSITY OF NEVADA PRESS *Reno & Las Vegas*

University of Nevada Press | Reno, Nevada 89557 USA
www.unpress.nevada.edu
Copyright © 2020 by University of Nevada Press
All rights reserved
Cover art © Andrei Gabriel Stanescu | Dreamstime.com and © Feverpitched | Dreamstime.com

LIBRARY OF CONGRESS CATALOGING-IN-PUBLICATION DATA
Names: Geraci, Victor W. (Victor William), 1948– author.
Title: Wine by design : Santa Barbara's quest for terroir / Victor W. Geraci.
Description: Reno ; Las Vegas : University of Nevada Press, [2020] | Includes bibliographi-
    cal references and index. | Summary: "In the later-half of the twentieth-century the Santa
    Barbara, California wine industry became a vital part of the global wine community through
    a process of Wine By Design that utilized science, technology, and agribusiness capitalist
    tenants. This history, set in the context of nineteenth- and twentieth-century state, national,
    and global wine history, illuminates a story of how a regional wine industry became part of
    the national and international wine industry"—Provided by publisher.
Identifiers: LCCN 2019048354 (print) | LCCN 2019048355 (ebook) | ISBN 9781948908443
    (paperback) | ISBN 9781948908436 (ebook)
Subjects: LCSH: Wine industry—California—Santa Barbara County—History. | Wine and
    wine making—Economic aspects—California—Santa Barbara County. | Viticulture—
    California—Santa Barbara County.
Classification: LCC HD9377.C2 G46 2020 (print) | LCC HD9377.C2 (ebook) | DDC
    338.4/7663200979491—dc23
LC record available at https://lccn.loc.gov/2019048354
LC ebook record available at https://lccn.loc.gov/2019048355

The paper used in this book meets the requirements of American National Standard for
    Information Sciences—Permanence of Paper for Printed Library Materials, ANSI/NISO
    Z39.48-1992 (R2002).

FIRST PRINTING

Manufactured in the United States of America

To all who have shared a bottle of wine with me, and to my grandfather Michaelangelo, who taught my father Victor the ways of the grape grower. He in turn taught the Sicilian ideal of family to my sons Matthew, Gregory, and Damien, and to his great-grandchildren Jordan, Victor, Karime, and Sophia.

Contents

Preface

Throughout history grape growers and winemakers have made a Herculean effort to ensure that their consumers had ample supplies of wine for their health, religious ceremonies, celebrations, and mealtime needs. Over time as European explorers came to the New World, they brought their wine culture with them and tried to establish vineyards for local use and to supplement the global wine trade. Often the attempts failed due to climate, pests, diseases, wars, and depressions. But strong cultural wine traditions and continuing demand encouraged vintners to not accept defeat and seek alternatives to make wines better, more plentiful, and profitable. Their answer to increased demand was easily solved by planting more vineyards at home and in their colonial empires. Thus, the early wine industry started a modern trend of meeting market needs by looking for the next new region to grow wine grapes. As their wine-making learning curve grew, they learned to match specific grapes to specific regions and created more efficient and profitable ways to produce, store, market, and distribute wines. In America the quest to establish a wine culture slowly gravitated to the new state of California, where wine entrepreneurs established regions like Napa, Sonoma, Mendocino, Los Angeles, and Santa Barbara.

The wine-by-design theme of this book evolved over twenty-five years of research and writing about viticulture and the history of the Santa Barbara County wine industry.[1] I began studying the region in the early 1990s as a graduate student at the University of California, Santa Barbara. In a 1994 Public History graduate seminar course, I and four other students conducted oral interviews, researched, and produced the tabletop book *Aged in Oak: The Story of the Santa Barbara County Wine Industry* for the Santa Barbara County Vintners' Association.[2] As a graduate student I expanded the research on the region and in 1997 completed my PhD dissertation, *Grape Growing to Vintibusiness: A History of the Santa Barbara, California, Regional Wine Industry, 1965–1995*. During my first academic job as assistant and later associate professor of history at Central Connecticut State University, I converted my dissertation into the book *Salud! The Rise of Santa Barbara's Wine Industry* that was published by the University of Nevada Press. Beginning with my new job as a specialist and associate Director of the UC Berkeley's Bancroft Library Oral History Center, I continued my research and conducted numerous oral histories, delivered conference and symposium papers, taught classes, reviewed viticulture exhibits and books for journals, and wrote articles and books about food and wine.[3]

My 2013 retirement from the Oral History Center provided the opportunity to refocus my work and rethink, synthesize, and expand my research on food and wine. This lead to the publication of my book *Making Slow Food Fast in California Cuisine*.[4] In 2016, as this book found its way through the publishing process, I began updating my original research on the Santa Barbara wine industry and realized that my first attempts needed updated materials and, most importantly, did not include over twenty years of growth and change. My understanding of the industry as a whole had also grown after decades of working on food and wine oral histories, documentaries, and research/writing at the Bancroft Library.[5] I now had new contexts in which to frame my earlier work, and reinterpretations of old materials helped put them in a more complex framework. This book is the result of past and new research; but, like all histories, the periodization and original stories leading up to the new history remain somewhat the same. Many of the themes and ideas that run the wine industry today have not changed, while others have evolved to adapt to new circumstances. *Wine by Design* is not a second edition of any previous work but a new book that utilizes past writings to set the context for a new story of the Santa Barbara wine industry.

Wine by Design Finds Santa Barbara

Wine's journey to the New World began with sixteenth-century explorers and seventeenth- and eighteenth-century colonization that brought European wine ways to the Americas. Despite the optimistic hopes of the new settlers, two hundred years of resolve failed to develop a viable commercial American wine culture. But, determined oenophiles never gave up hope and in the mid-nineteenth century they drew upon the ideals of capitalism and Manifest Destiny to spark a new excitement for developing an American wine industry. Many believed that the West Coast grape-friendly climate and geography finally provided the necessary ingredients for a successful wine industry.

As the American quest for wine reached the new state of California, entrepreneurs quickly took control of the industry and ushered in a new era built on the tenets of Gilded Age agribusiness and by 1900 California dominated the American wine industry. Regretfully, over the next fifty years California wine successes faltered as two World Wars, Prohibition, and the Great Depression again dampened the nation's wine hopes.

But the cultural passion for wine and its success as a trade item persisted, and a tenacious generation of entrepreneurs plotted a new course for American wine. Unwilling to give up, wine enthusiasts obstinately continued the wine quest in California and built an industry that from its onset could not keep pace with domestic demand. As the industry came into its own in the latter half of the twentieth century it was bolstered by the new military-industrial economy that allowed for unbridled economic opportunity. The only downside to the California wine success was the fact that over the next five decades growers and vintners failed to keep pace with ever-expanding consumer demands. At first they utilized the tried-and-true solution of simply planting more vineyards. But as cheap vineyard land disappeared, a new cadre of wine businesspeople sought state-of-the-art solutions to boost production and looked to new regions and consolidation to modernize the industry. As a result many began to view regions like Santa Barbara, California as part of the solution.

They shifted from traditional trial-and-error systems to a "wine-by-design" model whereby wine businesspersons utilized agribusiness techniques dependent upon science, technology, and marketing to achieve both vineyard and winery production goals while maximizing profits. Overall, this California adaptation of the capitalist tenants of agribusiness produced a modern wine industry that first dominated the American market and then became an integral part of the global wine industry.

By the end of the twentieth century the new California style became the global norm and many grape growers and winemakers became industrial capitalists who felt they could produce wine like a widget in a factory. So much so that in 2001 wine businessman and Napa vintner Ed Sbragia boldly told *Wine Spectator* magazine; "I think knowing more gives you more versatility. We can make a wine that fits the profile we want." In Santa Barbara, Alison Green, Firestone winemaker, likened the pursuit to the fashion industry where "you have to plan a year ahead for what people want."[6] In the new era of capitalist competition, many wineries became factories and aggressively chased consumer taste preferences by grafting to new varietals, creating artificial tastes, developing vertical and horizontal business structures, and created new marketing and distribution schemes.

Winemakers, for good or bad, had developed a vintibusiness style that ruled the day.[7] Both grape growers and winemakers now spoke of things like cool weather vineyards, temperature controlled fermentation, irrigation, chemical pest and disease control, trellis and canopy design, leaf pulling, grape thinning, new clones, and machines for picking, spraying, and pruning.[8] University-trained winemakers and vineyard managers employed new scientific discoveries and quickly learned how to act like megacorporations designed to bring efficiency and consistent quality to wine production.

In the case of Santa Barbara, local 1960s and 1970s farmers initially supplied grapes for the rapidly expanding northern California wineries and within a decade lamented that farmers never get rich. Many then shifted to creating their own premium wineries to profit from the American wine craze. As the demand for premium wine grapes continued throughout the 1990s and 2000s, premium wine-grape shortages sent corporate wineries on a second raid of the Santa Barbara industry. This time the vintibusiness industry bought wineries and vineyards instead of just grapes. The county had become the target for "Napazation" by large wine corporations seeking stable supplies of premium wine grapes.

Adding to the problem of corporate takeover of the region, Santa Barbara growers, estate wineries, and boutique wineries now faced an additional set of challenges. New environmental concerns, antigrowth factions, and escalating land prices hampered the region's growth. Early in his tenure as president and CEO of the Wine Institute, John De Luca identified the rising tension between the wine industry and environmentalists. In his words: "I have said on a number of occasions, people and grapes have one thing in common: they love to live in beautiful places."[9] By the year 2000 Napa had grown to 45,401 acres, Sonoma supported 57,149 acres, Monterey County grew to 42,259 acres, Santa Barbara had reached 17,566 acres, and the entire State now had over 425,695 acres of wine grapes. Statewide, most estate and small wineries, who had become dependent upon winery tourism and direct sales, were running out of inexpensive and unrestricted places to build their operations. As a result, opposition from environmentalists and land-use NIMBY (not in my backyard) proponents reshaped the industry and quickly pushed large commercial concerns to Monterey and San Luis Obispo Counties for cheap, unrestricted land.

As Santa Barbara County began to restrict its commercial and estate operations, small vintners shifted to new creative ways to expand their markets by embracing a business model based on the concept of the family wine farm and the allure of a rural destination. Legal and political battles between vintners, environmentalists, and anti-growth factions resulted in a compromise whereby the wine region retained established commercial wineries, who controlled the majority of the grapes, restricted the growth of estate wineries, and incentivized boutique non-vineyard wineries to open tourist operations in urban areas. Decades of struggles had slowly shifted the development of wineries and vineyards to more sustainable agricultural practices, more regulated winery growth, regulated events, and development of concentrated urban tasting rooms.

The new wine industry design promoted small premium wineries that had previously been unable to afford an estate vineyard tasting room or upscale rural retail space. They could now enter the industry by renting old industrial and commercial spaces and rely upon consumer direct sales. The shift pleased adversaries and small vintners got access to customers in high-density urban wine parks like the Lompoc Wine Ghetto, the town of Los Olivos, the Urban Wine Trail, the Funk Zone in downtown Santa Barbara, and Garagiste home production.

Santa Barbara had created a mixed wine industry that contained industrial operations, estate wineries, and small boutique labels to resolve environmental, land-use, and neo-Prohibition concerns. This Santa Barbara model, along with the larger industrial California model, utilized a *wine-by-design* philosophy that promotes good science, sustainability, mixed corporate and independent winery ownership, and nurturing of the concept of an American wine culture. In the end the region remained tied to the national and international wine industry while at the same time developing a thriving local wine industry. This history of the Santa Barbara wine industry, set in the context of the state, national, and global wine community, illuminates a regional story of the American trend of creating *Wine By Design*.

Notes

1. The *Wine by Design* title of this book is a phrase first used by Bruce Sanderson, "Wine by Design," *Wine Spectator,* 15 November 2001.

2. Otis Graham, Sarah H. Case, Susan Goldstein, Richard P. Ryba, Beverly J. Schwartzberg, and Victor W. Geraci, *Aged in Oak: The Story of the Santa Barbara County Wine Industry.* Cachuma Press. South Coast Historical Series Graduate Program in Public Historical Studies at the University of California Santa Barbara and published by the Santa Barbara County Vintners' Association, 1998.

3. Example of materials produced include: Victor W. Geraci, and Elizabeth S. Demers editors, *Icons of American Cooking* (Greenwood Icon Series), Santa Barbara: Greenwood Press, 2011; Victor W. Geraci, "Fermenting a Twenty-first Century California Wine Industry," *The Journal of Agricultural History*, 78:4 (Fall 2004): 438–65; Victor W. Geraci, *Salud: The Rise of Santa Barbara's Wine Industry* (Reno, Nevada: University of Nevada Press, 2004); Victor W. Geraci, "Wine, Women, and Song," in Gordon Morris Bakken and Brenda Farrington, eds., *Encyclopedia of Women in the American West*, Thousand Oaks, CA: Sage Publications, 2003; Victor W. Geraci, "Vintibusiness: The History of the California Wine Industry 1769 to the Present," in *California History: A Topical Approach*, ed. Gordon Morris Bakken, (Wheeling, Illinois: Harlan Davidson Inc., 2002); Victor W. Geraci "The Family Wine Farm: Vintibusiness Style." *The Journal of Agricultural History* 74: 2 (Spring 2000): 419–32; Victor W. Geraci, "The El Cajon, California, Raisin Industry: An Exercise in Gilded Age Capitalism," *Southern California Quarterly* 74 (Winter 1992): 329–54. Food and wine oral histories completed can be found at http://www.lib.berkeley.edu/libraries/bancroft-library/oral-history-center.

4. Victor W. Geraci, *Making Slow Food Fast in California Cuisine*, (New York: Palgrave Macmillan, 2017).

5. Principal investigator and historical consultant for the documentary *America's Wine: The Legacy of Prohibition*, 2008–2013, http://bancroft.berkeley.edu/ROHO/projects/prohibition/index.html.

6. Tad Weber, "Wine Making," *Santa Barbara News-Press,* 27 September 1987, A-1, A-11.

7. Vintibusiness is the vertical and horizontal organization of wine-grape farming, winemaking, distribution, and marketing of wine. Geraci, *Salud!*

8. Bruce Sanderson, "Wine by Design," *Wine Spectator,* 15 November 2001.

9. John A. De Luca, Ph.D., "President and CEO of the Wine Institute, 1975-2003," an oral history conducted in 1986-2007 by Victor Geraci, Ruth Teiser, and Carole Hicke, Oral History Center, The Bancroft Library, University of California, Berkeley, 2007.

Chapter One

Wine Begins Its Journey
to Santa Barbara

In 1946 Cretan novelist Nikos Kazantzakis published *Zorba the Greek* and aptly portrayed the depth of wine's mythical role in Western cultural and economic traditions. His chief character Zorba provided readers with a living paradigm of the beverage's cultural ability to temporarily release humans from the bondage of everyday existence and celebrate life. In one scene, Zorba, the simple Greek philosopher, warmed by an evening of wine drinking, lectured his new boss Basil, a middle-class Englishman, on "how simple and frugal a thing is happiness." He reminded readers that wine imparts a glimpse of happiness and the good life.[1] This observation stood in stark contrast to the serious capitalist Basil, who attempted to profit from reopening an abandoned lignite mine. Depending on your relationship with wine, the beverage can produce either happiness or capitalist profits. In the best-case scenario, it can provide both.

Much like the relationship between Zorba and his business-minded friend, the history of wine has become a tale of capitalist production and consumer experience. Though not entirely analogous, the story exemplifies over seven thousand years of the human need to escape an increasingly complex world and an agricultural industry's need to design efficient vineyards, production facilities, and distribution systems capable of providing profit for businesspersons.

While wine became a cultural means to distract and celebrate, it also became deeply rooted in Western civilization's economic and political story as entrepreneurs profited from the lucrative international wine trade. Historical geographer Tim Unwin believes that viticulture is "an expression of transformations and interactions in the economic, social, political and ideological structures of a particular people at a specific place."[2] Thus, by the seventeenth and eighteenth century European viticulture served as one of many symbols of class, and wine businesspersons instituted the mercantile ideas of capital, credit, science, new technology, and marketing. Early entrepreneurs then transported their business wine culture to their new homes in the Americas, where at first they struggled and were unsuccessful in building a wine industry. It would not be until the nineteenth century that they found success in California.

The struggles continued into twentieth-century America as the wine industry suffered through Prohibition, the Great Depression, and World War II. But wine businesspersons proved to be resilient and gave birth to a new cadre of winemakers that sought state-of-the-art solutions to boost production. In America, this history of wine manifested itself as a translocated struggle of a wealthy class searching for an artistic hobby, a nation attempting to both preserve Western European religious and cultural traditions and to forge its own identity, a wine-industry seeking profits, a consumer-focused middle-class seeking symbols of the good life, a rural population adhering to the Jeffersonian agrarian myth, temperance groups intent on legislating alcohol morality, and a nation searching for a national public health policy. Wine has served as the lubricant for the machines of human movement across continents and oceans and found success in California and, for the purposes of this story, Santa Barbara.

Between the 1960s and 2010s, the California Central Coast region of Santa Barbara became a model for the American wine-by-design movement. Ultimate consumer recognition for their new role as a premium wine region came in 2005 when Rex Pickett's buddy novel *Sideways* premiered as a movie.[3] Deeply imbedded into this story is the spirit of wine and the attitude of never giving up on simultaneously building an American wine industry and an American wine culture. The novel's chief protagonists, Miles and Jack, in many ways mirrored the spirit of Zorba and Basil. This time the setting was the wine-by-design region of Santa Barbara.

The amazing part of this modern Santa Barbara wine tale is the fact that for centuries wine history has continuously presented similar problems and solutions to the industry's vineyardists and winemakers. Like wine entrepreneurs of the past, they adapted science, technology, and market forces to overcome pests, diseases, taxes, wars, depressions, regulations, anti-alcohol proponents, waffling government intervention, consumer trends, and environmental concerns to keep the industry profitable and consumers happy.

PREMIUM WINES: BIGGER THE WINE THE SMALLER THE BARREL

For centuries class-conscious European consumers had demanded premium wine as a means to distinguish their social status from the masses who drank low-cost plonk. Disruption of the European wine trade by sixteenth- seventeenth- and eighteenth-century wars had crippled trade and left consumers with rising prices and dwindling supplies of their favorite French, Italian, and Spanish wines. Faced with these shortages European entrepreneurs then turned to their New World colonies to meet their needs. Thus, the early wine industry started a modern trend of meeting market needs by looking for the next new region to grow wine grapes. This expansion philosophy played out centuries later as San Francisco Bay Area (Napa, Sonoma, Mendocino) wineries, short on premium wine grapes, turned to areas like Santa Barbara to source grapes for their growing brands.

Grape growers, winemakers, and marketers had become fully entrenched in the politics and culture of Western Europe by the seventeenth century. In England the business of wine merchant (*négociant* in French) prospered as it was discovered that wines could be matured, transported, and stored in glass bottles with shaped corks. Merchants now shopped worldwide and governments established wine import taxes as a means to provide additional royal revenues. Consumers shifted to the new and exotic premium wines like champagne and port. They brought these traditions to the New World, and from the start the American wine industry faced global competition, distribution issues, and government attempts to regulate and tax their product.

By expanding production, wine capitalists successfully produced different and better wines with smaller price tags for a larger group of consumers. But this new trend could not keep pace with consumer demands and resulted in worldwide wine shortages. Exacerbating the shortage problem were differential customs and duties and shifting political boundaries. Despite the problems, international wine trade became profitable, and by the eighteenth century most wineries required high levels of capital investment. Much like today, only the wealthy class of landholders, merchants, and entrepreneurs could afford the long-term investments required by the premium wine industry, and also much like today, small producers found it difficult to compete outside their local region.[4]

QUEST FOR AN AMERICAN WINE CULTURE

European explorers and immigrants brought viticulture to the Americas during the Age of Discovery (1500–1750), and early explorers found that none of the Native American peoples had any knowledge of wine or for that matter any fermented spirits.[5] This was not an accident, for the native grape varieties made a very poor-quality wine. In response colonial settlers, with home country encouragement, introduced European vines (*Vitis vinifera*) countless times in an attempt to develop a successful wine industry in South America, Africa, Australia, New Zealand, the United States, and Baja and Alta California.

All thirteen of the original American colonies failed to establish a viable wine industry, forcing wine-drinking settlers to substitute new libations while they continued the search for a means to produce their own wine. In the few places where grapes would grow, yeoman farmers followed their European traditions and left grape growing and wine production to gentleman farmers. This helped deepen the American mystique of wine as a drink for a gentler class. Yet, many like President Thomas Jefferson hoped to cultivate the European tradition of a wine culture for all Americans. These hopes diminished as viticultural failures grew and post-revolutionary Americans turned to cheaper rum that quickly accounted for one-fifth of the value of all imports from England. Jefferson and many others worried that this new dependence on distilled spirits would diminish the vitality of the nation's health and pushed to intensify the quest for an American wine industry to moderate drinking habits.

Wine as a moderating alcoholic beverage has been a hope for many Americans throughout our history. Just before the American Revolution, all ages and social groups consumed alcohol and foreign travelers reported that America was a nation addicted to drinking. The national consumption rate had reached three and a half gallons per person (more than the present rate of consumption) per year. This astonishing rate of consumption forced many Americans to view wine as a means to moderate excessive drinking habits and led to historian William J. Rorabaugh labeling the nation as the *Alcoholic Republic*.[6]

As many American citizens began to worry that alcohol was destroying the moral fiber of the developing republic, they worried that moderation ideals had failed to keep pace with increasingly destructive alcoholic behaviors. Their concerns resulted in early nineteenth-century reform measures aimed at moderation, through wine consumption and teetotalism. These early reformers started a national debate on the health and social values of fermented and distilled alcoholic beverages that lasts to the present day. While most people still believed that wine and distilled spirits were a food and medicine to be imbibed in moderation, extreme reformers focused on the evils of alcohol and attempted to force moderation or teetotalism on the public in general.[7] These concerns and struggles have helped shape the modern American wine industry.

Yet, anti-alcohol activism did not lessen the consumption of spirits as consumers associated drinking with the American ideals of personal freedom and a modern lifestyle. Despite these newfound freedoms factory owners, needing a sober workforce, sought a means to decrease alcoholic consumption. To accomplish this they joined forces with middle-class urban Americans recently emboldened with the moral calls of evangelical leaders, women's temperance groups, and political leaders to bring about an era of temperance reform. The fiery rhetoric of extremists blamed economic decay, poverty, and social upheavals on all forms of alcohol. Many others favored abandoning distilled spirits for wine and they pushed for tax laws to incentivize moderation. Regretfully, high prices kept wine out of the reach of most Americans as wine prices skyrocketed to one dollar per gallon, or four times the price of whiskey. Making matters worse was the fact that high wine prices increased import duties and worsened the American balance of trade. Luckily for the wine industry, the moderation approach brought a new commitment to establish an American wine industry for production of cheaper wine. Despite these concerns hopes remained high and journalist Hezekiah Niles prophesied that in time the United States would produce all its own wine.[8]

Attempts to Build an American Wine Industry

Wine industry failures in the original colonies worried those seeking to establish an American industry. But these fears lessened as early colonial failures gradually gave way to limited commercial successes in the new western territories of Ohio and Kentucky, where the climate was more suitable for grape growing. The renewed optimism prompted President Jefferson to predict that Americans could "make as great a variety of wines as are made in Europe," just "not exactly the same kinds, but doubtless as good."[9] This faith in the ability of America to produce wine encouraged wealthy entrepreneurs to continue their quest.[10] But the successes were limited and, like vintners throughout history, they turned to new regions.

Moving West and Modernizing American Agriculture

As the American Republic struggled to grow a wine industry, many farmers, winemakers, scientists, and entrepreneurs looked toward the new western territories along the Pacific Ocean. Hopes for an American wine industry continued, and in 1851 Illinois senator Stephen A. Douglas enthusiastically stated that the "United States will, in a very short time, produce good wine, so cheap, and in such abundance, as to render it a common and daily beverage."[11] Many agreed with this optimistic view as they observed vintners and entrepreneurs move beyond regional trial and error to action plans that disseminated information, funded research, formed organizations, vigorously marketed their product, lured investors, sought government support, and relied on university programs and experimental stations. Despite all the optimistic hype, W. J. Flagg's 1870 *Harper's Monthly* magazine article correctly identified the problem: "The question of wine-drinking in America revolves itself into the question of grape-growing in America."[12] America needed to find a home for the wine industry.

Important for grape growing was the new national commitment to large-scale agriculture. From colonial times to the mid-nineteenth-century agriculture had always been at the heart of the American economy and the majority of Americans engaged in agricultural occupations. This changed as Manifest Destiny, the industrial revolution, and the exponential growth of cities pushed and pulled the nation in new directions and forcefully pushed agriculture into the industrial era. The agricultural shift for wine sped up in 1862 when the newly established United States Department of Agriculture directly sought ways to assist in the development of an American wine industry. Dreams of building a wine industry now turned to California, with its history of Spanish wine successes, Mediterranean climate, agricultural geography, cheap land, and ample man-made water supplies.

CALIFORNIA BECOMES AMERICA'S VINEYARD GARDEN OF EDEN

Since statehood in 1850 many considered California to be an exceptional state, a national jewel, and an important global agricultural region, and in a short time California lived up to the expectations of industrial agriculture. By the early twentieth-century geographers like M. K. Bennett made observations that California had become a model for specialized, commercialized, and mechanized agriculture with high yields per acre.[13] Another geographer, James Parsons, believed that: "In the popular mind it is somehow different, a state with distinctive qualities both of the physical environment and of the human spirit which give it a personality of its own."[14] The California wine identity quickly became tied to these visionary dreams and in many ways, became part of the present-day highly political and contentious culture wars of Blue versus Red State politics in a modern version of *Gemeinschaft* versus *Gesellschaft* battles of the past.[15]

The conflict was clear: the common man seeking to cultivate grapes and produce quality wine in a sustainable manner versus corporations trying to steal and plunder the land for profit while delivering manufactured wine. Despite the war of agricultural ideas, it did not take long for wine to become part of the state's sense of regional identity. For this story the rural versus urban ideological struggles would play a large part in how the Santa Barbara wine region would develop.

Like all agricultural stories one must begin with geography and climate. The geographic history of California is a complex story deeply set in plate tectonics theory. By the 1960s earth scientists formulated a theory of plates, or floating land masses, that moved across the earth's surface driven by volcanic action and earthquakes. Over millions of years these actions created the continental regions that we experience today. Writer John McPhee described how California had been "assembled" by thousands of violent earthquakes that brought landmasses from far parts of the world to fashion the region.[16]

Parts of the original North American lithospheric plate acted as the prow of a ship as it floated on the hot mantle and slipped into and acquired other masses of land, creating California as we know it today.[17]

In essence, parts of California have slid into place and divided the state into three parts, creating a profile that from the Pacific Ocean moves eastward (inland) about forty miles to the coastal ranges and drops down to flat sea level in the Great Central Valley and then butts up to the Sierra Nevada range, the highest mountain range in the lower forty-eight states. Millions of years of volcanic eruptions, earthquakes, weathering, and erosion left the state with large swaths of flat, rich soil and deposits of valuable minerals like gold and silver in the Sierra batholith. In this tumultuous process the San Francisco Bay became the largest estuary in the Western Hemisphere and one of the world's best harbors, while the Central Valley flatlands favored large commercial agriculture, and coastal regions enticed growing of cool weather crops and wine grapes.[18]

California has a classical Mediterranean or West Coast subtropical climate, with dry and hot summers that are drier, except along the coastal fringe, and hotter than those of Italy, Greece, or Spain and more comparable to those of North Africa or Israel. Yet, on the coastal hill areas like Napa, Sonoma, Mendocino, Santa Cruz, Monterey, and Santa Barbara, geography created microclimates that offer drastic differences to interior temperatures and create perfect conditions for premium wine-grape cultivation. The coastal hills funnel maritime fogs with their cool, moist air to the west sides of the hills, leaving the eastern hillsides warmer and sunnier. Thus, creative farmers had the ability to cultivate artichokes, brussels sprouts, lettuce, cauliflower, and broccoli on cooler western-facing locations, and grapes and fruit orchards on the warmer eastern sides. Statewide, the geography and climate produced four regions capable of producing cool-climate premium wine grapes—San Francisco Bay Area, Monterey, Santa Barbara, and Temecula.

From the start, business people promoted this sense of identity and nick-named California the Golden State for its 1849 gold rush, ample sunshine, and fields of golden grain. Over the next few decades, wine became a large part of this new sense of regional identity and California earned this sense of place, or what wine writer Matt Kramer labeled "somewhereness," based upon its geography and Mediterranean climate that allowed it to become one of the top food and wine producers of the world.[19]

CALIFORNIA DEVELOPS TERROIR

For hundreds of years French gastronomes spoke of terroir as a means to describe the effects that environmental and social conditions, including soil, topography, and climate, had on agriculture and the specific regional taste of foods and wines. Derived from the French term *le goût de terroir,* loosely translated as "taste of the earth," food enthusiasts expanded the term's meaning to provide a means to allow people to have a common language when describing their regional foods and wines and their effects on the social and cultural lives of the region's residents. University of Vermont nutrition and food science professor Amy B. Trubek describes this human side to terroir as the development of cultural values through farming, cooking, and eating. Adapted by many food enthusiasts, Trubek's definition rightly supports the idea that terroir is more than the mere need for sustenance and believes that every "American deserves a chicken in his or her pot."[20] Her anti-industrial food stance gives quality, sustainable food the dual role of nourishing our bodies and helping us to define our social environment. For the purposes of this book, terroir also refers to its business implication whereby businesses use terroir terminology to differentiate their product from competitors' products as a means to increase sales. Over the centuries this business description grew to include specific agricultural techniques, processing practices, political policies, cultural, religious, and ethnic preferences. In essence each distinct geographic region of a country could impart both the cultural unique flavor and aroma of a region's social environment and a business marketing description used to sell a product.

From this sensory profile, locations became known for their agricultural products and our regional landscapes became inseparable from an individual's sense of identity. English historian Simon Schama reminds us that "even the landscapes that we suppose to be most free of our culture may turn out, on closer inspection, to be its product."[21] Food and wine are products of terroir annexed through the cultural, economic, and political mindset of humans. Terroir both creates and is created by the humans and environment of people in a specific location.

For this California and Santa Barbara wine story, a cool Mediterranean climate with grape-friendly soils determined the terroir, agriculture, industry, and lifestyle of citizens. It also served as a lure to waves of both immigrants and American migrants that dates back to the 1849 gold rush. During the post–World War II years, the state underwent a massive Sunbelt population growth, and by the 1990s 95 percent of the state's thirty million citizens gravitated to urban centers, in part due to the pull effect of the Cold War military-industrial complex. Overall, the state benefited from a rapid rise in America's consumer wealth and the new era of conspicuous consumption.[22] This growth, in turn, created new mass markets, which opened opportunities for new agricultural industries best able to benefit from the economies of size offered by large-scale production. The California wine industry learned to use the components of terroir in a wine-by-design scheme composed of science, technology, and marketing to efficiently produce a quality marketable product in a profitable manner.

After over two hundred years of mixed results, American commercial grape growers and wineries had finally found a perfect home and it did not take long for wine entrepreneurs to design a profitable industry. Yet, historian Erica Hannickel warns of a dark side to this new wine commercialism. She describes the California viticultural industry as having boosterish narratives guided by pastoral Republicanism and Manifest Destiny that left most people with a flawed version of American terroir. A version without the warts of environmental degradation, racism, capitalist greed, and class hierarchy. She argues that California's capitalist wine culture had "acted as both a civilizing practice and one that strengthened America's grip on the continent" and that "Viticulture was thus part of the elaborate, ever-evolving ideology that sanctioned imperial growth in the nineteenth and twentieth centuries."[23] Through it all California agriculture became a capitalist terroir story with deep ties to consumerism, industrial food, California cuisine, and an American wine culture.[24]

Notes

1. Nikos Kazantzakis, *Zorba the Greek*, trans. Carl Wildman (New York: Simon and Schuster, 1981), 80.

2. Tim Unwin, *Wine and the Vine: An Historical Geography of Viticulture and the Wine Trade* (New York: Routledge, 1991), 3; Carlo Cipolla, "European Connoisseurs and California Wines," *Agricultural History* 49, no. 1 (Spring 1975): 294–310.

3. Rex Pickett, Sideways: *The Ultimate Road Trip. The Last Hurrah* (New York: St. Martin's Griffin, 2004).

4. Unwin, *Wine and the Vine*, passim.

5. Ibid., 59.

6. Ibid., 41.

7. Ibid.

8. Ibid.,104.

9. Joni G. McNutt, *In Praise of Wine: An Offering of Hearty Toasts, Quotations, Witticisms, Proverbs, and Poetry throughout History* (Santa Barbara, CA: Capra Press, 1993), 108.

10. Paul Lukacs, American Vintage: *The Rise of American Wine* (New York: Houghton Mifflin, 2000), passim.

11. Rorabaugh, William J., *The Alcoholic Republic: An American Tradition* (New York: Oxford University Press, 1979).

12. Lukacs, *American Vintage*, 35.

13. M. K. Bennett, "Climate and Agriculture in California," *Economic Geography* 15 (April 1939): 158–63.

14. James J. Parsons, "Uniqueness of California,"*American Quarterly* 7, no. 1 (Spring, 1955): 45.

15. *Gemeinschaft* and *Gesellschaft* (generally translated as "country vs city") was coined in the late nineteenth century by the German sociologist Ferdinand Tönnies to classify social ties or networks. Today, it is used by many as urban versus rural communities.

16. John McPhee, *Assembling California* (New York: Farrar, Straus and Giroux, 1993), passim.

17. Ibid., 6–11.

18. Ibid., 12-39; Brian J. Sommers, *The Geography of Wine: How landscapes, Cultures, Terroir, and the Weather Make A Good Drop* (New York: Plume, 2008), passim.

19. Matt Kramer, *Making Sense of California Wine* (New York: William Morrow and Company, 1992). Kramer first used the term "somewhereness."

20. Amy B. Trubek, *The Taste of Place: A Cultural Journey into Terroir* (Berkeley: University of California Press, 2008), xiii–xviii.

21. Simon Schama, *Landscape and Memory* (New York: Vintage Books, 1995), 9.

22. Edward L. Ullman, "Amenities as a Factor in Regional Growth," *Geographical Review* 44, no. 1 (January 1954): 119–32.

23. Erica Hannickel, *Empire of Vines: Wine Culture in America* (Philadelphia: University of Pennsylvania Press, 2013), 5–13.

24. Victor W. Geraci, *Making Slow Food Fast in California Cuisine* (Cham, Switzerland: Palgrave Macmillan, 2017), passim.

Chapter Two

Santa Barbara's First Wine Industry

SPANISH VITICULTURAL TRADITIONS

As we have seen, wine making was off to a slow start in the new American republic. However, determined wine supporters refused to give up on the possibilities of producing quality American wines. Many looked to the American territories in the old Spanish Southwest where religious and commercial wine making had peaked as Spanish soldiers, Franciscan Priests, and Spanish entrepreneurs planted vineyards in Alta and Baja California. It did not go unnoticed that Spanish wine making had flourished in Alta California and that colonizers had planted vineyards from European rootstock. Their small regional industry supplied wine for the Catholic mass, wine for daily use, and provided a local commercial trade commodity for presidio, pueblo, and mission settlements.

These viticultural successes increased throughout the eighteenth century as European vines flourished in the hot and dry Southwest, where they were freed from eastern severe winters, humid summers, disease, and insects. By 1744 a Franciscan priest in modern-day Texas recorded that local vineyards produced an abundant grape crop and "a rich wine in no way inferior to that of our Spain."[1] This led Southwest traders to start an American commercial enterprise of buying and selling El Paso and Rio Grande Valley wines. Further west in California Father Junípero Serra began building the mission San Diego in 1769 and his followers quickly established a wine trade between the presidios, pueblos, and the twenty-one missions of Alta California. By 1779 the Spanish settlers established vineyards in San Juan Capistrano and San Diego, and within a few years the Mission San Gabriel (today Los Angeles County) became the *Viña Madre* (Mother Vineyard) for grapevine cuttings.

START OF THE SANTA BARBARA WINE TRADITION

Early Spanish settlers in Alta California brought wine and grape-growing traditions to Santa Barbara Country. In 1769 Spanish explorer Gaspar de Portolá investigated the Santa Ynez Valley in the mountains east of the Santa Barbara Pueblo and Presidio. Father Juan Crespí, diarist for the Portolá expedition, praised the triangular valley's fine soil, rolling grassy hills, and abundance of water. Five years later Spanish explorer Juan Bautista Anza also praised the valley's agricultural possibilities.[2] By 1782 these observations induced mission priests to begin importing cuttings from the Mission San Gabriel in an attempt to guarantee supplies of sacramental wines for the region's three missions—La Purísima Concepción, Santa Inés, and Santa Barbára.[3]

Over the next fifty years, additional small church and private commercial wineries developed in the area. One such example were the vineyards of José Antonio de la Guerra y Noriega, commandante of the Presidio of Santa Barbara (1815–1846), whose vineyards yielded an estimated six thousand gallons of wine per year. José M. Ortega, presidio soldier, also planted vineyards and along with de la Guerra gained a statewide reputation for winemaking.[4] In the chain of twenty-one missions, priests took on the responsibility of making wine, and priests at the Mission Santa Barbára planted three vineyards—Viña Arroyo in Mission Canyon, La Cieneguita vineyard near present-day Cieneguitas Road, and the San José vineyard near the San José Creek in nearby Goleta. The San José vineyard contained 2,262 vines on seven and one-half acres, while the other two combined totaled around 3,695 vines.[5]

The Spanish government encouraged viticulture through incentives built into its land settlement policies. As early as 1794 Spanish Governor Borica granted six-leagues of land in the Santa Ynez Valley to the Ortega family with the stipulation that a vineyard be planted.[6] These Spanish land-holding traditions continued after the Mexican colonization law of 1824 and the Reglamento of 1828 that secularized hundreds of land grants throughout California.[7] Most grantees utilized the land to raise cattle for the hide and tallow trade while maintaining small subsistence agriculture for everyday food and wine needs. The resulting wealthy landowning class (Dons), of these great coastal ranchos, secured most of their wine supply from production at local vineyards, making wine a vital part of the California and Santa Barbara agricultural scene from the beginnings of European settlement.[8]

After 1833 mission wine production vanished as Mexican secularization laws stripped priests of the use of their vineyards and California's wine energy shifted to local commercial operations. As a result, over the next fifty years most of the wine production centered on the pueblo of Los Angeles where Americans like Joseph Chapman, William Chard, and Lemuel Carpenter had established a cottage wine industry with production of around thirty thousand gallons per year. It was not long until the commercial wine making venture of Frenchman Jean Louis Vignes, known as the "Noah of California," gained national attention.[9]

GRAFTING AMERICAN CAPITALISM TO SPANISH WINE TRADITIONS

After decades of failures and limited commercial successes California statehood provided an opportunity for pre–Civil War wine entrepreneurs to bring together the entire American wine making experience (east and west) and catapulted American, more specifically California, wines into the international marketplace. This westward flow of wine started when Germans, from the Philadelphia Settlement Society, established a flourishing 1860s Missouri wine industry in climates more suitable to grape growing. From this Missouri wine success grew a new generation of wine pioneers that would help bring American technology, research, trial-and-error knowledge, capital, and business ingenuity to what the Spanish had proven to be suitable climatic conditions for European wine grapes.

At first, the fledgling California wine industry, built on Spanish traditions, faced competition for American wine supremacy from wine producers in Missouri, Texas, Florida, Alabama, South Carolina, Virginia, Oregon, Washington, Ohio, and New York. Initially, the older established regions felt secure as California and its regional wines made minimal inroads into their markets during the Civil War years. This changed as post–Civil War eastern growers and producers faced stepped-up competition from the west. At first, eastern growers responded by expanding their viniculture and viticultural production by outsourcing grapes from other markets, increased vineyard acreage, and in some cases shifting to nonalcoholic use of grapes. Simultaneously, French wine imports decreased due to their vineyard destruction by the phylloxera louse (accidentally imported on American vines). To fill the gap Missouri and Kansas wine producers expanded their businesses.

SANTA BARBARA'S FIRST COMMERCIAL WINE INDUSTRY

When California shifted to United States sovereignty in 1850 over eight hundred land-grant cases appeared before the United States Land Commission. About six hundred of these cases were resolved, while the rest of the land reverted to the public domain. Historical records reveal that Santa Barbara County's forty-four land grants supported numerous successful vineyard plantings in or bordering the Santa Ynez and Santa Maria Valleys.[10] Included in these land-grant vineyards were Alamo

Pintado, Los Alamos, Casmalia, Corral de Quati, Cuyama, La Laguna, Nuestra Señora del Refugio, Punto de Laguna, Tepusquet, Tinaquaic, Todos Santos, Sisquoc, Santa Maria, Suey, and La Zaca Rancho.[11] Additional vineyards included the Missions Santa Bárbara, Purisma, and Santa Inés. Overall, the transformation of the ranchos to the Yankees resulted in the cultivation of thousands of acres of rich soil for planting wheat and grapes.[12] Despite diversifying, California agriculture remained small and continued as a regional economic endeavor.[13]

As the mission and Spanish-Mexican eras ended and California celebrated statehood, many of the local wineries, established by mission priests and military commanders of the Santa Barbara Presidio, passed into private commercial hands. In June of 1871 James McCaffrey, graduate of the California Mechanics' Institute, purchased the San José vineyard in the Goleta District of Santa Barbara County. He quickly added 3,300 vines and built a twenty-five-by-forty-five-foot adobe winery complete with wine presses and open top fermentors. Upon his death in 1900, McCaffrey's widow sold the winery to Michele Cavaletto, an immigrant from the Italian Piedmonte region, who ran the winery until the passage of Prohibition.[14]

By the late 1860s Santa Barbara County ranked third in California for wine production as the region's small wine entrepreneurs produced 5 percent of the state's wine. Topping the list was Albert Packard, a Rhode Island lawyer, who purchased 250 acres and established what was probably the first large successful commercial winery in Santa Barbara. Packard chose to plant his vineyard on the west side of the city (west of de la Viña Street between Carrillo and Cañon Perdido Streets) where the property's previous owner, Felipe de Goycochea, second commander of the Santa Barbara Presidio, had established a vineyard in the late eighteenth century.

Packard understood European wine-grape growing and applied the technical and scientific knowledge of the time. He knew that premium wines required a cool growing region and was quoted in a local newspaper as saying that "the wine making season is several weeks later here than elsewhere in California, owing to our proximity to the sea coast."[15] Packard also believed that he could make a fortune with viticulture by planting European varietals from Spain. As the vines came into production in 1865 he constructed his two-story adobe La Bodega winery with a capacity of eighty to ninety thousand gallons. With the help of Ed Breck, a Boston winemaker, and a Mr. Goux, a Bordeaux, France, winemaker, Packard produced his wines under the El Recodo (The Corner) label and shipped most of his wine to Los Angeles, San Luis Obispo, and as far away as Texas. Packard produced a quality claret that initially commanded prices double that of the Los Angeles average.[16] His success did not last long and by the turn of the century, while not documented, local speculation suggested that Anaheim disease had destroyed the vineyard much like it had destroyed the vineyards of Los Angeles.[17]

Despite the Packard setback, Santa Barbara County moved forward in its quest for a modern wine industry, and by the 1890s an estimated forty-five vineyards, on about five thousand acres, had been planted in the region.[18] While many were behind the coastal range in the sparsely settled Santa Ynez Valley, optimistic winemakers had not given up on the southfacing coastal shelf in and around the small town of Santa Barbara.[19] Small vineyards dotted the city itself and prospered, as can be seen by the huge Montecito vine, planted (legend has it) in 1812, that produced six tons, of grapes per harvest. Agricultural speculators cut the vine down in 1876 to serve as a display at the Philadelphia Centennial Exhibition where they used the stump to promote the region's agricultural enterprises. A larger Carpinteria vine planted in 1842 developed a trunk with a circumference of nine feet and by the 1890s was said to have produced ten tons of grapes per year. Yet, the south-facing coast of Carpinteria proved to be inhospitable to ambitious grape farmers like Colonel Russell Heath, whose ten thousand vines and two-story winery ended in failure as coastal moisture nourished destructive mildew in the vines and grapes.[20]

Perhaps the most successful commercial vineyard in the area was planted twenty-two miles off the coast of Santa Barbara on the Santa Cruz Island. In the 1880s French immigrant Justinian Caire planted a vineyard with premium European varietals like Zinfandel, Cabernet Sauvignon, Pinot Noir, Petite Syrah, Muscat, and Riesling on his island property. Caire managed his six hundred acres of grapes with Italian workers, and by 1910 his winery produced 83,000-gallons of wine per year and had loyal customers between Los Angeles and San Francisco.[21] Prohibition ended the profitable enterprise.

Out of this mixed record in Santa Barbara County local observers inferred a hopeful message. An 1883 history of Santa Barbara and Ventura counties featured this promotional piece:

> There are in the two counties not less than 400,000 acres of land which are capable of producing grapes of good quality. The warm and protected valleys of the Santa Maria, Santa Inez, and Santa Clara, with their lesser tributary valleys, with the sloping lands which surround them, form the natural home of the vine, and could, if occasion demanded, produce sufficient wine of a high quality to supply the utmost demands of commerce. In these sheltered and fruitful regions there is found, in the highest degree, the conditions for successful viniculture.[22]

Historian Hubert Howe Bancroft, in 1888, wrote that the Mission Santa
Bárbara had been "famous for its choice wines and profuse hospitality."[23]
Bancroft went on to note that Santa Barbara County produced greater crop
yields than Napa and Sonoma Counties, and that the only disease to strike the
area had been mildew. In his words: "It will probably not be long, before some
of the large ranchos of this district [Santa Ynez] will be subdivided and offered
for sale. Rumor mentions La Zaca, Corral de Cuati, and Jonata Ranchos. . . .
Experts in wine making rank the Jonata and College Ranchos as first-rate vine
land. The soil and climate seem well adapted to grapes."[24]

But these Santa Barbara hopes were not so much over optimistic as prema-
ture. Wine entrepreneurs with investment capital were to settle on lands and
wineries near the fast-growing region of San Francisco where ocean and rail
transport connected the industry to the eastern United States and the world. By
contrast, Santa Barbara County at this time was inaccessible and thinly settled.
In 1870 the city held only 2,898 citizens and its only trade routes were through
the Stearns Wharf steamer service and the treacherous San Marcos stage road to
Santa Ynez and Santa Maria Valleys. This changed in 1887 when the Southern
Pacific Railroad connected the area to both Los Angeles and San Francisco.[25]
California's wine entrepreneurs would for many decades concentrate their larger
commercial efforts in an arc around the cities of Los Angeles and San Francisco.[26]

Despite these numerous startups, it would be new plantings in California's
Los Angeles basin, Central Valley, and Napa that would grow to control the
battle for dominance of the American wine industry. In the greater American
wine industry three states grew to prominence—in order of total production
they were: California, Ohio, and New York.[27] By the end of the nineteenth
century, California had captured the lead in American wine production by
wedding eastern and midwestern wine-growing knowledge with western climate and Spanish traditions.

CHAOS BRINGS THE NEED FOR *WINE BY DESIGN*

The two-century race to grow a wine industry resulted in antebellum wine
entrepreneurs engaging in a vicious wine competition between regional industries in Missouri, Ohio, New York, and California. Eastern vintners accused
California wineries of selling their wines under counterfeit French and German
labels, which was often true, and counterattacked by placing California labels
on their inferior wines.[28] To get American customers to purchase domestic
wine, California growers and winemakers maximized their production and

profits by picking grapes before they were ripe, ignored sanitary concerns by failing to clean green and rotten berries out of bunches, ignored basic cleanliness standards in the fermentation process, used barrels previously used for other purposes, and sent wine to market too early. Unscrupulous wine men also stretched their production by adding sugar to low quality grapes and used free-run juice for white wine and bitter, low-quality second-press juice with skin and seed residue for red wines. Overall, wine quality deteriorated throughout the industry; yet, wineries were still unable to meet domestic needs. Amazingly, many of these inferior wines sold for prices above their French counterparts.

As an agricultural endeavor the wine industry learned from and followed the example of Gilded Age farmers and food processing industries.[29] They increased production through a wine-by-design technique that included mechanization use of new scientific knowledge and technology, and adopted new industrial practices for processing, transportation, and marketing. Additional support for agricultural businesses came from federal support of university research and legislators that produced landmark legislation that supported the nation's movement toward industrial agriculture. Governmental support also came at the state level in 1862 when the California State legislature passed the Wine Adulteration Act to enforce truth in labeling. At the ground level many farmers responded by sharing their knowledge through conversations, journals, treatises, and the formation of trade associations. The spirit of innovation, long characteristic of wine making, was intense in California.

To overcome past questionable practices, a new generation of reputable California winemakers and grape growers sought advice on how to improve their products and dominate the market. Many turned to George Husmann's (Missouri viticulturist, nurseryman, writer, and professor of horticulture, 1863) book *An Essay on the Culture of the Grape in the Great West* and his 1866 publication *The Cultivation of the Native Grape, and Manufacture of American Wines*. Husmann so believed in the possibilities of a superior California wine region that in 1883 he took his growing expertise to the Napa Valley and planted his own vineyard.

Theodore Hilgard, German Belleville, Illinois, lawyer and judge, moved to California with his son Eugene and became the champion of increasing wine quality through science and "rational winery practice."[30] The junior Hilgard later became a professor of agriculture and viticulture and director of the College of Agriculture Experiment Stations at the University of California, Berkeley. The father and son recognized the advantages offered by the region's moderate climate, close proximity to urban populations, and its trade opportunities through the San Francisco Bay. As a result, a premium wine industry began to concentrate in the Bay Area around San Francisco.[31]

Further commitment to improve the industry with science and technology continued throughout the 1880s and led to what wine historian Paul Lukacs refers to as the "machines in the garden."[32] F. T. Bioletti and UC staff at the University of California Experiment Station pushed for a scientific wine industry and in 1880 helped create the Board of State Viticultural Commissions to support their cause. This commission quickly convinced industry leaders to have faith in scientific grape-growing and wine-production practices with promises of consistent quality wine that consumers would embrace. Further enhancing the new industry was the commission's promotional efforts at marketing California wine at state fairs and at United States, and world expositions. As businessmen the bottom line of consistent quality and more profits ruled the day and in a short time this philosophy became the centerpiece for the state's leap to national and international wine prominence.

Yet, in a strange twist of events, it would be Mother Nature (plant pests and disease) that helped rectify much of the state's quality issue and consolidate the industry. Phylloxera, which favored California winemakers briefly in the 1870s by destroying virtually all French vines, had by the 1880s turned upon and destroyed California's vineyards. At the same time Anaheim disease (vine virus) destroyed the Los Angeles industry. In the long run, pests and disease actually benefited the industry by purging the state of its inferior Mission grape and allowing forward-thinking wine entrepreneurs to replant with more favorable European wine-grape varietals. The pestilence also acted as a mechanism to rid the state of many marginal and disreputable growers and producers. Get-rich-quick winegrowers either could not afford or refused to spend money to restart their businesses. As a result, the troubled Los Angeles industry shifted the wine industry's entrepreneurial energy to the northern part of the state where cool-climate, premium wine grapes flourished. The few remaining vineyards of Southern California shifted to table grapes, raisins, and sweet wines.[33]

BIRTH OF CALIFORNIA VINTIBUSINESS

Unlike its eastern and southern predecessors, California wine making had successfully survived Mother Nature and the economic spikes and peaks accentuated by three depressions that flattened the national economy near the middle of each of the post–Civil War decades. They had survived by utilizing university science and vertically integrated business structures, and their ability to meet these same challenges in the future would underscore their long-term success.

By the 1880s grape growing and wine making, like American agriculture in general, restructured as winemakers embraced the modern agribusiness era. This wine market reorganization brought about two forms of wine enterprises. First were wealthy entrepreneurs who gravitated to the industry and approached their new endeavor like any other business enterprise in the Gilded Age—vertical and horizontal integration, incorporation, and mergers—and created vintibusinesses. Second would be successful businesspersons who entered the field as a retirement or hobby enterprise, in what insiders today refer to as boutique or artisan wineries. The eventual loser in this new shift was the concept of the small family wine farm.

The era of corporate wine production and distribution began in earnest in 1894 when seven well-financed San Francisco wine merchants founded the California Wine Association (CWA). Their goal was to vertically integrate the entire wine supply chain from vine to store and produce bulk consistent-quality wines in enough quantity to supply national and international markets. The impetus for the organization came from Percy Morgan, English accountant and financier, who created the monopoly as an entity capable of controlling supplies and stabilizing fluctuating prices. As the director of CWA, Morgan cared less who drank or why they drank wine as long as members profited. Under his leadership the California industry quickly moved from local to national and international markets and as a result elevated Morgan to the status of a Gilded Age "captain of the wine industry."[34] Over the next few years, the organization grew to include over fifty wineries that in 1895 produced eighteen million gallons that grew to twenty-three million in 1900, thirty-one million in 1905, and topped at forty-five million gallons in 1910.[35] CWA grew to control two-thirds of the state's total wine production, and wine historian Paul Lukacs credits Morgan with "the introduction of wine as a manufactured commercial product, one with a consistent character and brand identity in the marketplace."[36] Truly a story of *Wine By Design* that between 1890 and 1910 helped establish California vintibusiness.[37]

Most California winemakers started the twentieth century with high hopes. The state's population soared to over 1,485,000 and national wine consumption grew to .3 gallon per capita, per annum. By 1910 this demand, low by European standards, was enough to consume the fifty million gallons the industry produced and retailers supplemented their supply deficit with large amounts of foreign imports. The state's share of the national wine market had grown from 50 to 88 percent and its only serious rivals were European wines.[38]

But this trend toward bigger-is-better and monopolized markets would face a new enemy. By the end of the century, Napa led the state in premium wine output, with Sonoma second, and Los Angeles third. Premium Bay Area wines could now be purchased in the eastern United States, Asia, South America, and Europe. Yet, deeply embedded in this industry success story is the basis for the almost complete collapse of the entire wine industry in the 1920s. The wine industry had fallen under the control of investors and financiers more interested in profits than maintaining an American wine culture. Lukacs believed that "large scale commercial winemaking obscured wine's essential identity, making it appear to many Americans to be but another form of alcohol."[39] Dreams of wine as a drink of moderation faltered.

Notes

1. C. W. Hackett, ed., *Historical Documents Relating to New Mexico, Nueva Vizcaya, and Approaches Thereto, to 1733*, vol. 3 (Washington, D.C.: Carnegie Institution of Washington, 1923–1937), 406.

2. James V. Mink, *The Santa Ynez Valley: A Regional Study in the History of Rural California* (master's thesis, University of California, Los Angeles, 1949), 2–20.

3. Ralph Auf der Heide, "The Vineyards," *Santa Barbara Magazine*, Winter 1977,, 6–14.

4. Paul W. Gates, *California Ranchos and Farms 1846–1862; Including the Letters of John Quincy Adams Warren of 1861, Being Largely Devoted to Livestock, Wheat Farming, Fruit Raising, and the Wine Industry* (Madison: State Historical Society of Wisconsin, 1967), ix; Walker A. Tompkins, Santa Barbara History Makers (Santa Barbara, CA: McNally and Loftin, 1983), 9–12.

5. Number of grapevines per acre varies by landscape, variety, and mechanization. An average would be around six hundred vines.

6. Gary L. Peters, "Trends in California Viticulture," *Geographical Review* 74 (October 1984): 463; *Gates, California Ranchos and Farms*, ix. A league is about 4,428 acres.

7. Pinney, Thomas. *A History of Wine In America: From the Beginnings to Prohibition* (Berkeley: University of California Press, 1989).

8. Robert G. Cowan, *Ranchos of California: A List of Spanish Concessions, 1775–1822, and Mexican Land Grants 1822–1846* (Fresno, CA: Academy Library Guild, 1956), passim.

9. Ibid., 243–58. An excellent description of the Los Angeles wine industry can be found in Thomas Pinney, *The City of Vines: A History of Wine in Los Angeles* (Berkeley, CA: Heyday, 2017).

10. *Gates, California Ranchos and Farms*, xix; Cowan, *Ranchos of California*, passim; Beverly Bastian, "Imperfect Titles, Invalid Claims: The California Land Commission and the Californios," (PhD dissertation, University of California Santa Barbara), passim.

11. Vada F. Carlson, *This Is Our Valley* (Santa Maria, CA: Santa Maria Historical Society, 1959), 1–100 passim; Tompkins, *Santa Barbara History Makers*, passim.

12. Gates, *California Ranchos and Farms*, ix.

13. Mink, *Santa Ynez Valley*, 80.

14. Stella Haverland Rouse, "Pioneer Family Preserved Early Goleta Winery," *Santa Barbara News-Press,* 4 October 1984, D-4 and D-9; Richard S. Whitehead and Mary Louise Days, "San Jose Winery: A Landmark of Mission Times," in *Those Were the Days: Landmarks of Old Goleta,* ed. Gary B. Coombs (Goleta, CA: Institute for American Research, 1986), 79–88.

15. Tompkins, *Santa Barbara History Makers,* 127–30; Stella Rouse, "1865 Was a Vintage Year for Santa Barbara Winery," *Santa Barbara News-Press,* 11 October 1986, B-5.

16. Since the 1700s "claret" is the name that British wine lovers gave to the red wines from Bordeaux, France.

17. Tompkins, *Santa Barbara History Makers,* passim 127–30; Stella Rouse, "1865 Was a Vintage Year for Santa Barbara Winery," *Santa Barbara News-Press,* 11 October 1986, B-5; Elias Chiacos, "Westside Was a Huge Estate Winery," *Santa Barbara News-Press,* 18 July 1990, B-1.

18. Colman Andrews, "Wine Country Gambler: Brooks Firestone's Southern California Strategy Pays Off," *Los Angeles Times Magazine,* 19 July 1987, 8–13.

19. Mink, *Santa Ynez Valley,* 52–55.

20. "Olden Days: Pioneer Settler Tried Many Crops," *Santa Barbara News Press,* 14 September 1969.

21. Helen Caire, "Santa Cruz Vintage," *Noticias* 35 (Spring/Summer 1989): 142–51.

22. Jesse D. Mason, *History of Santa Barbara County, California* (Oakland, CA: Thompson and West, 1883), 422.

23. H. H. Bancroft, *California Pastoral 1769–1848,* vol. 34 of *The Works of Hubert Howe Bancroft* (San Francisco, 1888), 194.

24. Mason, *History of Santa Barbara County,* 301.

25. Mink, *Santa Ynez Valley,* 2.

26. Otis L. Graham Jr., Robert Bauman, Douglas W. Dodd, Victor W. Geraci, and Fermina Brel Murray, *Stearns Wharf: Surviving Change on the California Coast* (Santa Barbara, CA: Graduate Program in Public Historical Studies University of California, Santa Barbara, 1994), 25.

27. Pinney, *History of Wine in America,* 373–81.

28. Leon D. Adams, *The Wines of America* (San Francisco: McGraw-Hill, 1990), 20; Vincent P. Carosso, *The California Wine Industry: A Study of the Formative Years* (Berkeley: University of California Press, 1951), 86–102.

29. Eric E. Lampard, *The Rise of the Dairy Industry in Wisconsin 1820–1920* (Madison: State Historical Society of Wisconsin, 1967), passim.

30. Lukacs, Paul, *American Vintage: The Rise of American Wine* (New York: Houghton Mifflin Company, 2000).

31. Maynard A. Amerine, "The Napa Valley Grape and Wine Industry," *Agricultural History* 49 (January 1975): 289–91.

32. Lukacs, *American Vintage,* 169.

33. Victor W. Geraci, "The El Cajon, California, Raisin Industry: An Exercise in Gilded Age Capitalism," *Southern California Quarterly* 74 (Winter 1992): 329–54.

34. Lukacs, *American Vintage,* 47–57.

35. Ibid., 58.

36. Ibid., 59.

37. Pinney, *History of Wine in America,* chapters 11, 12, and 13; George M. Walker and John Peragine, *Cucamonga Valley Wine: The Lost Empire of American Winemaking,* American Palate (Charleston, SC: History Press, 2017).

38. Doris Muscadine, Maynard A. Amerine, and Bob Thompson, eds., *The University of California/ Sotheby Book of California Wine* (Los Angeles: University of California Press, 1984), 383, 414, 419; Pinney, *History of Wine in America,* 374.

39. Lukacs, *American Vintage,* 87.

Chapter Three

False Starts and the Road to Rediscovering Santa Barbara

By the early twentieth century, the California wine industry seemed postured to become a major player in the domestic and global wine market, and entrepreneurs and large industrial corporations moved to provide wine for their seemingly ever-expanding market. But over the next three decades, vintners saw their product become illegal, become legal again with limitations, a depression, and the conversion of the American economy from peace to wartime status. Although the industry initially suffered, it slowly adapted and rebuilt to a point of readiness for the Cold War consumer era. While a small California industry survived, the Santa Barbara industry fell victim to the chaos of Prohibition, repeal, depression, and war and for all intents and purposes ceased to exist.

PROHIBITION

At the beginning of the twentieth-century many American citizens bemoaned what they felt was the societal degradation caused by alcohol. To conquer this new national enemy, they set out to wage war on large alcohol-related corporations and usher in the great social experiment of Prohibition. After decades of resistance the Temperance Movement pressured Congress in 1913 to allow dry (nonalcoholic) states to design and enforce their own alcohol commerce laws, and by 1919 thirty-three states prohibited alcohol. Wineries throughout California, including Santa Barbara, faced new challenges to their *Wine By Design* approaches to growing, making, and selling their product.

With the passage of the War Prohibition Act of 1918, designed by agricultural officials to save foodstuffs for World War I, many feared the possibility of restrictions or Prohibitions on alcohol. Their fears proved correct in 1919 as Congress passed the Eighteenth Amendment, over the veto of President Woodrow Wilson, prohibiting "the manufacture, sale, or transportation of intoxicating liquors within the United States." Minnesota congressman Andrew J. Volstead, aided by the Anti-Saloon League, quickly followed up with the Volstead Act that provided enforcement provisions for the new amendment. American wine drinkers and producers were stunned and for better or worse Prohibition slowed down American alcohol consumption, ended an era of working-class saloons, served as one of the more successful alliances of upper and middle classes to legislate morals and habits, and in a strange twist increased wine consumption.

As the nation officially turned dry, many Americans turned to legal home wine making and most of the homemade wine came from California grapes.[1] Limited wine production for vinegar, sacramental wine, medicinal wines, industrial alcohol, cream of tartar, flavorings, and home wine making could be secured with permits issued by the federal government. As a result home fermentation of wine skyrocketed, and, most importantly, wine production jumped from an estimated 50 million gallons per year before Prohibition to 76.5 million gallons per year during Prohibition as home winemakers could make 200 gallons per year for family use.[2] Herbert Hoover's Wickersham Commission counted over 45,000 legal permits in California alone and in 1931 concluded that "it appears to be the policy of the government not to interfere with it."[3] Per-capita national wine consumption climbed from .47 gallons per year in the years before Prohibition to .64 gallons of wine per capita, per year during Prohibition and showed some persistence in that increase at .53 gallons per year right after repeal.

Although wine consumption increased, the commercial wine industry collapsed as bonded American wineries fell from 700 in 1919 to below 140 in 1932. Wine production in Santa Barbara came to a screeching halt. Grape growers, on the other hand, prospered as red grape prices jumped from twenty-five dollars to over eighty-two dollars per ton. Realizing that Prohibition had killed the formal wine industry, vineyardists sought stability for their remaining grape market, and in 1926 anxious California grape growers formed the California Vineyardists Association to stabilize grape prices, secure markets, and enhance distribution systems throughout the nation and the world. In a short time they had signed up over 750 of the state's grape growers.

The long-term effects of Prohibition haunted the wine industry for decades. To meet the needs of home winemakers California wine-grape growers had grafted much of their vineyard land to thick-skinned varieties that could be easily transported to eastern home winemakers. These inferior varieties produced poor-quality sweet and dry table wines that drinkers learned to accept. As a result many premium vineyards and wineries fell into disuse, and for many wine became just another form of alcoholic beverage.

REPEAL

Good news came as the 1932 Presidential election left no doubt that most of the nation was tired of Prohibition. A wet California legislature, a wet United States Congress, and a wet President Franklin D. Roosevelt argued for easing up on Prohibition enforcement. Through an executive order Roosevelt approved 3.2 percent beer, a 12 to 14 percent watered-down, sweet carbonated sacramental wine, and gave doctors the right to prescribe wine. As a result wine production tripled between 1932 and 1933.[4] The best Christmas present for the wine industry came on December 5, 1933 as the nation officially repealed Prohibition.[5]

In 1900 the nation's wine consumers had preferred dry wines by a two-to-one ratio, and as a result of Prohibition consumers had been nudged toward sweet high-alcohol wines by a four-to-one margin. By 1933 the American demand for high-alcohol wine resulted in a doubling of sweet wine producers in the hot Central Valley of California. This preference for sweet wines continued throughout World War II and peaked at a high of three out of every four bottles of wine produced.[6]

This new trend worried anti-alcohol forces, who, after losing their Prohibition amendment, now doubled-down on their quest to stop what they saw as the ravages of alcohol on the social fabric of the nation. The new statistics also worried producers from the international wine community, who feared that the American Prohibition movement would damage future imports of their table wines. So much so that even Benito Mussolini, Italian premier and dictator, and others, warned winemakers in 1932 that after Prohibition Americans would have to reeducate themselves so as to be able to "enjoy the noble and delicate pleasure afforded by light, tasty, and refined wines."[7]

But the real blow to the wine industry was that the repeal amendment permitted each state to establish its own liquor laws. This legal precedent would forge all future growth for the industry. Thus, the wine industry faced forty-eight (later fifty) different sets of regulations for transport, sale, taxation, license fees, and distribution. Making matters worse was the fact that just after repeal nineteen states remained dry—Mississippi being the last to repeal Prohibition in 1966. Also of concern was the resurgence of hard-core Dry supporters, later labeled neo-Prohibitionists. This new anti-alcohol movement grew and quickly continued to wage war against alcohol and its marketing and distribution. For the wine industry to again gain global and national prominence, many local, state, and federal neo-Prohibitionist roadblocks would have to be overcome. One bright hope for the future remained, as small niche premium wineries not only survived but began to prosper.[8]

The problem became more complicated as some states allowed the sale of wine in grocery stores, while seventeen others created state or municipal monopolies (package stores) for the sale of alcoholic beverages. To appease pro- and anti-alcohol forces, Assistant Secretary of Agriculture Rexford Tugwell adapted the age-old position that wine could promote alcohol moderation and proposed that wine be exempted from federal taxation. This moderate proposal met the wrath of Missouri Congressman and Prohibitionist Clarence Cannon, House Appropriations Committee member and lifelong Prohibitionist. Cannon used his congressional power to block any help for the wine industry for thirty years until his death in 1964. Remarkably, his political clout allowed him to force the Department of Agriculture to strike the word *wine* from all of their publications and in essence created a government policy whereby wine was no longer considered to be an agricultural product.[9]

Things did not look good for the industry, and Leon Adams, wine writer, believed that by the 1930s most Americans thought of wine "as a skid-row beverage" and that the industry was only interested in profit margins.[10] The situation worsened as members of the industry openly battled over issues of bulk wine versus premium wines, sweet versus dry wines, high alcohol versus low alcohol, and, most importantly, over the question of whether wine is a food or alcohol. Just as the wine industry moved to rebuild, anti-alcohol forces vowed to continue their quest to restrict alcohol and save Americans from moral deprivation. In a short time they convinced state and federal politicians and policy makers to place wine under the jurisdiction of the Bureau of Alcohol, Tobacco, and Firearms. This political move branded wine as a dangerous substance that needed to be regulated.

In less than one century, America and California had created, lost, and won back a wine tradition and wine culture. The rest of the twentieth century would be spent rebuilding the industry and creating California, including Santa Barbara, as a premium international wine industry. But more bad news laid on the horizon as the nation faced a Great Depression and World War II.

POST-PROHIBITION WINES IN SANTA BARBARA

After repeal it would take decades for the state's wine industry to replant vineyards, modernize production facilities, and reeducate wine drinkers accustomed to cheap, sweet bulk wines. During this period Santa Barbara County's wine industry struggled out of this devastation with a false start by two local commercial winemakers. The first was Umberto Dardi, an Italian farmer, who on October 9, 1933 obtained bond number 3577 to produce 1,100 gallons of wine on his property near Kellogg and Patterson streets in Goleta, a neighboring community to the city of Santa Barbara. The enterprise ended in a double tragedy in August of 1937 when Dardi declared bankruptcy and not long after both he and his daughter died in a bizarre wine making accident.[11]

The second wine enterprise, while not a human tragedy, also ended in failure. In April of 1935 Benjamin Alfonso received bond number 4228 to operate the Old Santa Ynez Winery on land that was once part of the College Rancho in Santa Ynez Valley. His wooden structure with cement floors and tin roof contained a press, crusher, storage tanks, and over 3,000 gallons of fermentation tank capacity. Despite the impressive start Alfonso never really got the business off the ground. During 1936 and 1937 Bureau of Alcohol, Tobacco, and Firearms (BATF) records revealed that the winery had large amounts of spoiled wines, continually failed to file required bond forms, and had been forced to destroy numerous leaking tanks. The winery closed in 1940 when Alfonso faced BATF charges of illegal wine making. That same year Alfonso sold the land and thus ended Santa Barbara County's first attempts at post-Prohibition wineries.[12]

DEPRESSION

With Prohibition gone California's now-legal wine trade became one of the few industries to successfully expand during the Great Depression. To help achieve this goal, wine enthusiasts in 1935 formed the Wine Institute in San Francisco as a means to help reestablish California's wine industry by re-educating consumers and modernizing marketing. Industry members welcomed the institute and by the end of the year the organization boasted a membership of 188, or 80 percent of the state's wineries. Further cooperative rebuilding of the industry came in 1938 when the California Department of Agriculture utilized the California Marketing Act to establish the Wine Advisory Board that mandated membership for all of the state's wineries and assessed a per gallon tax to pay for a national wine marketing campaign. It was also at this time that the University of California at Berkeley's viticulture and enology programs moved to the one thousand-acre Davis, California, experimental farm and campus. Under the leadership of viticulturist A. J. Winkler and enologist Maynard A. Amerine, the program began helping grape growers and wineries rebuild and revise the marketing and scientific roots of the wine industry.

After initiating their marketing campaign, winery and grape grower cooperative associations then moved to lobby state and federal lawmakers for policies favorable to the industry. Their first goal was a reduction of the Federal Alcohol Control Administration's (FACA) alcohol taxes. Relief from the tax came in 1938 when legislators moved to allow the industry to prorate grapes under the California Agricultural Prorate Act.[13] With taxes reduced and market issues addressed, over 10,000 growers and 250 wineries entered the 1938 Federal Prorate Plan financed by Bank of America and the federal government's Reconstruction Finance Corporation. Under the plan participating wineries and growers made brandy from excess grapes and stored it in a public pool with a guaranteed percentage. This proved to be a good move as World War II and post-war shortages drove alcohol prices sky-high and most participants profited from these layover investments.[14] In the end the prorate strategy saved many growers from facing bankruptcy.[15]

WORLD WAR II

Yet, these methods fell short and in the long run it would be the beginning of World War II that reenergized the industry and boosted the demand for California wine. The post-Depression industry had relied heavily on bulk wine sales (80 percent of all wine produced) and this favored large growers, winemakers, and cooperatives. To survive, most smaller wineries adapted the advice of Dr. Frederic Bioletti, viticulture professor at the University of California, to establish their market share by emphasizing the sale of smaller quantities of higher-priced premium wines. Thus, over the next few decades innovators like Andre Tschelischiff, Carl Bundschu, the Beringer Brothers, Roy Raymond, Louis Martini, and Robert Mondavi established better vineyard practices, planted superior grape varietals, and utilized new technology. Their pioneer efforts encouraged others to adopt the new premium wine-by-design scheme. Despite these attempts to revive the wine industry, many industry leaders still worried as to how the nation's over 380 reopening wineries would overcome cooperage shortages, consumers short on cash, different state wine regulations, outdated equipment, and poor quality vineyards.

But larger problems loomed on the horizon as marketing for small and large wineries alike faltered under the repeal distribution policies that attacked the concept of "farm wineries."[16] These post-Prohibition discussions focused on whether wine was a food or an alcoholic beverage and could wines, grown and produced on family wine farms, be sold at their source like any other agricultural product. To resolve the issue California state policy makers moved to allow small, family-operated wine farms to promote themselves through tasting rooms and direct retail sales. This worked for the California market but set the stage for a future national confrontation over direct sales across state lines as each state developed its own post-repeal wine marketing policies and regulations.

World War II decimated the French, Italian, and Spanish industries and thus blocked most of their international wine trade with the United States. The upside is that this trade disaster provided the opportunity for California wineries to dominate the domestic premium wine market. But, in order to achieve this goal California wineries had to seriously increase their vineyard acreage and shift to higher-quality premium grapes and wines.

Their new international role began as early as 1936 when the Federal Alcohol Administration Requirement #4 mandated certified labels for varietal bottled wines to make them more competitive with European wines. The mandate also required wines to contain 51 percent of a grape variety in order to carry the name of the grape varietal on the label. This action forced many in the industry to begin switching from bulk to bottled wines. The adjustment continued in 1943 when the War Production Board converted the last of seven hundred bulk wine-tank railroad cars for use in the war effort, forcing wineries to bottle more wine at the local level. Further support for the premium wine industry came with the government wartime purchases of raisin grapes, that made up 54 percent of all grapes crushed for wine, in an effort to preserve foodstuffs for the war effort. This new policy also mandated that only premium wine grapes could be used in bottled wines. Together these actions greatly increased wine quality throughout the industry.

Over time World War II served as the vehicle to help the industry develop national brands, increase acreage of premium grapes, establish the practice of at-winery bottling, and brought about a massive influx of capital for modernization. The reversal from bulk and sweet wines to dry wine had begun and by 1944 Ed Rossi, president of Italian Swiss Colony, predicted that dry wine would surpass sweet wine sales.[17] His prediction would become reality in a few decades.

POST-WAR REBIRTH

Hopes for a renewed California premium wine industry were dependent upon being able to capitalize the expansion and conversion to modern techniques, and corporate America came forward to foot the bill. Federal regulations to preserve grain products for war needs had forced many corporate distilleries to reduce production, and in an attempt to protect corporate profits they diversified their holdings to include winery ownership.[18] In 1942 National Distillers bought Italian Swiss Colony for $3.7 million, and in 1945 Schenley Corporation (New York Liquor Company) purchased the Di Giorgio family three-thousand-acre Del Vista Wine Company for over $10 million. Thus began what observers later called the "The Whisky Invasion." By the end of World War II, industrial food corporations and agribusiness had become deeply entrenched in the business fabric of the California wine industry.

In order to achieve profitability, these new corporate wineries expanded their operations through a consolidation surge that over the next decade reshaped the entire California wine industry.[19] This new era of concentration patterned itself after the general agricultural trend toward larger farms, reduced numbers of farmers, new technology, mechanization, and increased efficiency and production. As the trend accelerated John H. Davis, director of the Moffett Program in Agriculture and Business at the Harvard Business School, addressed the issue in a 1955 Boston speech. In the talk, titled "Business Responsibility and the Market for Farm Products," Davis coined the term "agribusiness" to describe this centralizing process. He predicted that agribusiness embodied the spirit of a Second Agricultural Revolution where vertical integration of production and marketing would run business-farms of the future.[20] In California the redesigned wine industry embraced agribusiness.

In a move that appeared to consolidate the industry overnight large liquor companies in the eastern United States, such as Seagram's, Schenley, and National Distillers, made major investments in California wineries, and in the years after World War II they controlled one-half of the nation's commercial wine production. This led UC Davis viticulture and enology professors Maynard Amerine and Vernon Singleton to make a prediction in 1965 that: "California winemaking would soon be almost entirely in the hands of a few wineries as their numbers diminished and the survivors grew larger."[21]

The "bigger is better" philosophy resulted in a drop to 271 bonded wineries in 1960 down from a 1936 high of 1,300 wineries.[22] Fortunately, the liquor companies lacked wine-making knowledge and had little patience to rebuild the industry. Thus, over the next decade the state's wineries gradually reverted back to ownership by resident wine-making entrepreneurs. On the plus side this merger fever had saved the industry with an influx of much-needed capital for expansion and rebuilding of an industry ravaged by war, Prohibition, and depression.

As wineries fell back into the hands of wine businesses, they began the process of reeducating American wine consumers in the benefits of lighter premium wines. In many ways this seemed like an uphill battle as American consumption of flavored sweet wines had increased from 100 million gallons in the mid-1940s to 145 million gallons by the mid-'50s. This sweet-wine preference forced table wine producers like Robert Mondavi to actively engage in a public relations drive to reverse the trend. To do so Mondavi endorsed the formation of the Premium Wine Producers Board (advisory to the Wine Advisory Board) to initiate comparative tastings and help consumers differentiate premium wine by quality and price.[23]

Switching drinkers from sweet, high-alcohol wines got another boost in 1958 when federal alcohol regulations legalized "pop" wines, which had enough carbon dioxide to emit a small pop upon opening the bottle. This led the way to the popular light fruit wines of the late 1960s, and by 1971 consumers purchased $346 per million spent to purchase wine, up from $301 in 1969.[24] Not to be forgotten in this new market were women who now viewed themselves as different than men in all aspects, including consumption of alcoholic beverages.[25] Key to this wine revolution was increased wine consumption and a gradual consumer shift from cheaper, sweet, high-alcohol wines to premium, dry table wines.

In some ways Mussolini had been right about the effects of Prohibition and the reeducation of American consumers continued. Since Prohibition had destroyed American wine connoisseurship and created a nation without wine authorities, consumers relied heavily upon trial and error to find what tasted good to them. As curious consumers, with money to spend, they wandered through store isles unable to match quality and price value. To remedy this problem the wine industry took it upon themselves to lead the wine education charge and within a short time they were joined by a new generation of newspaper and magazine wine writers.

All the wine industry changes in marketing and education seemed to be working, and between 1964 and 1974 the number of California bonded wineries grew from 231 to 311 facilities and wine-grape acreage more than doubled from 136,758 acres in 1965 to a 1974 high of 322,044 acres. The increase was led not by regional small pioneers, but by the eight largest wine companies that increased their hold over the market from 42 percent in 1947 to 68 percent in 1972.[26]

BACCHUS ARRIVES ON SANTA BARBARA'S MOUNTAIN DRIVE

Despite the commercial setbacks the wine tradition was far from dead in Santa Barbara. Hidden in the foothills behind the city, along the winding road appropriately named Mountain Drive, could be found a flourishing outpost of the 1950s Bohemian lifestyle that kept the local wine dream alive over the next two decades. In the 1940s Bobby Hyde, the developer of the Mountain Drive community, bought a fifty-acre parcel of land along the winding road and he began to sell sections to young men and families that he found compatible with his bohemian lifestyle. Wine lover Bill Neely, a potter and summer park ranger, and architect Frank Robinson joined Hyde and the trio helped rebuild a local nontraditional wine culture.

Mountain Drive residents celebrated with frequent festivals and parties based on the spirit of Bacchus. The year's main event was an October grape stomp that began with a motorcade to San Luis Obispo County to pick wine grapes. Upon return the community leaders would select a wine queen who would then inaugurate the stomp dressed only in a gilded crown of grape leaves.[27] "The way the [Mountain Drive] wines were being made," confessed one participant, Stan Hill, "was too haphazard," though he also admitted "it was a hell of a lot of fun, stomping around in the vat with a bunch of naked cuties . . ."[28] Neely went on to experiment with plantings of Folle Blanch, Semillon, Corbeau, and other cuttings from UC Davis's Department of Enology, but, his vineyard succumbed to fire, gophers, and rocky soils. Hill, on the other hand, had limited success with Cabernet Sauvignon and Pinot Noir grapes. The Santa Barbara region still awaited the re-arrival of a commercial wine industry.

CALIFORNIA'S WINE REVOLUTION

As Mountain Drive residents experimented with wine making, post–World War II California commercial wineries reentered the national and international wine marketplace, and within one generation California wine increased in both quality and prestige and quickly became a viable part of the world wine market.[29]

The crucial moment of self-realization for the California industry came with the famous bicentennial (1976) blind tasting of French and California wines in Paris, France. In what *Time* Magazine called "The Judgment of Paris," French wine experts named Stag's Leap Wine Cellars 1973 Cabernet Sauvignon and Chateau Montelena's 1973 Chardonnay superior to Bordeaux and Burgundy competitors.[30] Most importantly, the tasting inspired American winemakers to raise their standards and in the words of wine writer Paul Lukacs "begin thinking of 'world class' as a goal."[31]

The blind tasting in Paris heightened the intensity of a series of planned and incidental industry growth factors. But the greatest changes came during the wine renaissance of the 1960s and 1970s as consumers shifted their taste preferences and wine drinkers with disposable incomes drank more wine.[32] Winemakers successfully reset American attitudes on wine by redefining "the best" to be the new California style that utilized science to produce fruit flavored wines based on quality grapes. Their work payed off as U.S. per-capita wine consumption jumped from 1.51 gallons in 1963 to a 1971 high of 2.37 gallons per adult.[33] The new wine movement was so successful that over the next two decades California moved the world industry from generic blended wines to the California style of varietal designated and vintage dated wines based on the philosophy that quality grapes make quality wines. This rise in consumption sent California wine-makers scrambling to make more affordable premium wines and created an ever-increasing need for more acreage of premium wine grapes.

In order to purchase reasonably priced acreage wineries, entrepreneurs now looked beyond the traditional counties of Napa, Sonoma, and Mendocino to new vineyard lands in the Central and South Coast regions of California.[34] Many began to look seriously at the successful history and traditions of Santa Barbara County and its affordable acreage. Assisting in the rapid expansion was the fact that federal, state, and local tax deductions helped investors and wineries expand. As an investment many were drawn to vineyards and win-eries not because they offered high profit margins but because tax incentives offered considerable growth potential in an inflationary period. This attracted professionals (doctors, dentists, lawyers, retired corporate officers, investors, and entrepreneurs) and their capital to launch the business techniques of large businesses to a fragmented industry.[35]

Notes

1. Doris Muscadine, Maynard A. Amerine, and Bob Thompson, eds., *The University of California Sotheby Book of California Wine* (Berkeley: University of California Press, 1984), 50.
2. Ibid.
3. Ibid., 51.
4. Ibid., 62.
5. Stanton Peele, "The Conflict between Public Health Goals and the Temperance Mentality," *American Journal of Public Health* 83 (June 1993): 805–10.
6. Paul Lukacs, *American Vintage: The Rise of American Wine* (New York: Houghton Mifflin Company, 2000), 103.

7. Letter, Seymour Berkson to T. V. Ranck, Rome, 11 December 1932, Rome. Than Van Ranck Collection, box 9 (New Haven: Yale University Sterling Memorial Library).

8. Lukacs, *American Vintage*, 77.

9. Ibid., 106.

10. Ibid., 107.

11. University of California, Davis, Special Collections Archives—Bureau of Alcohol, Tobacco, and Firearms Records for the Bonded Winery Number 3577, Umberto Dardi.

12. University of California, Davis, Special Collections Archives—Bureau of Alcohol, Tobacco, and Firearms Records for the Bonded Winery Number 4228, Benjamin Alfonso.

13. The California Agricultural Prorate Act allowed for cooperative marketing as a means to level out boom and bust cycles.

14. Burke H. Critchfield, Carl F. Wente and Andrew G. Frericks, "The California Wine Industry during the Depression," an oral history interview conducted by Ruth Teiser in 1972, Oral History Center, The Bancroft Library, University of California, Berkeley, 1972.

15. Otto E. Meyer, "California Premium Wines and Brandy," an oral history interview conducted by Ruth Teiser 1971, Oral History Center, The Bancroft Library, University of California, Berkeley, 1973.

16. Leon Adams, "California Wine Industry Affairs: Recollections and Opinions," an oral history interview conducted by Ruth Teiser in 1986, Oral History Center, The Bancroft Library, University of California, Berkeley, 1990.

17. Edmund A. Rossi, "Swiss Colony and the Wine Industry," an oral history interview conducted by Ruth Teiser in 1969, Oral History Center, The Bancroft Library, University of California, Berkeley, 1971.

18. Ibid.

19. Charles L. Sullivan, *Napa Wine: A History from Mission Days to Present* (San Francisco: The Wine Appreciation Guild, 1994), 234–305.

20. Alan E. Fusonie, "John H. Davis: His Contributions to Agricultural Education and Productivity," *Agricultural History* 60 (Spring 1986), 97–110.

21. Thomas Pinney, *A History of Wine in America: From Prohibition to the Present* (Berkeley: University of California Press, 2005), 347.

22. Lukacs, *American Vintage*, 111.

23. Pinney, *History of Wine in America*, 344.

24. Gavin-Jobson Publication, *U.S. News and World Report, The Wine Marketing Handbook, 1972*: 14–15.

25. Catherine Gilbert Murdock, *Domesticating Drink: Women, Men, and Alcohol in America, 1870–1940* (Baltimore, MD: Johns Hopkins University Press, 1998), 161.

26. Bunce, "From California Grapes to California Wine," 57.

27. Lin Rolens, "When the Magic Was on Mountain Drive," *Santa Barbara Magazine*, January/February 1992), 40–47; Elias Chiacos, ed., *Mountain Drive: Santa Barbara's Pioneer Bohemian Community* (Santa Barbara, CA: Shoreline Press, 1994), passim.

28. Stanley Hill, interview by Teddy Gasser, 10 January 1987, interview in the collection of Santa Barbara Historical Society.

29. Lukacs, *American Vintage*, 85.

30. Frank J. Prial, "Wine Talk: A Coda to the 1976 France vs. California Rivalry That Changed Some Attitudes," *New York Times,* 22 May 1996, B-5; "20 Years Ago . . . a Taste of History," *Wine Enthusiast,* June 1996, 45.

31. Lukacs, *American Vintage*, 86.

32. Gavin-Jobson Publication, *U.S. News and World Report, The Wine Marketing Handbook, 1980*, 74.

33. Gavin-Jobson Publication, *U.S. News and World Report, 1972, The Wine Marketing Handbook*, 14, 89; Frank Braconi, Morton Research Corporation, *The U.S. Wine Market: An Economic Marketing and Financial Investigation* (April 1977, A Morton Report, Merrick, New York): 4–5; K. S. Moulton, "The Economics of Wine in California," in *The Book of California Wine*, ed. D. Muscatine, M. Amerine, and B. Thompson, (University of California, Berkeley, CA, 1984)380–405.

34. Sullivan, *Napa Wine*, 234–305, passim.

35. Ibid.; Irving Hoch and Nickolas Tryphonopoulos, *A Study of the Economy of Napa County, California* (University of California, California Agricultural Experiment Station Giannini Foundation of Agricultural Economics Research Report Number 303, August 1969), passim.

Chapter Four

The California Wine Revolution
Looks to Santa Barbara

Napa Seeks Premium Wine Grapes

In order to meet wine-grape shortages, Bay Area wineries rapidly expanded their vineyard acreage. This became problematic as they competed with post-war urban expansion that also needed land for development. The land grab by wineries and developers resulted in escalating land prices in the regions best suited for wine grapes. After a half decade (1960–1965) of unprecedented urban sprawl, environmental activists countered the loss of prime agricultural lands.[1] Acting at the county level, they patched together laws that exclusively zoned land for agriculture based on farmers' arguments that they provided a sense of community, helped secure economic diversity, preserved historic and aesthetic values, and secured open space for recreational and health benefits.[2]

Despite the initial efforts the threats of urban sprawl reached statewide and an unusual collaboration of farmers and environmental activists temporarily joined forces to lobby state legislators to curb the loss of agricultural and open space lands. They started by addressing the mid-1960s California property tax method that taxed property at its highest and best value. This meant that a five-acre vineyard could be taxed as a subdivided parcel capable of fifteen homes or more. Unable to pay their taxes, many agricultural landowners sold their properties. Faced with this untenable situation, California legislators passed the California Land Conservation Act of 1965 (Williamson Act) and the Property Tax Assessment Reform Act of 1966.[3] These laws established a statewide voluntary county participation program, based on property tax incentives, to save valuable farmland.

Initially these policy measures slowed the conversion of California farmland for urban and suburban development and increased sales of agricultural land for vineyards and wineries. According to Santa Barbara County agricultural real estate agent Dean Brown, this allowed many investors in Santa Barbara to utilize agricultural acreage as a system of depreciation on full costs of vineyard investment and three years of zero income tax by claiming tax write-offs while waiting for vine production to begin. Thus, vineyard investment became a tax loophole for hedging against the 1970s' increasing inflation rates faced by large landholders, cattle ranchers, and agribusiness.[4]

For some this tax solution served as a means to transfer agricultural lands from ranchers and farmers to a new generation of gentleman farmers from the cadre of doctors, dentists, lawyers, business executives, and agricultural entrepreneurs seeking the 1960s version of the good life—the wine industry. In a short time high-income investors purchased land, planted grapes, and under the existing tax laws avoided paying taxes by simultaneously writing off all invested income and capital improvements as losses. If investors sold the land several years later, it was taxed at the lower capital gains tax rate. The window of opportunity for these advantages only lasted until the 1976 Tax Reform Law amended the Internal Revenue codes to exclude vineyard investments as a form of tax write-off.[5] Without the generous tax advantages, many investors moved their money to other more profitable financial schemes and again farmers found it more difficult to find investors. Faced with not being able to sell their land, many farmers converted some of their own land to the new agricultural "hot crop"—vineyards. In no time at all ranchers and grain growers converted parts of their ranches from row crops, dairies, and fruit and nut orchards to vineyards.

By the 1970s the demand for premium wine-grape vineyards reached a fevered pitch as U.S. wine consumption doubled and dry table wine sales topped 50 percent of all wines consumed. The reeducation of American consumers to switch to dry wines had worked, and marketers had to quadruple foreign wine imports from 14,369,000 gallons in 1964 to a 1971 total of 51,394,000 gallons to meet domestic demands.[6] Economic reports from the early 1970s solidified the idea that the United States' wine industry was woefully short of premium wine-grape acreage. In a 1973 comment about the problem, Professor Maynard Amerine predicted that "150,000 acres of new vineyards are to be planted throughout the state in the next several years and the variety of grapes to be grown on each acre will be matched to the climate and soil conditions of that acre to yield the best quality grapes."[7] Amerine's prediction proved correct.

The search for new wine-grape lands heightened throughout California and economic projections from the Bank of America and the Wine Institute provided market growth data that encouraged developers, grape growers, bankers, insurance companies, and gentleman farmers to move into action.[8] Prompted by these business possibilities, investors reached out to researchers from the University of California, Davis, and California State University, Fresno, for the research and development reports to guide the establishment of the new vineyards. The problem was that the California wine industry needed more premium wine-grape acreage in regions where real estate prices and other economic opportunities offered reasonable profit margins. Keeping with centuries-long traditions California wineries began a decade-long search for new California wine-grape regions.

REDISCOVERY OF SANTA BARBARA VITICULTURE

Economic historian Alan L. Olmstead chronicled how regional American agricultural industries become location specific as a result of "induced innovations" brought about by marketplace factors.[9] In the case of the California wine industry wine-grape shortages sent viticulturists out on a statewide journey to find the regions capable of supporting premium varietal wine grapes. Many growers of the 1950s and 1960s automatically turned to the state's past records and combed new and old economic and research reports looking for indicators left by fellow farmers, business investors, and universities. The physical and cultural wine terroir of Santa Barbara was being rediscovered.

A few early 1960s pioneers found that Santa Barbara County provided a promising cool climate and an economic infrastructure needed for success. Two regions within the county, Santa Maria Valley and Santa Ynez Valley, surfaced as prime locations for wine-grape vineyards. The county's agricultural economy ranked twentieth among California's fifty-eight counties and in 1965 had brought in an all-time high of $71.2 million to the general economy.[10] Demographic studies showed that the region's fast-growing population could support local wine sales. Between 1960 and 1965 Santa Barbara County population growth increased by 40 percent, making the county the third-fastest-growing county in Southern California (behind Orange and Ventura Counties).[11] The good news continued as projections for the future pointed to new growth as the University of California built its Santa Barbara Campus and the Air Force developed missile facilities at Vandenberg Air Force Base in Lompoc. The 1966 Security First National Bank report projected that Santa Barbara County would grow at a rate substantially higher than the state and that Goleta, Carpenteria, and Santa Ynez would become the county's high-growth areas. Although the report made no mention of viticulture, it was apparent that Santa Barbara County was economically ripe for all types of business and agricultural expansion.

In January of 1965 the Santa Barbara County Agricultural Extension Service, in conjunction with Marston H. Kimball, UC Davis Bioclimatologist, issued an extensive report on the climate of Santa Barbara County.[12] The study utilized La Zaca, Lompoc, Solvang, Santa Ynez, Los Alamos, and Sisquoc Ranch weather data to support favorable climatic conditions for wine-grape growing. The report's narrative explained that mild temperatures were the rule in Santa Barbara County and that precipitation came in a concentrated period between November and April. It also boasted that sunshine was abundant throughout the county, although low cloudiness during the night hours of summer brought cooling effects to the coastal points and western valleys of Santa Ynez and Santa Maria.[13]

Additional support came from the fact that the report described favorable grape-growing conditions because of the geography and maritime climates of the Santa Ynez and Santa Maria River Valleys. The Santa Ynez Mountains, with elevations up to 4,000 feet, paralleled the coast line from Point Arguello to the eastern edge of the county and the Santa Ynez River's westward flow emptied between the San Rafael Mountains and Purisima Hills (elevation 1,200 to 1,700 feet) to the north. The southern Santa Ynez Mountains (elevations from 800 to 2,600 feet) encircled present-day Lake Cachuma and the Los Padres National Forest to the east, and formed a series of low hills to the west as the river empties into the Pacific Ocean near Surf, California. These features allowed the maritime moderating climate to work its way up the long narrow Santa Ynez River Valley that widens at Lompoc. The Santa Maria Valley, on the other hand, was described as a triangular area about twenty miles long and fifteen miles wide with its apex near the town of Sisquoc with its base along the San Luis Obispo Bay. The report described how the Cuyama River flows westward and empties into the Santa Maria River, which is also joined by the Sisquoc River. Grape growers reading the report benefited from the precise climatic data including frost, fog, precipitation, temperature, growing season, heat summation, and elevation statistics.[14]

Most importantly, the report's intricate climate map pinpointed areas capable of growing grapes based upon data gathered by the University of California at Davis.[15] Readers could easily identify the coastal zone, which ran between eight and thirty miles inland up the two river valleys, that would be perfect for grape growing. Direct ocean influences, including summer fogs, modified temperatures 75 to 85 percent of the time in the upper Santa Maria Valley (Garey to Sisquoc Ranch) and western valley floors of Santa Ynez (Lompoc to Solvang). By 1965 county farmers had available data that could support decisions to plant University of California Amerine/Winkler Index Region I and II premium wine-grape varietals.[16] A few wine-grape pioneers in the northern part of the state quickly realized that the economic infrastructure and climatic data all supported wine-grape expansion into Santa Barbara County. In response, banks, insurance companies, and private investors began to diversify their portfolios with investments in Santa Barbara County agriculture and wine.[17]

Notes

1. James D. Hofer, "Cucamonga Wines and Vines: A History of the Cucamonga Pioneer Vineyard Association" (master's thesis, Claremont University, 1983), passim.
2. Donald Joseph de la Peña, "Vineyards in a Regional System of Open Space in the San Francisco Bay Area: Methods of Preserving Selected Areas" (master's thesis in City Planning in the College of Environmental Design; University of California, Berkeley, 1962) passim.
3. Rebecca Ann Conard, "The Conservation of Local Autonomy: California's Agricultural Land Policies, 1900–1966" (PhD dissertation, University of California, Santa Barbara, 1984), vi.
4. Dean Brown, interview by Victor W. Geraci and Jeff Maiken, 25 October 1995, Santa Ynez, California, tape recording, Special Collections, University of California, Santa Barbara, Santa Barbara, California.
5. Bunce, "From California Grapes to California Wine," 62.
6. Wine Institute Statistical Survey, 1974. Total of all wine marketed in 1964 was 175,918,000 gallons and doubled to 349,403,000 gallons in 1974. Frank Braconi, Morton Research Corporation (Merrick, NY: A Morton Report, April 1977): 14–18, 37–57, 89–98.
7. Ibid.
8. The Bank of America released wine industry reports from its agricultural economics division in 1970, 1973, and 1978.
9. Alan L. Olmstead, "Induced Innovation in American Agriculture," *Journal of Political Economy* 101 (February 1993): 100–18.
10. Economic Research Division of Security First National Bank, Ventura, Santa Barbara, and San Luis Obispo Counties (Los Angeles: Economic Research Department Security First National Bank, July 1966), 34.
11. Ibid., 25–29.
12. Agricultural Extension Service, "The Climate of Santa Barbara County: Plant-Climate Map and Climatological Data" (Santa Barbara, CA: University of California Agricultural Extension Service, 1965), passim.
13. Ibid., 6.
14. Ibid., passim.
15. Ibid., 23. Table 5, "Effective-Heat Summation, Degree Days for Grapes." Based on H. E. Jacob and A. J. Winkler's "Grape Growing in California," California Agricultural Extension Service Circular 116, November 1950; A. J. Winkler, "The Effect of Climatic Regions," *Wine Review* 6 (1938): 14–16.
16. M. A. Amerine and A. J. Winkler, *Grape Varieties: For Wine Production* (Berkeley, CA: University of California Division of Agricultural Sciences, 1963).
17. Lynn Samsel, Diane I. Hambley, and Raymond A. Marquardt, "Agribusiness' Competitiveness for Venture Capital," 7 (July 1991): 401–13.

Chapter Five

Santa Barbara Pioneers
Plant Wine Grapes

During the decades of the sixties and seventies, California premium wine-grape shortages forced Bay Area wineries to look elsewhere for fruit and started a quest for wine-growing lands in central and south coast regions. The initial search began as early as 1962 when Paul Masson and Wente wineries looked to resurrect historical wine-growing regions of Salinas.[1] But, the urgency of this land shortage sent wineries as far afield as San Luis Obispo, Santa Barbara, Temecula, and the Central Valley. As a result, satellite vineyards began to appear in new regions and northern wineries quickly negotiated contracts for their fruit.

The quest for new vineyard land increased and spread throughout thirty-two of the state's fifty-eight counties. Between 1965 and 1980 the number of California wineries grew from 227 to 380. This surge included ten new wineries in Santa Barbara, thirteen in Santa Cruz, ten in Santa Clara, and seven in Monterey.[2] Between 1970 and 2000 Bay Area wineries also expanded locally as new sources of investment money from corporate wineries and individual investors helped Napa grow from 15,000 to 43,000 acres and Sonoma grow from 15,000 to 52,000 acres.[3]

Consumers with disposable incomes, ideas of middle-class social mobility, and medical touts of the health benefits of wine pushed sales to new record highs. Again, demand became so high that marketers relied upon foreign imports to supplement American production shortages. There was plenty of opportunity for domestic growth.

SANTA BARBARA RESPONDS TO CONSUMER DEMANDS
Between 1964 and 1978 viticultural pioneers planted wine-grape varietals in Santa Barbara County's Santa Maria and Santa Ynez Valleys. After accumulating

capital in nonagricultural businesses, these nonindustry investors gambled their personal resources and skills as architects, retired business executives, ranchers, real estate developers, doctors, and dentists to build a wine region. In a relatively short time, their gamble produced 5,836 acres of wine grapes.[4] The new Santa Barbara pioneers included men like Uriel Nielson, James Flood, Harold Pfeiffer, Bob Woods, Louis Lucas, Dale Hampton, and Bob and Steve Miller, who established large commercial wine-grape vineyards in what would become the Santa Maria appellation. Close behind were the smaller individual, corporate, and family vineyards of Boyd Bettencourt, Giff Davidge, Pierre La Fond, A. Brooks Firestone, Marshall Ream, Jack McGowan, Richard Sanford, Michael Benedict, Fred Brander, and Bill Mosby in the Santa Ynez Valley.

COMMERCIAL VITICULTURE FOR THE SANTA MARIA VALLEY

In the early 1960s the area's first two pioneers, Uriel Nielson and Bill Dematei, both from Central Valley grape-growing families, planted over 100 acres of vine-yards in the Santa Maria Valley. The two had first noticed the region in the late 1930s where as students at the University of California, Davis, they had worked on a research project that had mapped California coastal climates best suited for premium wine-grape growing.[5] After World War II both men studied the cli-mates of French wine-grape regions and compared their results with the micro-climate records they had collected while at UC Davis. Their study concluded that the cooler Regions I and II Santa Maria and Santa Ynez Valleys of Santa Barbara County provided the best opportunities for wine grapes.[6] Then in 1964 the two acted on their research data and purchased land in Santa Maria for the purpose of experimenting with premium wine-grape varietals like Cabernet Sauvignon, Pinot Noir, Chardonnay, Johannisberg Riesling, Sauvignon Blanc, and Sylvaner.[7]

Nielson and DeMattai hired Bill Collins, an experienced Delano, California, grape grower, as the vineyard manager for the project. Collins, like his employ-ers, believed that the region was "one of the rare places in the world where high quality wine grapes" could be grown.[8] More importantly, he believed that the region could produce "better quality wine than those produced in Napa Valley." Collins's faith in the region was given a boost when Christian Brothers Winery quickly contracted for the vineyard's grapes. In Collins's words, "If a rancher said he was going to start a vineyard, he would find a winery representative at his door the next day offering to contract for his future production."[9]

The project's initial yields exceeded four tons per acre, and northern win-eries paid $400 per ton for the grapes. With production costs averaging about

$1,000 per acre, Collins felt that a "family with forty acres of high-quality grapes," could "make a hell of a good living."[10] Thus, he predicted that numerous local growers would follow suit after this initial project. A short time later a PG&E monthly bill insert quoted Collins as predicting that the region would someday have over 5,000 acres of vineyards producing premium wine grapes.

Not far away a third pioneer decided to enter the Santa Barbara vineyard business. In 1952 James Flood III purchased the 37,000-acre Rancho Sisquoc with capital acquired from the sale of his 200,000-acre Rancho Santa Margarita to the United States government for establishment of the present day Camp Pendleton Marine base, just north of San Diego.[11] From the outset Flood looked for ways to diversify the cattle ranch operation and increase the land's overall productivity, and in 1963 he hired Harold Pfeiffer as ranch manager and the two immediately considered growing wine grapes.[12] In the early sixties a promising series of negotiations with Almaden Winery had inspired Flood to ready his Sisquoc Mesa lands for vineyards. He was so sure of the possibilities of the deal that he installed an irrigation system. His high hopes diminished when Almaden changed hands and scrubbed the deal, forcing Pfeiffer to convert the 1,000-plus acres of irrigated lands to sugar beet production. They did not give up on the idea of premium vineyards.

A few years later neighbors DeMattei and Nielson began planting their vineyards and Flood began to rethink the possibility of vineyards on his ranch. Flood and Pfeiffer both felt they had the perfect microclimate for wine-grape growing, and in 1968 they planted grape test plots with cuttings from the Nielson-DeMattei vineyard. They utilized the mesa area of the property, just above the Sisquoc riverbed, because of its almost frost-free microclimate and low 300 foot riverbed elevation that allowed fog and air movement preferred by many wine-grape varietals.[13] Expansion of the vineyard continued in 1968 and 1969 when Pfeiffer purchased more grape clippings from DeMattei and Nielson and established a nursery that was used to plant twenty-nine acres in 1970, forty-eight acres in 1971, twenty-eight acres in 1972, and in 1974 a final plot of eighty-seven acres.[14] Joe Carrari, Paul Masson vineyard manager, provided practical vineyard advice for the project.

Between 1972 and 1973 most of the Nielson-DeMattei crops went chiefly to the Napa Oakville Winery and then in 1974 they signed a six-year contract with Bob Meyer of Geyser Peak. A decade of success prompted both men to hire Ed Holt as the new vineyard foreman and plant the 200 acre Rowan vineyard on the upper mesa. But the largest of the Santa Maria pioneering efforts was yet to come.

In the late 1960s George A. Lucas and Sons, agribusiness family from Delano, California, decided to expand their 1,500-acre grape-farming operation into Santa Barbara County. Louis Lucas, upon graduating from college, ran the family's table- and raisin-grape business in Bakersfield, California, and toyed with the idea of expanding the family operation by including wine grapes. During 1967 and 1968 his new interest in premium wines from European varietals led to his joining the American Society of Enologists and Viticulturists. With new information in hand, he then decided to find inexpensive quality land with appropriate climate for wine-grape growing and with his brother George began a series of scouting trips through the south and central coast. Their forays revealed that the Santa Maria Valley had the characteristics they sought.[15]

The brothers brought in business partner Dale Hampton, an eight year family employee and high school friend from Delano, and the three spent 1969 researching the area's soil and microclimates, studying existing grape test results, evaluating water resources, and reading about California's two-century-long tradition of winemaking.[16] They decided that any new location had to be capable of utilizing the newest in technology and wine-grape science, and in their words they "didn't want to follow the same train of thought everybody else did."[17]

Their final research led them to Santa Barbara County's Tepesquet Rancho lands in the Santa Maria Valley. Irrigation proved to be no problem as local water-well test-holes affirmed the ranch's ability to provide ample water. Local real estate agents confirmed the availability of cheap land ready for planting and directed the brothers to the favorable PG&E report. Additional support for the overall project came from the 1970 Bank of America Wine Industry Report that had projected a decade of wine industry growth.[18] The brothers spoke with DeMatei (Luis's Delano Little League coach) and Nielson (old ranch neighbor from Delano) and both supported the proposition. The final push came when Brother Timothy, Christian Brothers winemaker, who had been purchasing grapes from the Nielson Vineyard, told the Lucases that he "would consider paying Napa Valley prices" for their grapes.[19]

The family corporation moved into action and put some properties together to form the Dalmatian Vineyards Associates as a limited partnership stock company.[20] They attempted to form lease options, purchase land, rent parcels, form termed leases, or whatever was possible to create an economically feasible project that would attract investors and "looked like farmers had done it."[21] Attempts to get Dean Witter, E. F. Hutton, and other major investors to underwrite the project faltered, and the funding ended up with the small firm of Beckman and Company from San Jose, California. The company agreed to serve as broker to the project on a best-effort basis.

With funding secured the Lucas brothers then planned a model Region I to Region II vineyard. Their business plan included the newest science and technology, like automated irrigation systems, virus-resistant grape stock varieties, machine harvesting to reduce labor costs, frost protection systems, metal trellises, five twenty-acre-feet reservoirs, and numerous one thousand foot deep wells. The deep gravel soil was free of phylloxera and oak tree fungus and thus only required heat-treated rootstock with varietals like Cabernet Sauvignon, Pinot Noir, Pinot Chardonnay, and Johannisberg Riesling. Their ambitious prospectus offered a limited number of investors a 10 to 60 percent per year profit and a 12 percent tax deduction for years one through three.[22] But the deal failed to attract enough investors and rather than proceed they sent everyone's money back. The brothers believed that they were "about five years ahead of their time."[23]

Not willing to give up, the brothers then decided to figure out another way to plant their vineyards and sought the expertise and resources of family and private investors. Alfred Gagnon, a senior partner in a consulting firm, had invested in the original project and upon receiving his $50,000 refund decided that it "must have been a good deal for somebody if they felt they could do it for themselves."[24] This led Gagnon in 1969 to further investigate the properties and agree to come on board in a 50 percent limited partnership that utilized Gagnon's money and expertise and some farm equipment supplied by the Lucas brothers.

A gigantic boost for the deal came in 1970 when Beringer Winery signed a five-year renewable contract for the grapes. At this news financial institutions jumped at the opportunity to provide additional funds for the project. Eventually the plan raised $3.5 million and Dale Hampton became the vineyard manager of the 1,200-acre Tepusquet vineyard. The project gave Hampton recognition and over the next few years he consulted on the 350-acre Paragon Vineyards for Jack Niven and the 190-acre Delon White vineyard, both in close proximity to the Tepusquet Ranch. Santa Barbara had now restarted a commercial wine-grape industry.[25]

A great deal of the expertise necessary to plant much of the newly expanding Santa Barbara industry would come from the ranks of the Tepusquet venture. With vineyard development experience under their belts Dale Hampton, Joe Tucker, and Garth Conlan formed the Coastal Farming Company in Santa Maria. As general partners Hampton oversaw field operations, Tucker, became the irrigation expert, and Conlan acted as the business officer.[26] Over the next few years Coastal Farming either created or consulted on an additional two thousand acres of vineyards in Santa Barbara County.[27]

Another small planting of vines took place on the Santa Maria Suey Ranch, owned and operated by the Newhall Farming Company. The Newhall family purchased the Suey Ranch in 1921 after William Randolph Hearst acquired their central coastlands for his mini-empire. Bob Woods, hired as general ranch manager in 1966, initially sought ways to diversify the 3,500-acre ranch and investigated dry-farming, cattle ranching, lemons, avocados, and sugar beet ventures. Woods then began to explore the idea of vineyards and in the late 1960s decided to try grape-growing when Bay Area winery owner Ed Mirassou and his son Peter visited the Suey Ranch. The Mirassous used statistics from the UC Davis Viticulture and Enology program to convince Woods to plant test plots of sixteen wine-grape varieties from the UC Davis wine-grape nursery. Woods later admitted that he "didn't know anything about grapes," and literally "had never drank wine."[28] Yet, by 1969 they had planted 25 acres of Pinot Noir and a few acres of Cabernet Sauvignon in their Rancho Viñedo Vineyard. The experiment produced positive results, and by 1973 the vineyard covered over one thousand acres. This was not the only wine-grape foray in the region. In 1971 investors planted the 90-acre Camelot Vineyard and the 533-acre Katherine's Vineyard, both located eleven miles east of Santa Maria on Santa Maria Mesa Road. The region began to catch the attention of entrepreneurs interested in wine-grape vineyards.

More was yet to come as financial institutions like Prudential Insurance sought profitable agricultural investments. Entrepreneur Harley D. Martin used the successful planting reports and the favorable 1970 Bank of America report in his prospectus that convinced Prudential to loan him $2,900,000 to form a limited partnership for the creation of the Sierra Madre Vineyard, Inc. With the money Martin purchased one thousand acres of the Suey Ranch in Santa Maria and contracted the Coastal Farming Company to plant 850 acres of wine grapes. Mismanagement of the vineyard resulted in the project's failure and Prudential Corporation convinced Superior Court Judge Arden T. Jensen to place the property in receivership so as to protect the company's assets. In 1975 the court named Coastal Farming Company as receiver and they quickly brought 630 acres of the premium wine grapes back into production. All the grapes from the project were shipped northward for inclusion in less expensive wines.[29]

Cold War military base expansions on the Pacific Coast led to the condemnation of the Central Coast agricultural holdings of the Broome Family (Point

Magu—air base and state park). Bob and Steve Miller, fourth-generation members of the Broome Family, wished to stay in agriculture and spent a good part of the late 1960s investigating over three hundred ranch sites statewide to replace the family's holdings. Their search lead to the 1968 purchase of the 35,000-acre Rancho Tepusquet from the Allan Hancock family (La Brea Interstate Bank) in the Santa Maria area where the Cuyama and Sisquoc Rivers intersect.[30] Between 1968 and 1972 the Millers planted row crops on the land and closely watched the development of neighboring vineyards at Rancho Sisquoc, Nielson's 110 acres, and the Lucas's Tepusquet Vineyards. In 1974, based on their neighbors' successes, the Millers planted 640 acres of wine grapes.[31]

The Millers wanted a state-of-the-art operation and hired Dale Hampton to plan and plant their vineyard. Bob Miller later reflected that; "one of the things he pioneered [first at Tepusquet, then at Bien Nacido Vineyards and other vineyards] was the concept of using metal stakes in the vineyard."[32] People began to call it a "Cadillac Vineyard." That's when they decided on the vineyard name of Bien Nacido—a Mexican slang expression for being born with a silver spoon in your mouth.[33]

Coastal Farming partner Garth Conlan convinced the Millers to plant UC Davis registered grapevines and enrolled them as a producer of "certified increase nursery stock."[34] Not only would this meet the need for future cuttings but the registry qualified the vineyard for free advice from the UC Davis Viticulture and Enology Department.[35] Further consultation for the new vineyard came from Vince Patrucci from the California State University, Fresno, campus. They had created a *Wine by Design* vineyard, and by the mid-1970s grapes from those first years went north to Wente, Martini, Sonoma Vineyards, ZD, and Fetzer. In the nearby Los Alamos Valley, Italian immigrant Mary Vigoroso followed the movement with her planting of 350 acres of Pinot Noir, Cabernet Sauvignon, Zinfandel, and Chardonnay grapes intended for sales to large northern wineries.[36]

SANTA YNEZ VITICULTURAL ENTERPRISES

Just south of Santa Maria, in the adjacent Santa Ynez Valley, agricultural speculators planted smaller vineyards to help alleviate premium wine-grape shortages. These corporate, individual, and family operations helped meet the demand for premium wine grapes but like their Santa Maria neighbors were more susceptible to the cyclic characteristics of the viticultural marketplace.

The region joined the wine-grape movement in 1967 after a false start by Daniel J. Gainey, Minnesota Josten Jewelry partner and Santa Ynez Arabian horse breeder. Gainey directed his ranch manager Don Bryant and assistant manager Barry Johnson to study the possibilities of wine-grape growing in the region and soon thereafter launched a study for a vineyard project on his 1,800-acre Santa Ynez ranch. As part of the planning, they established a ten thousand cutting grapevine nursery for the projected vineyard. In 1968, as planting time approached, Gainey decided that he was not sure about grape growing and sold the cuttings to another nearby vineyard venture.[37]

Not far from the Gainey Ranch, Boyd and Claire Bettencourt faced rising taxes and the common 1950s–1960s threat of losing the family farm. Determined not to lose their second-generation dairy, they searched for various means to diversify production and keep the ranch ledger in the black.[38] Their neighbor Giff Davidge, who later became their partner, referred them to the PG&E brochure where Collins had projected that vineyards could do well in Santa Barbara County.[39] Inspired by the report the Bettencourts visited the Salinas, California, area and investigated newly established vineyards in that region.

The Bettencourts then visited Boyd's UC Davis classmates Nielson and DeMattai to discuss the initial results from their Santa Maria vineyard. Bolstered by their positive research the Bettencourts cautiously proceeded into the wine-grape business. The initial planting included fifteen acres of vines with the addition of five more acres per year for the next two years. Nielson and DiMatteis's vineyard manager, Bill Collins, served as the vineyard consultant, and they utilized many of the nursery vines from the aborted Gainey project. By 1969 the twenty-five acre vineyard began production and they negotiated contracts with Paul Masson for all of the grapes.

In 1971 Richard Sanford and Michael Benedict planted their mixed-variety Sanford and Benedict Vineyard at the western end of the Santa Ynez Valley near Santa Rosa Road. Sanford, born in Palos Verdes Peninsula, graduated from UC Berkeley in 1965 with concentrations in geography and geology. He then spent three years in Vietnam as a Navy destroyer navigator and after his tour of duty he traveled through Burgundy. During his travels he began to dream of a life in viticulture and toyed with the ideas "of vertical integration of the wine business" and "growing a crop, manufacturing a product, and then marketing it."[40] He had no viticultural experience and thus went through the agonizing decision of whether to go to UC Davis for a master's degree in enology or just plant a vineyard and learn through trial and error. Prompted by the 1970 Bank of America's 11 percent growth prediction, tax advantages, and being "a little bit crazy," Sanford decided to go directly into business.[41]

Sanford then began his search for a region to grow Chardonnay and Pinot Noir grapes in a climate that could match that of France's Bordeaux and Burgundian regions. The geographer/geologist found that the Santa Ynez Valley offered the long, cool growing seasons with maritime influence that matched both Burgundy and Napa. With partner Michael Benedict, botanist, and backed by financial investors, Sanford planted 110 acres of grapes nine miles west of Buellton along the Santa Ynez River on the 738-acre ranch that was once part of the original Santa Rosa Land Grant.

In the 1950s Dean Brown, third-generation Betteravia (Santa Maria) cattle rancher, purchased the 2,200-acre Rancho Corral de Quati. The cattle ranch created tax problems for Brown, so in the late 1960s and early 1970s he looked for ways to diversify the ranch's production and take advantage of the 1970s tax laws.[42] After numerous conversations with his friend Giff Davidge, Brown became interested in the idea of grape growing and its tax advantages. He then hired Dale Hampton to plant and manage the vineyard and figured out ways to write off soil ripping, soil fumigation, plants, stakes, irrigation system, and labor. By 1972 the 100-acre vineyard included Cabernet Sauvignon, Chardonnay, Riesling, and Pinot Noir cuttings from UC Davis and grapes from the vineyard were sold to Martini and Geyser Peak. More importantly, Brown's initial success convinced other neighbors to follow his lead.

Leonard Firestone, automobile tire industrialist and ambassador to Belgium, sought an agricultural business venture and in 1971 he purchased 550 acres of the Rancho Corral de Quati. He immediately looked for ways to utilize his new investment. The previous owner, Dart Industries, had recently completed a feasibility study by Vince Patrucci that recommended growing wine grapes on the ranch. Patrucci's report predicted that the area could produce Cabernet Sauvignon grapes capable of prices ranging from $1,000 to $1200 per ton.[43] Additional good news came when Coldwell-Banker Real Estate agents T. Hayer and Richard Dick commissioned California Farm Management (San Joaquin Valley) to conduct an agricultural feasibility study of the Corral Di Quati.[44] This study, along with evidence from the Sisquoc's thirty-two-acre test plot, the Bettencourt-Davidge vineyard success, and Dean Brown's 100-acre La Zaca Vineyard success, all pointed to the idea of grape-growing in the region.

Firestone then directed his son A. Brooks (recently retired after twelve years with the family-owned Firestone Tire and Rubber Company) to investigate and complete an in-depth report on the ranch's agricultural possibilities. The younger Firestone studied data from UC Davis's survey and neighbor Dean Brown's ten-year weather study. Overall, the study found that subterranean springs provided ample water and that a western maritime influence, between the San Raphael and Santa Ynez mountains afforded the ranch a UC Davis Regions I and II grape-growing classification. Firestone's study also revealed that the area averaged sixteen inches of rain per year, with little or no rain during harvest times, and that its sand to gravely-loam soils made for the perfect growing medium for wine grapes.[45] The most convincing evidence, for both Firestones, came from the trial-and-error success that had prompted local farmers to rate the area "brilliant" for wine grapes. Both Firestones believed that these farmers looked "like they know what they're doing."[46] Convinced by these feasibility studies, Leonard Firestone began planting 260 acres of classic wine-grape varietals—Chardonnay, Sauvignon Blanc, Gewürztraminer, Riesling, Merlot, and Cabernet Sauvignon—and placed Brooks in charge of the project. Brooks used this opportunity as a way out of what he considered the rat race of the large corporate life. Since Firestone Tire and Rubber Company had gone public in the 1970s, his role in the family business seemed unsure; in the words of Brooks, "We just didn't fit."[47] Fortunately, he was able to utilize his father's investment in Santa Ynez as an opportunity to create an active farming career.[48]

Further Santa Ynez planting continued throughout 1972 as Marshall Ream, vice chairman of the Atlantic Richfield corporation studied the region. While on a vacation with his wife at the Alisal Guest Ranch in Santa Ynez, he discovered where he wanted to retire and in a short time, he became interested in an 1,800-acre ranch that the realtor predicted was perfect for wine grapes.[49]

Seeing an opportunity Ream brought together an investment group to plant a vineyard and take advantage of the tax benefits offered by wine grapes. Statewide market indicators, like the wine-grape successes in Monterey County and the B of A report helped him convince investors John Cushman (Los Angeles realtor), John T. McDonald (Stanford economics professor), Carl L. Kempner (managing partner of Hamershlauh/Kempner Company), Joseph Harnett (former Standard Oil president), Thomas J. Simpson (agricultural developer and consultant), and Charles E. Westwood (Montana cattleman and real estate investor) to join the partnership.[50] Together, the group purchased 1,500 acres and planted 200 acres of wine grapes.

Not all of the new vineyards started on the large scale of Firestone and Ream. In 1972 Pierre Lafond, Montreal architect, decided to plant seventy-two acres of vines on his 105-acre Santa Ynez Valley ranch. LaFond needed wine grapes for his Santa Barbara winery (established in 1962) that had been producing non-grape wines with purchased fruit. In Lafond's words, "I couldn't buy enough grapes to make my wine."[51] He then entered the expansion frenzy from a different perspective—he would grow wine grapes for his established winery. Lafond plotted a plan whereby he could "gradually but steadily improve our ability to make fine wines."[52] Bill Collins became the vineyard manager for the Lafond Valley View Vineyard in Santa Ynez.

Vineyard growth continued in 1973 when Bob Woods, retired from the Newhall Corporation's Suey Ranch operations, moved his family to their Rancho Viñedo property. The retired ranch manager ran a small herd of Angus cattle and in 1973–1974 planted twenty-seven acres of Chardonnay, Pinot Noir, and Gamay grapevines. His "idea was [to] have half of the ranch in white grapes and half in red grapes." In his words, "The knowledge was deficient around these areas as to what we should grow, what would sell, and what would be beneficial."[53] Wood's decision to grow Pinot Noir was "based on the fact that everybody else was Cabernet Sauvignon and this was [another] red." He claimed that it was a personal decision made after he "flipped a coin."[54] Woods also knew that he could not compete with the huge Lucas and Newhall ranches for Cabernet Sauvignon vineyards. Through trial and error and pure luck, Woods picked a perfect microclimate for a Pinot Noir and Chardonnay vineyard. His Rancho Viñedo vineyard received little if any frost, needed little irrigation, and enjoyed a long, cool growing season. He sold most of the fruit from those first years to northern wineries through San Francisco grape broker Joe Ciati.

Another 1973 entry into this planting spree included Jack McGowan, ex-McDonald-Douglas executive. McGowan hired Hampton to plant and maintain vineyards on land adjacent to Alamo Pintado Road just outside the community of Solvang. The initial planting included just over twelve acres of Cabernet Sauvignon on the lower acreage, three and one-half acres of Merlot, and nine acres of Cabernet Sauvignon on the upper La Questa vineyard.

Dr. Bill Mosby moved to the Santa Ynez Valley in 1958 and opened a dental practice in the nearby town of Lompoc. Throughout the 1960s and '70s both he and his wife Jeri planned on an agricultural retirement on their ranch and carefully watched as vineyards popped up throughout the county. In 1969 their first planting of sixty acres of row crops had ended as a flood swept the crop away. Undaunted by their first agricultural disaster, they decided to try viticulture. Bill approached his old college fraternity brother Bob Gallo, from the Gallo wine family, who sent them experimental cuttings. In 1971 the Mosbys planted test-plots of Merlot, Cabernet Sauvignon, Gewürztraminer, Chardonnay, Sangiovese, and Nebbiolo grapevines. The experimental plots prospered, and the Mosbys searched for additional land that could support premium wine grapes.[55]

In 1976 the Mosbys found a favorable vineyard location and purchased 206 acres of the Rancho La Vega (Spanish for "the meadow") south of Buellton and planted eighteen acres of Gewürztraminer and Chardonnay grapes. The ranch carried with it the mystique of past rancho days as the Mosbys learned that Dr. Roman de la Cuesta and his new wife Micaela had received the ranch in 1853 as a wedding present from her father Francisco Cota. The property still contained the original adobe homestead and its attached carriage house. Thus was born Vega Vineyards, a family venture to sell wine grapes to wineries.

Long Beach dentist Walter Babcock and his wife Mona purchased 100 acres of land near Lompoc in 1978 as an agricultural escape from city life. The Babcocks, like the Mosbys, sought the quiet agricultural life of Santa Ynez and planted lima beans the first year. Conversations with neighbors like the Bettencourts, Firestones, and Branders convinced them that grapes would be a more profitable and glamorous agricultural enterprise. So in 1979 the Babcocks planted thirty acres of vineyards and embarked on a new enterprise. Within a few years they expanded the vineyard to fifty acres.[56]

In 1979 Robert and Donna Marks purchased 110 acres in the Buellton area as a family retreat and hobby farm. Their Rancho Dos Mondos provided lumberyard owner Robert space to build a runway for his private airplane and an opportunity for the family to experiment as "sundown farmers."[57] Early agricultural endeavors with wheat, garbanzo beans, and African Daisy flower seeds proved to be far too labor intensive and unprofitable. In an attempt to diversify, in 1980 the family planted three acres of Chardonnay and family and friends spent their spare time planting, pruning, picking, and maintaining the vineyard. Eventually the vineyard grew to include eighteen acres, and they hired one part-time agricultural worker.

The surge of small vineyard planting continued into the early 1980s. In 1981 Paul Albrecht, Long Beach investor, planted his small, four-acre 11 Oaks Ranch vineyard at the intersection of Alamo Pintado and Baseline Avenue, two miles north of Solvang, adjacent to Carey and the La Questa Vineyard. Two years after this planting, Betty Williams planted her thirty-nine-acre Buttonwood Farm across from the 11 Oaks Ranch and Carey vineyards. By the end of the 1970s, Santa Barbara's Santa Ynez and Santa Maria Valleys contained a number of premium wine-grape vineyards, most of which shipped fruit to northern wineries.

The Wine Revolution Continues

Throughout the 1970s and into the mid-1980s, increases in premium wine consumption continued to encourage many wine-grape growers to court the dream of producing fine wines with their own fruit. This transition from grower to producer or grower/producer was motivated by the favorable market signs reflected in the 1973 Bank of America report, fair trade laws, a 1977 Morton Research Corporation evaluation of the wine market, and the 1977 move by the Santa Barbara County Board of Supervisors to allow wineries on Preserved Farmland.[58]

The 1973 Bank of America report documented that between 1967 and 1972, American premium wine consumption had increased by 65 percent. This spectacular five-year increase was due in part to a shift in the public attitude toward appreciating wine as a fashionable and pleasurable beverage, and of course reflected population growth and rising incomes that allowed for purchases of luxury items.[59] The 1970 B of A report had projected consumption of 400 million gallons by 1980 and the 1973 report upgraded this figure to 650 million gallons.[60] Californians drank more wine than the rest of the nation and wine consumption increased at a faster pace than beer and distilled spirits.[61] Clearly American tastes for dry table wines exceeded previous forecasts.[62] The B of A report credited part of this shift to a change in the age make-up of the nation's population as more people reached legal drinking age (18 to 21 depending on individual state laws).[63] Californians ranked third behind the District of Columbia and Nevada in per-capita consumption. Sales also increased as more restaurants and grocery stores sold wines and the fact that people were being educated in the art of drinking wine.[64]

In an attempt to meet consumer needs, wine brokers increased the amounts of wine imports. California's share of the U.S. wine market was just under 71 percent in 1972 and the report projected continued increases in foreign imports.[65] On the brighter side, devaluation of the dollar in February of 1973 made French, German, and Spanish wines more expensive but did little to affect the supply of cheaper Italian wines. Overall, plenty of room existed for expansion of wine sales from all California wine regions.[66]

"Grape Farmers Never Get Rich"

A Brooks Firestone, Santa Barbara County Winemaker

By the mid-1970s many Santa Barbara County growers began to lament that their premium wine grapes were blended into bulk northern wines. It had become painfully apparent that wineries, not grape growers, profited most from the expanding industry. Operating profit margins for wineries jumped over 40 percent, while grape costs declined and the cost of materials as a percent of sales decreased from 62 percent to less than 50 percent.[67] Santa Barbara growers also feared a settling out of the marketplace as Napa acreage and wine-grape tonnage nearly tripled.[68] The pressing question for the fledgling Santa Barbara grape growers was how to get the highest possible price for their grapes. Most began to realize that a local wine industry would help establish the region's reputation and in the long run secure the best prices for local fruit.

Santa Barbara growers also realized that a decade of statewide planting of wine-grape vineyards could lead to a bust in the market and diminish their marginal grape profits. The 1973 B of A report had conceded that grape growing was a risky proposition and the history of the wine-grape industry had always been one of boom and bust—under-planting and over-planting. The report also warned that sometime between 1978 and 1980 the supply of grapes for crushing would far exceed the amount required.[69] Yet, despite these warnings Santa Barbara County vineyard planting continued with Cottonwood Canyon Vineyards in 1973, Ballard in 1974, Brander in 1975, and Sweeney Canyon in 1979. Many of the original pioneers, like Lucas, Miller, Bettencourt, Ream, and Firestone, feared the possibility of market gluts and dreamed of permanent wine-grape contracts or better yet, their own wineries to ensure usage of their estate grapes.

Cost-efficient vertical integration of vineyards and wineries became a reality in the last part of the 1970s as marketing reports confirmed the success of bringing vineyards and wineries together. The 1977 Morton Research Corporation's wine market report showed that vertically integrated wineries were more competitive and maximized their profits by utilizing their own grapes and the report cited a general trend toward vertical integration within the industry.[70]

The 1978 Bank of America report also provided a positive outlook for the California wine industry and blamed the early 1970s recession for the 1973–1974 industry slowdown. On the bright side, the report confirmed the fact that wine consumption and grape prices continued to rise within their reported predictions of the 1970 and 1973 reports. The study further projected that the three-billion-dollar retail wine industry would continue to grow at a 6 percent rate well into the 1980s. Lastly, the report blamed the short downturn on nothing more than a "settling out" of inefficient wineries and grape growers. Those who failed to read the market signs correctly had made the "big mistake" of not realizing that they had to process, market, and sell all of their new products in an efficient manner.[71] Overall, the report called for a merging of grape growing and wine making to ensure profitability.

By the late 1970s many wineries responded by vertically integrating their vineyards with wineries. From large corporate vintibusinesses like Coca-Cola and Gallo, to family enterprises like Mondavi, wineries and vineyards state-wide began to integrate.[72] By the 1980s northern wineries had doubled winery acreage and the percentage of wine grapes grown by farmers had decreased from 70 percent to 35 percent. The bottom line for growers and winemakers was that the United States had undergone a strong growth in wine demand and that projected average growth rates of 8.6 percent per year far exceeded the state's estimated production capacity. Experts based these figures on the presumptions that the economy would remain stable, wine prices would not outstrip disposable personal income, and the projected consumer increase in wine usage would continue. Faced with this data the Santa Barbara County wine industry quickly moved into a new era of establishing wineries and gaining recognition for its vineyards and wines.

Within Santa Barbara County many grape growers, on a smaller scale, attempted to create stable wine-grape sales through production of their own wines and limited contract sales to other wineries. Grape farmers quickly realized that profits lie in winemaking and not grape growing and in response many Santa Barbara grape growers built smaller vertically integrated farms and wineries to take advantage of the 1930s idea of the family wine farm with sales directly to consumers. This Santa Barbara evolution toward vertical integration was the reverse of northern wineries, where established wineries purchased vineyards.

Notes

1. Thomas Pinney, *A History of Wine in America: From Prohibition to the Present* (Berkeley: University of California Press, 2005), 211.
2. Ibid., 239.
3. Ibid., 339.
4. California Grape Acreage Reports, 1965–1990.
5. This was the same project that produced the University of California, Davis, Heat Degree Day Index that established five types of viticultural growing regions in the state.
6. Stephan Bedford, oral history interview conducted by Victor W. Geraci, 24 February 1994, Santa Maria, California, tape recording, Special Collections, University of California, Santa Barbara, Santa Barbara, California.
7. Ibid.

8. Pacific Gas and Electric Company, "Finest Dry Wine Grapes: New Tepusquet Vineyard Blessed with Ideal Climate." Hereafter referred to as the PG&E Report.

9. Ibid.

10. Ibid.

11. Ed Holt and Harold Pfeiffer, oral history interview conducted by Richard P. Ryba, 21 April 1995, Santa Maria, California, tape recording, Special Collections, University of California, Santa Barbara, Santa Barbara, California.

12. Becky Sue Epstein, "Way with Wines," *Santa Barbara News-Press,* 1 December 1988, E-1, E-10.

13. Ed Holt and Harold Pfeiffer, oral history, and Stephan Bedford, oral history.

14. Ed Holt and Harold Pfeiffer, oral history.

15. Undated news clipping from the personal files of Dale Hampton. "Major Grape Venture Announced For Region," "1200-Acre Vineyard Slated for Tepusquet Mesa." *Santa Maria Times.*

16. Bob Miller, oral history interview conducted by Richard P. Ryba, 15 September 1994, Santa Barbara, California, tape recording, Special Collections, University of California, Santa Barbara, Santa Barbara, California.

17. Dale Hampton, oral history interview conducted by Victor W. Geraci and Susan Goldstein, 10 February 1994, Santa Maria, California, tape recording, Special Collections, University of California, Santa Barbara, Santa Barbara, California.

18. Bank of America Economics Department, *Outlook for the California Wine Industry* (San Francisco: Bank of America, 1970), passim.

19. Louis Lucas, oral history interview conducted by Richard P. Ryba, 29 June 1994, Santa Maria, California, tape recording, Special Collections, University of California, Santa Barbara, Santa Barbara, California.

20. Ibid. The vineyard was named for the Dalmatian Islands off Yugoslavia where the Lucas family came from and where family members had raised grapes for more than four centuries.

21. Ibid.

22. Dalmatian Vineyard Associates Performa, undated news clipping from the personal files of Dale Hampton.

23. Dale Hampton, oral history interview conducted by Victor W. Geraci and Susan Goldstein, 10 February 1994. Louis Lucas, oral history.

24. Ibid.

25. Louis Lucas, oral history.

26. Coastal Farming Company Limited Partnership Agreement, Dale Hampton personal files.

27. Tad Weber, "1986 Called A Vintage Year," *Santa Barbara News-Press,* 2 October 1986, B-1.

28. Bob and Jeanne Woods, oral history interview conducted by Richard P. Ryba, 12 April 1995, Santa Maria, California, tape recording, Special Collections, University of California, Santa Barbara, Santa Barbara, California.

29. Ibid.; "Receiver Appointed to Preserve Assets of S.M. Vineyards," *Santa Barbara News-Press,* 10 April 1975; "Prudential Insurance Sells Sierra Madre Vineyard," *Los Padres Sun* (Santa Ynez, California), 17 August 1988.

30. Jeff Wilkes, oral history interview conducted by Susan Goldstein, 3 March 1994, Santa Maria, California, tape recording, Special Collections, University of California, Santa Barbara, Santa Barbara, California.

31. Bob Miller, oral history.

32. Ibid.

33. Ibid.

34. Jeff Wilkes, oral history.

35. Bob Miller, oral history.

36. Chris Hodenfield, "Tramping out the Vintage: In Los Alamos Valley, Harvesting Grapes Is Filled with Simple Pleasures and Financial Perils," *Lost Angeles Times*, 8 December 1985.

37. Barry Johnson, oral history interview conducted by Susan Goldstein, 28 January 1994, Santa Ynez, California, tape recording, Special Collections, University of California, Santa Barbara, Santa Barbara, California.

38. Cork Millner, *Vintage Valley: The Wineries of Santa Barbara County* (Santa Barbara, CA: McNally and Loftin, 1983), 95.

39. Boyd Bettencourt, oral history interview conducted by Beverly Schwartzberg, 2 February 1994, Santa Ynez, California, tape recording, Special Collections, University of California, Santa Barbara, Santa Barbara, California; Pacific Gas and Electric, "Finest Dry Wine Grapes: New Tepusquet Vineyard Blessed with Ideal Climate." Mailed out as a flyer to PG&E Customers.

40. Carol Caldwell-Ewart, "Sanford Winery: Managing Costs Profitably," *Pacific Wines and Vines*, November/December 1993, 40; Richard Paul Hinkle, "Searching for the Holy Grail," *Wines and Vines*, July 1993.

41. Richard Sanford, oral history interview conducted by Victor W. Geraci and Otis L. Graham Jr., 7 March 1995, tape recording, Santa Barbara, California, Special Collections, University of California, Santa Barbara, Santa Barbara, California; Richard Paul Hinkle, "Searching for the Holy Grail," *Wines and Vines*, July 1993; "Trampling on the Vineyard," *Los Angeles Times*, 29 November 1991, H-21.

42. Dean Brown, oral history interview conducted by Victor W. Geraci and Jeff Maiken (Zaca Mesa), 25 October 1995, Santa Ynez, California, tape recording, Special Collections, University of California, Santa Barbara, Santa Barbara, California.

43. A. Brooks Firestone, oral history interview conducted by Richard P. Ryba, 18 February 1995, Santa Ynez, California, tape recording, Special Collections, University of California, Santa Barbara, Santa Barbara, California.

44. T. Hayer, oral history interview conducted by Richard P. Ryba, 29 June 1994, Santa Ynez, California, tape recording, Special Collections, University of California, Santa Barbara, Santa Barbara, California.

45. Dan Berger, "Firestone's Family Values," *Los Angeles Times*, 20 January 1994.

46. Ibid.

47. Bob Wiedrich, "Firestone's Tire-to-Vine Trek Not So Implausible," *Chicago Tribune*, 12 March 1990, Section 4, Business.

48. Hayley Firestone Jessup, oral history interview conducted by Victor W. Geraci, 3 February 1994, Santa Ynez, California, tape recording, Special Collections, University of California, Santa Barbara, Santa Barbara, California; Catherine Boulton Firestone (Kate), oral history interview conducted by Victor W. Geraci, 3 February 1994, Santa Ynez, California, tape recording, Special Collections, University of California, Santa Barbara, Santa Barbara, California.

49. Millner, *Vintage Valley*, 109–14.

50. Jeff Maiken and Sheryl Duggan, oral history interview conducted by Sarah Case and Victor W. Geraci, 27 January 1994, Santa Ynez, California, tape recording, Special Collections, University of California, Santa Barbara, Santa Barbara, California.

51. Wesley Mann, "Vintner's Grape Plans Back on Track," *Santa Barbara News-Press,* 7 May 1982, B-10; Kathleen Sharp, "A Heady Time for Vintners," *Santa Barbara News-Press,* 27 September 1987, E-1, E-2, E-3.

52. Mann, "Vintner's Grape Plans Back on Track," B-10, B-11.

53. Bob and Jeanne Woods, oral history.

54. Ibid.

55. Geraldine Mosby, oral history interview conducted by Susan Goldstein, 28 January 1994, Santa

Ynez, California, tape recording, Special Collections University of California, Santa Barbara, Santa Barbara, California.

56. Bryan Babcock, oral history interview conducted by Susan Goldstein, 2 February 1994, Santa Ynez, California, tape recording, Special Collections, University of California, Santa Barbara, Santa Barbara, California; Robert Lawrence Balzer, "Young but Mature: Babcock Wines Bear out the Promise They Showed in '87," *Los Angeles Times Magazine*, 5 March 1989, 36.

57. Donna Marks, oral history interview conducted by Beverly Schwartzberg, 8 March 1994, Santa Ynez, California, tape recording, Special Collections, University of California, Santa Barbara, Santa Barbara, California.

58. Mary Anne La Pointe, "County Grape-Growing Operations Now a Source of Premium Wines," *Santa Barbara News-Press,* 23 May 1977, B-1, B-2; "Winery Operations Allowed in Farmland Preserve Areas," *Santa Barbara News-Press,* 28 June 1977, B-1; Frank Braconi, Morton Research Corporation, *The U.S. Wine Market,* passim.

59. Frank Braconi, Morton Research Corporation, *The U.S. Wine Market: An Economic Marketing and Financial Investigation* (A Morton Report, Merrick, New York, April 1977), passim; Kenneth R. Farrell, "The California Wine Industry: Trends and Prospects," testimony presented at a public hearing to consider amendment of the state of California Marketing Order for Wine, San Francisco, California, March 2, 1966.

60. Farrell, "California Wine Industry," 3.

61. Jerry Belcher, "Wine Upstaging Other Libations," *Los Angeles Times*, 3 June 1980.

62. Frank Braconi, Morton Research Corporation, *The U.S. Wine Market: An Economic Marketing and Financial Investigation*, 37–57.

63. Farrell, "California Wine Industry," 5-6. Source: U.S. Department of Commerce, Bureau of the Census; Frank Braconi, Morton Research Corporation, *The U.S. Wine Market: An Economic Marketing and Financial Investigation*, 4–23.

64. Ibid.

65. Ibid, 8–10; Frank Braconi, Morton Research Corporation, *The U.S. Wine Market: An Economic Marketing and Financial Investigation*, 37–57.

66. Ibid, 11.

67. Braconi, Morton Research Corporation, *The U.S. Wine Market*, 71.

68. Charles Sullivan, *Napa Wine: A History from Mission Days to Present* (San Francisco: Wine Appreciation Guild, 1994), 399.

69. Ibid., 20.

70. Braconi, Morton Research Corporation, *The U.S. Wine Market*, 71.

71. Carl Cannon, "A Favorable Wine Projection Should Not Cloud the Heads of Investors," *Los Angeles Times*, 14 May 1978, 7:3; "Enthusiasm Chills for U.S. Wines," *Los Angeles Times*, 22 May 1984.

72. Carl Cannon, "Coke Unveils Wine Plan and It's a Corker," *Los Angeles Times*, 19 November 1978, 6:1.

Chapter Six

Santa Barbara Gains Recognition

As we have seen, wine grapes and wine came to Santa Barbara County with the missions and flourished until Prohibition devastated the commercial wine trade. Upon repeal the industry slowly reappeared as local pioneers first planted vineyards in the 1960s and 1970s and subsequently developed two forms of wineries that by the 1980s had developed premium vineyards and a regional wine industry. But the fledgling local wine industry confronted a disorderly market that was controlled by boom-and-bust cycles, shifts in consumer tastes, and both domestic and foreign trade struggles. Overcoming these problems required continuous efforts stretching from technology, to marketing, to vertical integration, political lobbying, consumer education, and new scientific approaches to pests and diseases.

Most Santa Barbara vintners realized that successful sales required branding techniques to elevate their name and label recognition. Jim Fiolek, vice president of marketing for Zaca Mesa winery, and others, believed that both medals and publications meant a boost in sales for small wineries.[1] Local wine entrepreneurs remembered how the 1976 Paris competition boosted California wine sales and sought this type of prestige and profits for the county. Building this recognition became an arduous and multifaceted campaign.

Bay Area winemakers had achieved world recognition by designing a California wine style by blending science and traditional handcrafted techniques to produce reasonably priced, high-quality, and consistent-tasting wines. In the 1980s Santa Barbara wineries built on these same foundations by stepping up their marketing game and adapting agribusiness techniques. To that end, local industry members marshaled in the establishment of three new American Viticultural Areas (AVAs), demonstrated the quality of their wines, marketed the region through their trade organization, the Santa Barbara County Vintners Association, and developed high-profile labels that were built on both winery and winemaker reputations. Winemakers developed a sense of place by branding their region, and consumers learned to recognize Santa Barbara premium vintages on shelves in grocery stores and wine shops.

SANTA BARBARA APPELLATIONS

For Santa Barbara grape growers and newly established wineries, a first step in recognition came with the designation of three AVAs. In the early 1970s most American wine consumers divided national wines into two simple categories—corked and capped. This changed as California vintners helped create new wine-savvy consumers who by the 1980s wanted to know more about their favorite wines. Most of all they wanted to know whether a bottle of varietal designated wine was worth the ever-increasing price tag. Industry members feared that premium wines could become "indistinguishable, at face value, from similar products" and become a commodity that consumers purchased based on price alone.[2] Regions like Santa Barbara, with a burgeoning reputation for artisan wineries and premium wines, feared their wines would be lumped with cheaper, lower-quality commercial products. They believed that appellation designations would encourage upscale, terroir-based wine drinkers to choose their products.

In the United States the Bureau of Alcohol, Tobacco, Firearms, and Explosives (BATF—today referred to as ATF) became the body that designated viticultural appellations. The ATF webpage describes their mission as follows:

> ATF is a law enforcement agency in the United States' Department of Justice that protects our communities from violent criminals, criminal organizations, the illegal use and trafficking of firearms, the illegal use and storage of explosives, acts of arson and bombings, acts of terrorism, and the illegal diversion of alcohol and tobacco products. We partner with communities, industries, law enforcement, and public safety agencies to safeguard the public we serve through information sharing, training, research, and use of technology.[3]

This is very different from the European system whereby independent government agencies determine regional labels to assist consumers in the selection of wines. It seems somewhat strange that in America the body that designates appellations is also the body that enforces regulations on the industry. Most ATF officials have little knowledge of what Rick Theis, Sonoma County Grape Growers Association, considered to be the fact that the "quality of the wine is determined in the vineyard, not in the location of the winery. Wineries and brands come and go but the land remains unchanged."[4] Thus, it became a marketing task of local wineries, grape growers, and trade associations to define, sometimes after the fact, the characteristics of AVAs. Santa Barbara County received three early designations and then spent decades building their reputation.

The ATF designated Santa Barbara's first region on 5 August 1981 when the agency recognized the petition of Newhall Land and Farming Company of Valencia to name the Santa Maria Valley an AVA. The petitioners argued that the funnel-shaped valley with well-drained fertile soil along the Santa Maria River had a sixty-year agricultural history and that grapes had been grown there since the 1970s. Over 90 percent of the grape growers had signed the petition and the agency agreed that the area had a unique viticultural and agricultural identity. After listening to nine supportive witnesses, the commissioners wrote in the Federal Register that "the Bureau of Alcohol, Tobacco and Firearms believes the establishment of Santa Maria as a viticultural area and its subsequent use as an appellation of origin on wine labels and in wine advertisements will help consumers better identify the wines from this area."[5] Santa Barbara had started a three-decade quest to brand their terroir as consisting of premium grapes and wine.

The ruling defined the AVA as being based on the Santa Maria River Valley with northern boundaries formed by the plummeting slopes of the San Rafael Mountains at a point near where Highway 166 intersected the section line just southwest of Chimney Canyon and the western boundary as being Highway 101. Agency officials agreed that the area encompassed 7,500 acres of vineyards and that growers had planted on the region's flat valley floors and sloping hillsides at elevations varying from 300 to 800 feet. Growers and winemakers further defined the locale as a cool Region I, based on the UC Davis scale of heat summation, with well-drained sandy loam to clay loam soils capable of nurturing Chardonnay, Pinot Noir, Merlot, Sauvignon Blanc, Cabernet Sauvignon, and Johannisberg Riesling grapes.[6]

Two years later, on April 15, 1983, the ATF in a unanimous decision recognized the Santa Ynez Valley as Santa Barbara County's second AVA, based on the petition initiated by the Firestone Vineyard in Los Olivos. The designation covered a 285-square-mile area and included 1,200 acres of vineyards. Regulators also recognized the AVA's historical grape-growing tradition that had been started in the early 1800s by priests at the Mission Santa Ines. Supporting documents described its geography as the area that surrounded the Santa Ynez River with the northern boundary as the Purisima Hills that separated the valley from the Los Alamos Valley. The Santa Ynez Mountains became the southern boundary that separated the valley from the South Coast and Lake Cachuma and the Los Padres National Forest formed the eastern boundary. The agency defined the western boundary as the place where the Santa Ynez Valley narrows and is separated from the Lompoc Valley by the Santa Rita Hills. Based on the Winkler and Amerine viticultural heat summation scale, regulators identified the AVA as a cool Region I to II growing area with a beneficial cooling maritime influence.[7]

On October 24, 1985 the Federal Commission recognized the petition by Taylor California Cellars in Gonzales, California, to create the Central Coast Viticultural Area as the third AVA to influence the region. The new viticultural boundaries swept from the Pacific Ocean on the west to the coastal mountain ranges on the east. The huge generic AVA included over one million acres with 51,209 acres of grapes and included vineyards in Monterey, Santa Cruz, Alameda, San Benito, San Luis Obispo, and Santa Barbara Counties. Designed as a catch-all AVA, the region provided wine-grape status for large commercial wineries like Taylor California, Wente Brothers, Mirassou, and Paul Mason.[8]

Santa Barbara County had achieved the first step toward wine recognition and earned the right to use geographic names on wine labels. Consumers could now choose to drink Central Coast, Santa Ynez, and Santa Maria wines.

SANTA BARBARA COUNTY VINTNERS ASSOCIATION

After observing Napa and Sonoma marketing techniques, Santa Barbara County vintners moved to promote and brand their region by modeling the marketing techniques of their northern counterparts. Local growers and winemakers realized that in order to survive in the wine industry they needed to organize and promote their region and they had encouraging words from Robert D. Reynolds, executive director of the Wine Growers of California. He predicted that Santa Barbara County vineyards would rank "very near the top."[9] Prompts like this convinced grape growers and wineries to adapt a Napa-like business strategy to secure their place in the larger California, United States, and world wine markets.

Initially, many of the local wineries participated in the California Central Coast Wine Growers Association that lumped Santa Ynez and Santa Maria with Paso Robles; but many wanted more-specific geographic recognition. In 1981 seventeen local growers and wineries, seeking an opportunity to sharpen their region's image, formed the Santa Ynez Valley Viticultural Association (SYVVA). Bob Lindquest, Qupé winemaker, became the first president and in 1983 Deborah Kenley Brown, Byron, organized their first vintner's festival at the Santa Inez Mission.[10]

No sooner had the alliance (SYVVA) come together than the members realized that the association excluded most of the region's Santa Maria vineyard land. This prompted a 1983 move by Rick Longoria, Richard Sanford, and fifteen other Santa Barbara County winemakers, wineries, and growers to expand the Santa Ynez Vintners Association into what would become the Santa Barbara County Vintners Association (SBCVA).[11] Initially funded with a 50-50 matching grant of $25,000 from the statewide Wine Commission members drew up an organizational mission statement "to support and promote Santa Barbara County as a premium wine producing and wine-grape growing region and to enhance the position of Santa Barbara County wines in the world marketplace."[12] Further funding for the association came from dues paid by members according to case production or numbers of acres in production and was supplemented with profits from vintner's festivals. To increase exposure the group started bringing in associate members to be more inclusive with the general tourist and service industry sectors.

Once established, the association sponsored promotional events to build regional recognition. Members believed that "wine tourism is the ultimate brand differentiator" and an important means for the region's small artisan wineries to sell directly to consumers.[13] In 1985, with mentoring from the Sonoma County Vintner's Association, SBCVA established the tradition of the yearly vintner's festival that over the years brought thousands of people to the local wine country for food from top restaurants, educational exhibits, enjoyment of popular musical entertainment, and locally grown foods. In the meantime the organization produced color brochure maps for tourists and sponsored wine tasting events in Washington, D.C., Los Angeles, and San Diego.

The initial programs proved to be successful and prompted members to seek an expanded role for the group. In 1987 the SBCVA board of directors under President Jim Fiolek hired Pam Maines Ostendorf, UCSB coordinator for the Industrial Affiliation Program in Engineering, as its first full-time executive director. Ostendorf moved into action and between 1987 and 1990 the SBCVA used its resources to produce posters, brochures, maps, sponsor seminars, and organized promotional and advocacy events aimed at consumers, journalists, industry members, community organizations, and governmental agencies. She continually promoted the idea "that we are the ideal wine country for Southern California and the fact that it's not like Highway 29 [Napa] on a Saturday."[14]

During the 1990s the SBCVA stepped up marketing and advertising campaigns. They hired a pamphlet distribution company to distribute their brochures in restaurants, hotels, gas stations, visitor centers, train stations, airports, and travel and car rental agencies. Ostendorf's office also established a series of press releases and press kits designed to draw California newspapers, filmmakers, and wine writers to the region. Ongoing projects included a biannual trade wine-tasting event and a server seminar series that educated hundreds of local restaurant and hotel servers, owners, managers, and chefs about Santa Barbara wines. Ostendorph made sure to keep the industry in the minds of local leaders with periodic community/governmental luncheons where she informed them of the contributions the industry made to the local economy. Advocacy roles for the association also included membership in professional wine organizations, government legislative and regulatory watches, and the building of a professional library to keep members apprised on new industry developments. The SBCVA also published a history of the Santa Barbara County Wine Industry in conjunction with the UCSB Public History Program.[15]

By 1999 the association grew to nearly one hundred members (wineries, growers, vineyard managers) and encouraged wineries within their ranks to promote themselves by organizing one-day, tourist-friendly wine trips based loosely on the region's two AVAs—Foxen Trail (Santa Maria AVA) and Santa Ynez Triangle (Santa Ynez AVA). The Foxen Trail included a one-day (twenty-mile) trip along Foxen Canyon Road to the Andrew Murray Vineyards, Cottonwood Canyon Vineyard and Winery, Foxen Vineyard, Bedford Thompson Winery, Fess Parker Winery, Rancho Sisquoc, Byron Winery, Firestone Vineyard, and Zaca Mesa Winery. The Santa Ynez Valley Triangle took visitors on a circuitous triangular route that brought together Gainey, Sunstone, Santa Ynez, Buttonwood, Curtis, Los Olivos, and Brander wineries. Santa Barbara County now had a successful trade organization.

QUALITY WINES BRING LABEL RECOGNITION

Trade association activities would be of little use without production of high-quality wine grapes and wine. By the early 1970s pioneers like Hampton feared that as over 310 northern wineries imported 92 percent of the county's grapes that chances for local recognition would be blended into oblivion.[16] Winemaker associations, government regulations, and advertising provided some relief for the problem, but real success came from the award-winning wines produced and marketed by the county's then twenty-two wineries.

Throughout history wine regions have risen and fallen based on their ability to produce quality wines and adapt to the marketplace. As a result, wine-grape growers and vintners learned to become responsive to the market signs of supply and demand, methods of production, labor, research and development, and consumer preferences. A wide range of wineries, like most industrial producers, offered varied levels of product quality so as to appeal to a wide range of consumers and their varied pocketbooks. Santa Barbara's small-scale premium wineries shunned the Gallo dominated bulk wine market and aimed for the middle and high-end product lines that afforded them the greatest profits. Economic stability for the local industry would, in the long haul, be dependent upon the ability of wineries to consistently produce and market quality, competitively priced premium wines.

Santa Barbara County rapidly developed a reputation for high-quality premium wines as local vintners, large and small, garnered awards. Larger commercial producers like Firestone and Zaca Mesa broke into national and international markets, and smaller local wineries gained acceptance in regional markets closer to home. Slowly, as their premium wines reached retail outlets, satisfied consumers began to recognize local labels. Many local wineries also attempted to break into the super-premium market where wine collectors pursued handcrafted wines from their favorite wineries and winemakers. In the end, wine writers recognized the region and oenophiles developed loyalties to their favorite wines and winemakers.

Vintners strengthened their brand recognition in the late 1970s and early 1980s by winning awards for their premium wines. Firestone Winery led the charge when a July of 1978 *New York Times* article featured the winery in its Sunday magazine. A few months later Anthony Austin, Firestone winemaker, won a double gold medal in London for the winery's Chardonnay. In 1978, 1981, and 1982, Zaca Mesa won state awards for every varietal that it produced, and in 1983 its Central Coast Cabernet was named one of the best red wines at the International Wine Center in New York.

Consumers, overwhelmed by shelves burgeoning with choices, had learned to look to wine writers for suggestions on new and exciting wines, wine regions, and up-and-coming winemakers. These writers, in their quest for wines to intrigue their readers, spread the word of a region's potential. In the late 1970s *New York Times* wine writer Frank J. Prial visited Santa Barbara and proclaimed that Firestone, Zaca Mesa, and Sanford and Benedict were wineries to watch in the future.[17] Wine travel guides also began to discuss and praise Santa Barbara wines and wine grapes. *Sunset's* 1970 edition of Bob Thompson's, *Guide to California Wine Country* did not mention Santa Barbara

County. But the 1977 edition noted, "Farther south, in Santa Barbara County, 6,000 acres of vines have been planted since 1971 and the Firestone family operates a pioneering winery." The 1979 *Sunset* version mentioned, "From the viewpoint of visitors . . . there has been a tremendous revolution in the state's wineries since 1968." Seven Santa Barbara County wineries were mentioned in the new edition.[18] Another big literary boost for the region came in 1984 when wine writers Doris Muscatine, Maynard Amerine, and Bob Thompson edited a book about California wine and Santa Barbara County received numerous mentions and accolades.[19]

By the early 1980s Santa Barbara wines had won recognition worldwide and wineries like Firestone, Zaca Mesa, and Santa Ynez Winery had garnered medals for their Pinot Noirs, Chardonnays, and Rieslings.[20] In 1981 Sanford Winery and Zaca Mesa had wines listed as "recommended" in *Wine Spectator* magazine where Zaca Mesa was a regular advertiser.[21] So extensive was Firestone's international recognition that the winery was honored by a visit of England's Masters of Wine.[22] In the latter half of the 1980s, it was not unusual to hear that local vintners took a double gold at the International Wine Competition in Toronto, international medals at the Quantas Cup Wine Competition in Australia, or four gold medals at the San Diego National Wine competition where they represented 3 percent of the wines entered and won 48 percent of the medals.[23] However, by the mid-'80s many worried that too many competitions and awards confused consumers in what Frank Prial referred to as shelf after shelf of wines "beribboned like so many generals."[24]

Additional accolades for the region came when President Ronald Reagan served local wines in the White House and established his western White House on a ridge overlooking both the Santa Ynez Valley and the South Coast. Brooks Firestone said that his business increased tenfold after the president served his wines and predicted that the region would now break into the lucrative Washington, D.C., market.[25] Surgeon James Carey of Carey Vineyards, a harsh critic of Reagan policies, realized the possibility of presidential recognition and put his politics aside when he sent a case of his estate bottled Adobe Canyon Chardonnay to the president.[26] Over the next few years guests and diplomats for Republican and Democratic presidents drank wines from Firestone, Zaca Mesa, Sanford, and Gainey, to name a few.

Wine writers now mentioned the region on a regular basis and *New West Magazine* nicknamed the region a "piece of paradise."[27] In 1987 Anthony Dias Blue, wine editor for *Bon Appétit* magazine, named Santa Barbara County "one of the better wine regions in the country."[28] Wine writer Matt Kramer described Santa Maria Chardonnay as "lush, rich, intense and succulent," "not easily bullied by breezes, heat or sunshine," "bottled sunbeams."[29] By the 1990s *Wine Spectator* described the ruggedly beautiful South Central Coast as "an adventure for wine drinkers and tourists alike," and deserving of the title of California's "Other Coast."[30]

NAME RECOGNITION FOR INDEPENDENT WINEMAKERS

Those who enjoy the luxury of specialty artisan wines tend to form followings, much like a music groupie, for the artist/winemaker that they patronize. An elite few collect expensive wines and speak a special jargon as they drop the name of their favorite wine artists and they relish the opportunity to rub elbows with winemakers who become celebrities. Most of them realized that every wine region making upscale wines needed a certain amount of this snobbish recognition to build a regional reputation.

Many Santa Barbara winemakers readily took up the artisan wine-mantle and delivered their artist message to a growing number of wine enthusiasts. These self-proclaimed wine geniuses clearly understood that Americans embrace field-specific superheroes with their hearts and support their endeavors with an open pocketbook. In many ways this is not dissimilar to the cliques and patronage systems that historically supported all artists. In the 1960s winery owners Robert Mondavi, Joe Heitz, Louis Martini, Karl Wente, and Dolph Heck became the superstars. By the 1980s a more savvy media realized that the industry was more than just owners and winemakers became the new superstars.[31]

Santa Barbara County's 1970s through 1990 regional wine recognition also included a group of talented artisans whose names became buzzwords for regional, state, national, and international upscale wine consumers. As we have seen, customers quickly learned to recognize wines from winemakers like Sanford and LaFond. But elite status also came to a number of independent winemakers who produced wines without physical wineries or vineyards. These winemakers conducted business through post office boxes and borrowed, leased, rented, and bartered facilities and equipment. Their trademarks were their high-priced, small-production, usually under five thousand cases, of premium, handcrafted wines that were marketed on the reputation of their personas.

These independent winemakers developed techniques to stay competitive with the larger commercial competitors. They overcame the millions of dollars in cost for technology and equipment by loosely modeling themselves after *négociant* winemakers in the industry's European past that had created what wine buffs referred to as "wineries without walls."[32] As a group they shunned commercial formulaic production techniques and emphasized the role of the winemaker as the one who oversees and controls all aspects of the winemaking process. They were a generation of what wine writer Dennis Schaefer referred to as a new breed of "active" winemakers. Many ignored the old vintner's adage claiming, "nature makes the wines" and portrayed winemakers as more than "just the caretaker" and mention of their wines became common occurrences in *Wine Enthusiast* and *Wine Spectator* magazines.[33] Santa Barbara's entrants in this independent category included the labels of Chris Whitcraft, Jim Clendenen, Bob Lindquist, Rick Longoria, Lane Tanner, and John Kerr, to name a few.[34]

Chris Whitcraft, native Long Island resident and pre-law, music, and philosophy graduate of California State University Fullerton, converted his wine expertise as a manager for Mayfare Wine and Spirits in Santa Barbara and radio wine show host to that of Pinot Noir winemaker. His local recognition for wine expertise started in 1978 when he helped establish the Santa Barbara Wine Festival and began his radio wine talk show. The wine bug bit him between 1978 and 1985. He made wine under the bond at Santa Barbara Winery and then in 1988 and 1989 moved to Brander's bonded facility. By 1990 his passion led him to the Miller Brothers' Central Coast Wine Warehouse and Bien Nacido Vineyard.[35]

Jim Clendenen drew acclaim for his purist Burgundian winemaking approach. After his 1980 graduation from the Law and Society program at UCSB, he accepted the assistant winemaker position at Zaca Mesa winery. He resigned the position in 1981 to work in Australia and Burgundy and the next year returned to Santa Barbara, where he joined Adam Tolmach, former Zaca Mesa enologist, and produced *Au Bon Climat* (French for "the good climate") traditional Burgundian Pinot Noir and Chardonnay wines. He started with a press and then leased equipment from Santa Monica lawyer Sam Hale's Los Alamos Vineyards.[36] By 1982 he produced 1,600 cases annually of Chardonnay and Pinot Noir.

The elite wine community took notice of Clendenen's Burgundian-style wines. In order to produce his "signature wines" he mimicked the Burgundian winemakers' philosophy and attitude toward life and took on their demeanor and behavior. Clendenen felt no need to own vineyards because he saw grapes as "merely the raw materials, the blank canvas that we imprint or stylize."[37] Therefore he opted to purchase grapes from selected vineyards with low yield production and emulated the Burgundian techniques of barrel fermentation, malolactic fermentation, and extended cellaring.[38]

Robert Lindquist gained his name recognition from his philosophy of "all the modern technology that is appropriate" within the bounds of traditional production techniques.[39] He established the *Qupé* label and described his style of wine making as being produced in "a modern Stone Age Winery." Lindquist entered the industry in 1979 as a twenty-two-year-old college social science graduate when he took a job as the manager of John Ream's, son of Zaca Mesa's Marshall Ream, wine shop in Los Olivos. After nine months at the shop, he was fired but landed on his feet as John's father hired him to be Zaca's first tour guide.[40] Over the next five years, he trained under winemakers like Ken Brown, Jim Clendenen, and Adam Tolmac.

Rick Longoria moonlighted his Longoria label while acting as the wine-maker for the Gainey Vineyard. The Longoria style based itself on the use of intensely flavored wine grapes to produce naturally flavored, fruit-tasting wines in the best California style. He began his career in the spring of 1974, one year after graduating from UC Berkeley with a degree in sociology. As a student at Berkeley he became familiar with regional Sonoma Valley wines while working at Buena Vista Winery, where he met and mentored under André Tchelistcheff. Two years later Longoria took the job of cellar master with Chappellet vine-yards in Napa. It was during this time that he realized that what appealed to him was the "diversity of the job," because "during the making of the wine, you become a chemist and craftsman combined."[41]

Longoria realized that he missed Santa Barbara County—he was born and raised in Lompoc—and in 1979 he took a job as winemaker at the new J. Carey Winery and with financial help from his father slowly established his private Longoria label. Then in 1985 Longoria, as head of a young family, sought the job security of an established winery and he accepted the winemaker position at Gainey Vineyard. Over the next decade he became a regional leader and mentor as he actively helped found the SBCVA, served as Gainey winemaker, maintained his personal label, and consulted for numerous small local win-eries. In 1996 he reached a new level of recognition when *Playboy* magazine ran a photograph of his Cuvee Blues blend of Cabernet Franc and Merlot and commented that it had the "kind of energy you feel when B.B. King is cooking with Lucille or when Buddy Guy is wailing on his ax."[42] Because of the article he received calls from as far away as Connecticut asking for a bottle of this wine. Longoria resigned from Gainey in 1997 and opened a new winery with partner Iris Rideau next to Buttonwood Farm and Foley Winery (previous Curtis Winery) on Alamo Pintado Road in Santa Ynez.

Lane Tanner proved that women could also achieve status as an independent winemaker. Tanner specialized in Pinot Noir and claimed to be "a real old traditionalist."[43] She believed that technology was good up to a point and that "winemaking is a simple process that machines can only refine so much."[44] She did everything herself and believed that her Pinot Noir was the most feminine, finicky, fickle, and incredibly responsive of all grapes.[45] In her words "grapes want to become wine" and she accepted the responsibility of being "the keeper of the grapes."[46]

John Kerr followed a circuitous route to becoming a winemaker. Upon returning from Vietnam military service in 1971, Kerr supported his college studies with a tasting room job at the Brookside Winery in Ventura.[47] Then in 1980 he followed his wife's archaeological career to Monterey and took jobs with Chalone Vineyard, Jekel Winery, and Ventana Vineyards. During this time he developed a winemaking philosophy that was a blend of traditional Burgundian styles, new university knowledge, and gut feelings.

Kerr reestablished his Santa Barbara wine career when his wife accepted a permanent archaeological position with the Forest Service in Santa Barbara County. He landed a consultant job with the newly established Babcock Winery and worked at Houtz and Brander wineries. From 1984 to 1995, while serving as assistant winemaker at Byron Vineyards and Winery and using the Byron bond, he produced wines under his J. Kerr label. Kerr specialized in Chardonnay and Syrah wines, and by 1993 his production grew to 1,300 cases and his Chardonnays took numerous awards in Orange County. After a long and arduous startup struggle, Kerr received recognition in 1994 when his 1991 J. Kerr Chardonnay took first place (out of 390 entries) in the American Wine Competition with a score of 98 and a Platinum Medal.[48] Like Longoria he eventually settled for the prestige and security of a corporate winery and accepted the title of winemaker for the Carey Winery in 1996.

Notes

1. Ken Sternberg, "Gold Medals Lead to Golden Sales: Winning Small Wineries Get a Boost," *Wine Business Monthly*, January 1999, 23–28.
2. Abby Sawyer and Jim Hammett, "American Appellations Earn Distinction as a Marketing Tool: Growers and Vintners Weigh Merits of Tying Appellation to Varietal," *Wine Business Monthly*, June 1998, 1, 13–19.
3. Bureau of Alcohol, Tobacco, Firearms, and Explosives (ATF) website, https://www.atf.gov

4. Abby Sawyer and Jim Hammett, "American Appellation…" 19.

5. Federal Register, 27 CFR Part 9, "Santa Maria Valley Viticultural Area," T.D. ATF-89; Ref: Notice No. 360, 5 August 1981: Federal Register 46 FR 39811, 5 August 1981.

6. Department of the Treasury, Bureau of Alcohol, Tobacco, and Firearms, Rules and Regulations, "Santa Maria Viticultural Area," 46:150 (5 August 1981): 39811–39812.

7. Department of the Treasury, Bureau of Alcohol, Tobacco, and Firearms, Rules and Regulations, "Santa Ynez Valley Viticultural Area," 48:74 (15 April 1983): 16250–16251; M. A. Amerine and A. J. Winkler, *Grape Varieties for Wine Production*, pamphlet number 154, Division of Agricultural Sciences, University of California (March 1963).

8. "Central Coast Viticultural Area," Federal Register 27 CFR Part 9, 50 FR 43128, 24 October 1985.

9. Bob Barber, "Winegrowers' Group Director Optimistic on County Grapes," *Santa Barbara News-Press*, 11 September 1986, D-7.

10. Pam Maines Ostendorf, oral history interview conducted by Victor W. Geraci, Oral History Center, The Bancroft Library, University of California, Berkeley, 2007.

11. Tad Weber, "Growers, Wine Makers May Team Up," *Santa Barbara News-Press*, 13 March 1987.

12. "Area Wines to Be Judged Saturday in Santa Maria," *Santa Barbara News-Press*, 15 July 1981, C-4; "County Wineries Healthy," *Santa Barbara News-Press*, 15 September 1985, A-9; Jenny Perry, "Sipping in the Summer Sun: Wine Festival Benefit," *Santa Barbara News-Press*, 26 August, 1986; Jenny Perry, "Wine Harvest Festivals Mean Merrymaking," *Santa Barbara News-Press*, 17 September 1986; Santa Barbara County Vintners Association, "SBCVA Mission and Policies" from membership form dated May 1993.

13. Laura Madonna, "Making the Consumer Connection: The Importance of Tourism to the Wine Business," *Wine Business Monthly*, May 1999, 1, 11–14.

14. Pam Maines Ostendorf, oral history.

15. Otis L. Graham Jr., Sarah Harper Case, Victor W. Geraci, Susan Goldstein, Richard P. Ryba, and Berverly J. Schwartzberg, *Aged in Oak: The Story of the Santa Barbara County Wine Industry* (Santa Barbara, CA: Cachuma Press, 1998).

16. Joe Shoulak, "A Heady Time for Vintners," *Santa Barbara News-Press*, 27 September 1987, E-1, E-2.

17. Frank J. Prial, "A Winery in the Making," *New York Times*, 23 July 1978, 36, 44.

18. Bob Thompson, *California Wine Country* (Menlo Park, CA: Lane Books, 1969; 1977; 1979), passim.

19. Doris Muscatine, Maynard A. Amerine, and Bob Thompson, eds., *The University of California/ Sotheby Book of California Wine* (Berkeley, CA: University of California Press/Sotheby Publication, 1984), passim.

20. Malcolm R. Hebert, "The Pick of the Vines," *Los Angeles Times*, 14 October 1979; "Pinot Noir: Put to a Rigorous Test," *Los Angeles Times*, 5 October 1980; "Area Wines to Be Judged Saturday in Santa Maria," *Santa Barbara News-Press*, 15 July 1981; County Wineries Are Big Winners," *Santa Barbara News-Press*, 20 July 1981; Harvey Steiman, "Scouting the Wine Country of the future from San Diego to the Sierra," *San Francisco Examiner and Chronicle*, 18 November 1981; "Zaca Mesa Winery King of the Grapes," *Santa Barbara News-Press*, 21 July 1982, B-5; Bill Griggs, "Summer of '84 Grape Production Could Bring Forth an All-Star Cask," *Santa Barbara News-Press*, 30 September 1984, D-2;

21. "New Releases," *The Wine Spectator*, November 1-16, 1983. Zaca Mesa advertisements were found in *The Wine Spectator*, June 1–15, 1981; July 16–31, 1983; September 1–15, 1983.

22. Larry Roberts, "Masters of Wine on First California Tour," *The Wine Spectator*, June 1–15, 1981, 19.

23. "County Vintners Take High Honors," *Santa Barbara News-Press*, 22 June 1987.

24. Frank Prial, "Wealth of Winners Tarnishing Gold of Wine Competitions," *Santa Barbara News-Press,* 31 August 1986, C-1.

25. Bill Griggs, "Vintner Bubbles about Capital Business," *Santa Barbara News-Press,* 12 February 1981, B-1.

26. Jerry Rankin, "Winemaker Forgets Political Wrath, Offers Reagan a Case of His Best," *Santa Barbara News-Press,* 3 April 1986, A-1, A-11.

27. Barney Brantingham, "Pieces of Paradise," *Santa Barbara News-Press,* 3 April 1979, B-1.

28. Joe Shoulak, "A Heady Time for Vintners," *Santa Barbara News-Press,* 27 September 1987, E-1, E-2.

29. Matt Kramer, "Gone With the Wind?" *Wine Spectator,* 31 July 1996, 31.

30. Jeff Morgan, "California's 'Other' Coast," *Wine Spectator, 15* May 1996, 49–59.

31. Judy Kimsey, "Winemakers: The Next Superstars: Individuals Lend Focus to Advertising," *Wine Business Monthly,* July 1999, 26–28.

32. Cliff Carlson, "Case Study: Emergence of 'Escargociants,'" *Wine Business Monthly,* June 1996, 51–52.

33. Dennis Schaefer, *Vintage Talk: Conversations with California's New Winemakers* (Santa Barbara, CA; Capra Press, 1994), 7–9.

34. Bob Senn, "Touring the Wine Belt: The Definitive Guide!," *Santa Barbara Independent,* 15 May 1997, 27–31. Senn includes Ken Brown, Bruno D'Alfonso, Bill Mosby, Bryan Babcock, Bill Wathen, Dick Dore, Bruce McGuire, Andrew Murray, Kathy Joseph, and Craig Jaffurs in this wine artist category.

35. Chris Whitcraft, oral history interview conducted by Beverly Schwartzberg, 3 February 1994, Santa Ynez, California, tape recording, Special Collections, University of California, Santa Barbara, Santa Barbara, California.

36. Jim Clendenen oral history interview conducted by Richard P. Ryba, 10 February 1994, Santa Maria, California, tape recording, Special Collections, University of California, Santa Barbara, Santa Barbara, California.

37. Schaefer, *Vintage Talk,* 56.

38. Dan Berger, "Winemaker of the Year," *Los Angeles Times,* 31 December 1992, H-18.

39. Schaefer, *Vintage Talk,* 210.

40. Robert Lindquist, oral history interview conducted by Sarah Case, 24 February 1994, Santa Maria, California, tape recording, Special Collections, University of California, Santa Barbara, Santa Barbara, California.

41. Tad Weber, "Wine Making," *Santa Barbara News-Press,* 27 September 1987, A-1, A-11.

42. "Pour Us Some Blues," *Playboy,* August 1996, 161.

43. Mark van De Kamp, "Local Vintners Sample the Taste of Technology," *Santa Barbara News-Press,* 21 April 1996, A-1, A-2.

44. Ibid.

45. Lane Tanner, oral history interview conducted by Susan Goldstein, 3 February 1994, Santa Ynez, California, tape recording, Special Collections, University of California, Santa Barbara, Santa Barbara, California.

46. Ibid.

47. John Kerr, oral history interview conducted by Sarah Case, 9 February 1994, Santa Ynez, California, tape recording, Special Collections, University of California, Santa Barbara, Santa Barbara, California.

48. J. Kerr Winery press packet release.

Chapter Seven

1990s: Santa Barbara Gains Vintibusiness Status

Santa Barbara County Helps Quench California's Wine Shortage

As we have seen, California wineries could not keep pace with domestic and international consumer demands and the average price of wine rose 43 percent and wines rated 90 plus, by wine publications, rose 52 percent.[1] Most importantly, California premium varietal wines began to outsell generic geographically named wines like Chablis and Burgundy. According to *Wine Spectator* writer Kim Marcus, "Welcome to the wine boom of the mid-1990s, a millennium-ending frenzy that is driving up prices and leaving shortages of top wines in its wake."[2] Mike Rudy of Deloitte & Touche accounting firm added: "If you can't make money now in the wine business, you can't make money."[3] Even better news came in 1995 when Dr. Arthur Klatsky, Kaiser Permanente cardiologist, announced that "taking one or two drinks per day probably adds three to four years to life expectancy as compared with not drinking at all."[4] Despite neo-Prohibition, consumption of premium wines increased and the industry continued to grow. Yet, efforts to ameliorate wine-grape and wine shortages through science and efficient business practices had failed to bridge the gap between consumer need (demand) and production (supply). By the mid-1980s over 70 percent of all California winery business plans projected an enlargement of their vineyards and facilities.[5] This in turn, forced many northern wineries to again seek expansion possibilities outside of the Bay Area.

The end result was the wine boom of the 1980s and '90s that brought about a statewide wine-grape vineyard increase from a 1990 total of 290,561 acres to a 1999 high of 374,752 acres, a 22 percent increase. In that same time period Napa grew from 31,623 acres to 40,186 acres, Sonoma 32,036 acres to 48,967 acres, and Santa Barbara County from 9,407 acres to 14,626 acres. The county had added 1,942 acres of Chardonnay, 1,046 acres of Pinot Noir, and 369 acres of Syrah. Even with the impressive growth of vineyards statewide grape shortages continued and wine prices increased about 10 percent. Wineries celebrated the growth while growers' profits stagnated since fruit only accounts for about 15 to 20 percent of the total cost of retail wine.[6] The 1980s and 1990s wine industry continued to grow as American consumers quaffed more wine than ever before. Overall, the California four-decade struggle to re-educate wine drinkers had worked, as can be seen by the fact that American 1970s per-adult consumption of nine bottles annually had by the 1980s increased to over eleven bottles.[7]

By 1999 Santa Barbara County had become California's fifteenth-largest agricultural county as the region's farms grossed over $650 million and wine-grape production ranked third with a value of $60.1 million, just behind strawberries and broccoli. The county's wine-grape vineyards averaged three tons per acre at an average of $1,400 per ton and many predicted that the region's wine industry had positioned itself to take the county's agricultural lead.[8]

Throughout this era of expansion, Santa Barbara County became internationally known for its premium Chardonnay and Pinot Noir wines. One way to track the region's brand recognition is through wine magazines like *Wine Spectator,* which at the time had the largest circulation of all domestic wine magazines. Their 100-point scoring system had become a standard to help enthusiasts connect with the best premium wines and best values. Traditionally, wines that score 90 or better are considered to be some of the best wines in the world and wines in the 80–89 category are considered to be great value wines. Santa Barbara wines scored well throughout the decade of the nineties as *Wine Spectator* rated ninety-one Santa Barbara County wines in the 90-plus category, including fifty-seven Chardonnays and seventeen Pinot Noirs. By 1993 winery names like Byron, Cambria, and Gainey had scored a 91 for their premium Chardonnays and consumers quickly learned to trust Santa Barbara County Chardonnay and Pinot Noir as globally competitive wines.[9] But, the big surprise for the decade came with a consumer interest in Rhône-style Syrah wines and in this category Santa Barbara Rhône Rangers collected seventeen 90-plus scores.[10]

Santa Barbara's three major varietals quickly became international stars. Wine drinkers sought out Chardonnay and Pinot Noir from Sanford, Byron,

Zaca Mesa, Steele, Santa Barbara Wine Company, Au Bon Climat, Gainey, Babcock, Nichols, Qupé, Lincourt, Fess Parker, Landmark, and Foley. The wine quality had improved so much that many enophiles began to whisper that certain vineyards like Bien Nacido should receive possible Grand Cru status because eighteen of the region's coveted wines had been sourced with grapes from Bien Nacido vineyards. Others also spoke of Sanford and Benedict and Sierra Madre vineyards being just as deserving. Since the county's twenty-three wineries utilized under 40 percent of all the grapes grown in the county there was an ample supply of wine grapes for small independent winemakers and wineries that classified themselves as garagisti, artisan, and boutique wineries.

A SECOND WAVE OF SANTA BARBARA WINE PIONEERS

Pressures to expand production outside Napa and Sonoma to the Central Coast intensified in 1988 when premium wine sales jumped 20 percent in price and dominated 45 percent of the total domestic wine market. Eileen Fredrikson, wine consultant and vice president for the San Francisco–based Gomberg, Fredrikson, and Associates, observed that cheaper land, recognized grape quality, and high profits drove wineries to the Central Coast. In Fredrikson's words, "This is the market you want to be in."[11] Michael Moone, president of Wine World, agreed and began a search for Central Coast vineyard land because in his words, "We can produce a good value wine when we farm it ourselves."[12] The solution to the domestic wine shortage problem, for a second time, evolved from vintibusinesses looking southward for less expensive Santa Barbara, Monterey, and San Luis Obispo vineyard lands.[13]

This shift southward for new wine-grape land grew in intensity as vintibusinesses realized the premium reputation developed by the region. Wine writer Matt Kramer in his book *Making Sense of California Wine* described how the "best wines are revelations of place," or what he referred to as "somewhereness."[14] The county's twenty-three wineries and 9,000 plus acres of vineyards now had somewhereness and became the target for "Napazation" by large wine corporations seeking stable supplies of premium wine grapes. In a short time Mondavi, Kendall-Jackson, and Wine World purchased over $36 million worth of Central Coast vineyards and wineries.

From 1987 through the 1990s, a second wave of wine pioneers took over established Santa Barbara vineyards and wineries, planted new vineyards, opened wineries, and produced a variety of new labels. The new push began in 1987 when Tepusquet vineyards fell on difficult financial times after Louis and George Lucas, with partner Al Gagnon, failed to negotiate their option to purchase the vineyard from Wells Fargo Bank.[15] Napa based Beringer Vineyards (Wine World Inc.—a division of Nestlé S.A. of Switzerland) saw this as an opening into Central Coast vineyards and offered $12 million for the 2,700-acre ranch including its 1,700 acres of developed vineyard land. Michael Moone, president of Wine World Inc. wanted the vineyard's premium wine grapes to upgrade their Napa Ridge Chardonnay label and hoped to place Beringer in a position to knock S. Korbel & Brothers, Glen Ellen Winery, Mondavi, and Kendall-Jackson Winery out of the competition for the region's grapes. The possibility of a Beringer takeover angered the Lucas brothers who feared that the corporate entity would not give proper recognition to Santa Barbara County and would bury its quality grapes in their Napa Ridge second label. Their distrust of Beringer went back to 1978 when the winery breached (for rumored quality problems) grape contracts and both sides engaged in a series of lawsuits and countersuits.[16]

With no love lost, Louis Lucas looked elsewhere for a partner or partners to help him execute his right of first refusal and strike down the Beringer offer.[17] He immediately looked to Kendall-Jackson Winery, which had grown dependent on Tepusquet fruit and produced sixty-three thousand cases a year of Chardonnay from the region. Jess Jackson, a UC Berkeley Law School graduate and San Francisco real estate lawyer, had started making Chardonnay in the 1970s with the business practice of the best middle-market wines possible.[18] Jackson showed an interest in the deal because he had considered expanding his Chardonnay production to over two hundred thousand cases. He recalled that he had "been pulling grapes out of this area since the seventies," and in his words, "I don't think they know how good they are."[19] The two formed a partnership that quickly dissolved when Jackson's Canadian financing failed to materialize.[20]

Jackson, not one to give up, reached out to Robert Mondavi winery as a possible partner. Over the past decade Mondavi had grown dependent upon the Cabernet Sauvignon and Sauvignon Blanc grapes from south coast vineyards. In a cooperative move the two partnered in 1987 and purchased 1,200 acres of the Tepusquet vineyard. The arrangement allowed both Kendall-Jackson and Mondavi to secure their grape needs and for the time being blocked Wine World's expansion efforts into the region.

The second phase of the expansion continued when Firestone Vineyards purchased the twenty-five acres of grapes and seven-thousand-case production facility of J. Carey Cellars.[21] A short time later Wine World, Inc., who had not given up on the region, purchased the 700-acre Cat Canyon vineyard near Santa Maria. This pushed locals to look for ways to preserve an independent Santa Barbara wine industry. To this end Dale Hampton put together a consortium with Douglas Cramer (Hollywood producer) and John Cushman III (real estate developer) to purchase the 630-acre Sierra Madre Vineyard from Prudential Insurance Company for $8.5 million. Hampton felt that the acquisition was necessary "to protect the premium wine producers of the county," and was the only way to ensure "the continuing quality and reputation of the Pinot Noirs and Chardonnays produced from the local appellations."[22]

Hampton's fears intensified the next year when Wine World Inc. purchased the 2,350-acre White Hills Vineyard as a centerpiece for its Chardonnay program. Wine World named their Paso Robles–centered enterprise Meridian Vineyards and hired Charles Ortman as winemaker.[23]

For those fearing a northern takeover, 1990 brought more bad news. First when Robert Mondavi Corporation purchased 600 acres of Santa Maria land, which included 175 acres of grapes and the twenty-thousand-case Byron Vineyard and Winery. Byron's owner, Ken Brown, believed that the county produced the state's best Chardonnay and Pinot Noir grapes and that "in five or ten years," the local industry would "see double the acreage in the county."[24] Brown had wanted to be part of this growth, but he lacked the capital to make it happen and the Mondavi buyout allowed him to remain as winemaker and expanded the facility's production to over fifty thousand cases. Then came the partnership of The Wine Group of San Francisco and Wine World Inc. as they purchased the 330-acre Corbett Canyon Vineyards (formerly Los Alamos Vineyards) for $4 million.[25]

Not all of the new growth emanated from corporate wine investors. Fess Parker, retired actor and Santa Ynez resident, followed Dale Hampton's advice and purchased the 714-acre Los Olivos Ranch for the new Fess Parker Winery and Vineyard. Parker hired Jed Steele as wine-maker for the new 11,700-square-foot winery and separate 4,800-square-foot wine storage building.[26] That same year Richard Doré and Bill Wathen founded Foxen Vineyard, and Norman Becko purchased the 80-acre Cottonwood Canyon Vineyard.

The Santa Barbara noncorporate expansion continued in the early 1990s when former Olympic competitor Gerry Moro started his own label. Soon thereafter Kathy Joseph established Fiddlehead Cellars dedicated to Sauvignon Blanc and Pinot Noir wines and Bob Lindquest joined his old friend Jim Clendenen and built a winery under a lease agreement with Bien Nacido

Vineyards. That same year Ken Brown, with cash from the Mondavi deal, acquired the 432-acre Nielson Vineyard with a goal of five-thousand-case production and a self-promise to stay out of the "corporate thing."²⁷ Ron Burk and Bob Espinola followed with their Costa De Oro Winery in Santa Maria and utilized cuttings from the prestigious Sierra Madre Vineyard. In the Santa Maria AVA, Lane Tanner (Firestone enologist, André Tchelistcheff student, and Hitching Post and Zaca Mesa winemaker) became the first female winemaker in the California Central Coast and dedicated all her energy to Santa Barbara County Pinot Noir.

Rapid expansion of the Santa Barbara industry continued throughout the early 1990s. English manufacturing executive and wine collector Robert Atkin purchased the 674-acre Benedict Vineyard for $2.5 million and the new influx of capital facilitated plans for a subterranean winery with a fifty-thousand-case capacity. Most importantly, Atkin pledged to sell grapes to Richard Sanford and rename the vineyard Sanford and Benedict. As a welcome back to his old vineyard, Sanford authorized sales of three tons of grapes (200 cases) to five local winemakers—Foxen (Bill Wathen and Dick Doré), Lane Tanner, Jim Clendenen, Bryan Babcock, and Rick Longoria. In a great marketing move, Sanford then collected one barrel from each participant and along with a barrel from himself sold the wine in a half-case mix of the best of the vineyard.²⁸ Sanford then struck out on his own with funding from partner Robert Kidder, chairman of Borden Corporation and former chairman of Duracell Corporation, by planting 150 acres of grapes on his 485-acre Rancho Rinconda.²⁹

As the growth continued some like Andrew Murray entered the Rhône Ranger category with his new vineyard in the Santa Ynez Valley AVA. That same year Bion Rice started Sunstone estate-grown wines. Douglas Braun founded Presidio Vineyard & Winery in 1991 with the idea of bringing European viticultural philosophy to Santa Barbara County by utilizing high-density, low-yield-per-vine vineyards planted low to the ground just west of the Santa Rita Hills near Lompoc. He certified the vineyard as organic and biodynamic for Pinot Noir, Syrah, and Chardonnay. Thomas J. Barrack Jr. established the Happy Canyon Vineyard on his Piocho Ranch in 1992 around the same time as Tom and Marilyn Stolpman's 120-acre Ballard Canyon Stolpman Vineyards.

Accolades for the region continued when Dan Berger, wine writer for the *Los Angeles Times*, named Jim Clendenen of Au Bon Climat as winemaker of the year. Berger praised his Burgundian-style Chardonnay and Pinot Noir for their rarely filtered "clean wine" excellence. In a short ten years, the Au Bon

Climat label had become a shining star in the newly recognized region.[30] This is important because wine experts since the 1950s had declared that Chardonnay and Pinot Noir had no future in America and that California was too hot to grow these premium varietals. Added to that is the fact that American consumers preferred heavily oaked Chardonnay and condensed Pinot Noir wines, which were much different than traditional Burgundian wines. But a new American Burgundian style of Chardonnay and Pinot Noir began to make inroads in markets like Oregon, California, and Washington. In a short time cool-climate Burgundian wines from Santa Barbara County became one of Burgundy's chief competitors in America.[31]

The flourish of new Santa Barbara small wineries continued throughout the 1990s. Facing the necessity of having to recapitalize, Austin Cellars Winery owners chose to sell to Art White, Napa and European wine researcher. In 1992 White formed the Santa Ynez Wine Corporation, with a silent partner, and purchased the Austin Cellars. The niche for the small, vertically integrated enterprise was centered on a converted home in the center of the Los Olivos tourist/art community. In White's words he was interested in "developing a close synergy between the businesses in Los Olivos, especially the restaurants, art galleries, and our wines."[32] With his wife, Nancy, winemaker Clay Thompson, and art gallery director Randy Viau, they created a two-room retail business that offered wine, gourmet snacks, Lennox plates, tourist gifts, paintings, sculpture, and wine.

California wineries quickly learned that the struggle to stand apart in a crowded premium wine industry required the development of a brand image. For years Zaca Mesa had watched its wine image decline, and in 1993 Jeff Maiken, general manager, mobilized the quest for a new marketing vision. The winery hired Daniel Gehrs, Congress Springs winemaker, and introduced an Alumni Winemaker Series. The wine series featured 1,500 cases of wine from famous alumni winemakers like Clendenen, Lindquist, and Tanner that had used their estate grapes in the past.[33] Another marketing boost for the winery came in 1996 when French president Jacques Chirac visited Washington, D.C., and the White House served Zaca Mesa's 1993 Syrah that *Wine Spectator* had scored at a 94 and named one of the top-ten wines of the year. When President Clinton ordered three cases for himself, owner John Cushman had found the winery out of the wine and filled the order from his private stock.[34]

In 1994 Steve and Cathy Pepe (employment lawyers) established their Clos Pepe Vineyard and Tom and Judy Beckmen (Roland corporation electronic music business), joined by their youngest son, Steve, planted their forty-acre

Beckman Vineyard near Los Olivos. That same year Stephan Bedford formed a partnership with David Thompson to start the Bedford Thompson Winery & Vineyard. David grew the grapes from his vineyard located in the hills of the Los Alamos Valley and Stephan made them into wine. Craig Jaffurs, aerospace cost analyst and home winemaker, with prodding from winemaker Bruce McGuire, made his first Santa Barbara County Syrah that received rave reviews from both *Wine Spectator* and *Wine Advocate.* Adam Lee and Dianna Novy left their native Texas and moved to the Sonoma County wine country and worked at small, family-owned wineries and learned everything they could about growing grapes and making wine. In 1994 they released the first Siduri Pinot Noir wines with grapes from Cargasacchi, Clos Pepe, and John Sebastiano vineyards.

The small winemaker energy continued through the end of the nineties. Steve Clifton sold most of his stake in Brewer-Clifton and with his wife Chrystal started the Palmina label to produce wines from Northern Italian varietals grown in Santa Barbara County. In the same year the husband and wife team of Geoff Rusack and Alison Wrigley Rusack planted seventeen acres of grapes on their Ballard Canyon ranch. After graduating from USC, Chad Melville, son of Ron Melville (Melville Vineyards & Winery), began a career as a winemaker. The younger Melville left a lucrative career as a stockbroker on the Pacific Stock Exchange and moved into a double-wide trailer to plant a vineyard and make wine on California's Central Coast.

The momentum continued in 1996 as Jim and Mary Dierberg, bankers and past owners of the Hermannhof Winery in Hermann, Missouri, planted two vineyards—their namesake Dierberg Vineyard and the Drum Canyon Vineyard. Joe Davis, UC Davis graduate, established the Arcadian winery in Lompoc and devoted all his energy to Central Coast, single-vineyard Chardonnay, Pinot Noir, and Syrah wines. John Clark with the viticulture expertise of his wife, Kelley Brophy Clark, focused on varietals they felt excelled in this region—Pinot Noir, Chardonnay, Rhône blends, and Zinfandel.

The 1990s steady stream of expansion, and new vineyards, wineries, and labels, was far from over. In 1996 Louis Lucas teamed up with longtime friend and retired superior court judge Royce Lewellen to form the partnership of Lucas and Lewellen Vineyards. They placed Cal-Poly-trained soil scientist Megan McGrath Gates, who mentored under Dan Gehrs, in charge of the winery and by 1999 they developed a business plan that included producing thirty-thousand-cases. Their mission was to develop a ground-to-glass ethos for their Lucas and Lewellen Toccata and Queen of Hearts labels and sell their excess grapes to other wineries. The operation grew to include vineyards in Santa Maria (Goodchild, High Nine, and Old Adobe Vineyards), Los Alamos (Los Alamos Vineyard), and Santa Ynez (Valley View Vineyard). During this same period the wine bug bit aerospace analyst Craig Jaffurs, who, after eight years of making garage-wines, doing cellar work for Bruce McGuire, and taking enology classes at UC Davis, started his own label.[35]

Napa's interest in Santa Barbara continued as Tim Mondavi proclaimed that the Mondavi Corporation was not done in the region and that "you ain't seen nothing yet."[36] In early 1996 Mondavi Winery increased its county hold-ings to 1,500 acres, roughly equivalent of its Napa holdings, when it secured deals to acquire 1,100 acres of land adjacent to its other county lands. The purchases included 350 acres of unplanted land in Santa Maria and the Sierra Madre Vineyard.[37] Despite the rapid growth in Santa Barbara, Monterey, and San Luis Obispo Counties, many Bay Area wineries continued to meet brand demands by purchasing premium bulk wines from other countries. Many win-eries now also looked outside the country for grapes and wines to sell. In 1996, following this trend, Firestone Vineyard and Winery sourced twenty-thousand cases of Merlot for its Prosperity Merlot label, and entered an agreement with Viña Santa Loria for a three-hundred-acre vineyard in Colchagua, Chile.[38]

Locals also continued to increase vineyard acreage and take advantage of the merger boom. Looking for expansion opportunities Fess Parker Winery and Vineyard purchased the 1,400-acre Camp Four Ranch near Santa Ynez for less than $7 million. In 1998 Joe Carrari sold his 196-acre Carrari Vineyards (off Highway 101) to the partnership of Royce Lewellyn and Louis Lucas. Carrari in turn used his proceeds to acquire the 3,400-acre Ferrero Family ranch just south of Highway 135, where he planned on converting 600 acres to vineyards.

NAPA COLONIZES SANTA BARBARA COUNTY

Many locals lamented these northern purchases of Santa Maria vineyards and the Napazation of the county. They predicted that it would eventually harm wine quality and reduce local profits and their concerns proved to be valid. Between 1988 and 1996 California's fifteen largest wine-grape growers cre-ated a "vineyard royalty" that increased their statewide vineyard ownership by 75 percent.[39] For Santa Barbara County this meant that Wine World, Robert Mondavi Winery, and Kendall-Jackson assumed ownership of over 6,300 acres of the county's nearly 14,000 acres of premium wine grapes.[40] The top indepen-dent growers of Santa Barbara County dwindled to include; Bien Nacido (589 acres), Firestone (448 acres), Rancho Sisquoc (408 acres), Zaca Mesa (224 acres), Carrari Vineyards (150 acres), Lucas Brothers (150 acres), Stolpman Vineyards (110 acres), Gainey Vineyards (85 acres), and small acreages maintained by wineries like Carey, Mosby, Buttonwood, Brander, Santa Ynez, and Santa Barbara.[41]

Not all participants in the Santa Barbara County wine industry feared the influx of northern vintibusinesses and many felt that this influx of northern money would only strengthen and build the reputation of the region. Jeff Newton, vineyard manager, believed that "the large wineries of Mondavi and Kendall-Jackson brought in the expertise and capital necessary to make the industry work."[42] Bryan Babcock added: "It is real healthy when people think enough of an area to come to the county and speculate in its soil and vineyards," and he believed that "it will only help in the long run."[43]

Santa Barbara grape growers, while split on the issue of "foreign capital," benefited from statewide grape shortages that forced tonnage prices upward. Average local grape prices jumped from $1,000 to $1,500 per ton reflecting an overall minimum 20 percent increase. Anthony Austin, of Los Olivos Austin's Cellar, felt that these escalated prices would "strengthen wine-grape's role in the county's overall agricultural picture."[44] Lon Fletcher, on the other hand, felt that as Napa purchased Santa Barbara County vineyards that they would "use us to pick up their quality," and result in lower grape prices as vineyard competition diminished.[45] Barry Johnson, Gainey Vineyard general manager, agreed with Fletcher and warned that there were "a lot of award winners from Napa that use a great deal of Santa Barbara County fruit."[46]

High demand and short supply encouraged the continued explosive growth of the county through the year 2000, and some began to consider Santa Barbara County to be the Silicon Valley for California's wine industry. Kendall-Jackson Vineyards secured county permission to build two compacted earth–filled reservoirs to store thirty-nine million gallons of water for its vineyards. Beringer Wine Estates soon followed with four earthen reservoirs and built a tasting room for its Meridian Vineyards wines in the downtown Santa Barbara Paseo Nuevo Shopping Center.[47] Beringer also had future plans for a giant facility in Santa Barbara to process the thousands of tons of grapes from the White Hills Vineyard that it presently trucked north to its Meridian Vineyard facility in Paso Robles. They hoped to start in 2001 with a 200,000-square-foot facility and expand to over 550,000 square feet over fifteen years.[48]

After the chaotic expansion many independent Santa Barbara County wineries, mainly situated in Santa Ynez, were able to secure alternative fruit supplies after their loss of Santa Maria grapes to northern wineries. Funding for the expansion emanated from a strong American and recovering California economy that permitted a new generation of professionals to retire and invest in the primal lure and glamour of the wine lifestyle. For some, survival came by selling the winery to an investor willing to modernize and expand the business.

A New Grape Vies for Stardom

A new industry-wide consumer shift in taste brought a rediscovery of Rhône wines, especially Syrah. As a result, many wine drinkers, wishing for a new experience, shifted their attention to Santa Barbara's fledgling Rhône premium wine producers. Alexis Lichine, wine writer, believed that the Syrah grape was brought to Europe in 600 BC from Asia Minor by Phoenician and Greek traders and that at that time Rhône grapes accounted for 3 percent of all of France's wine-grape plantings.[49]

The grape had appeared in California over 180 years ago and failed to catch consumer interest in large part due to Prohibition, depression, war, phylloxera, and Pierce's disease. It had just been in the last twenty-five years that a group of California Syrah pioneers, through trial and error and persistence, brought the French star of the Hermitage and Australia's Hunter Valley to the American consumer. Labeled "Rhône Rangers," by Mike Higgins, owner of the Oakland wine shop Vino!, they led a modern resurgence of Rhône varietals that by the 1990s included over 5,000 acres statewide.

Rhône wine grape varieties were first seriously considered in the 1970s as a means to help restart the wine industry. UC Davis viticultural professor Harold Olmo imported Syrah cuttings from the French Hermitage and convinced Christian Brothers iconic wine master Brother Timothy to plant four acres of Syrah in the Napa Valley. About the same time, Sacramento wine importer and retailer Darrell Corti began spreading the gospel of Rhône wines and in 1972 Gary Eberle, with Darrel Conti's encouragement, planted disease-free UC Davis Syrah stock in the cooler climate of Paso Robles. But it would be UC Berkeley graduate Kermit Lynch who reintroduced post-war consumers to French Syrah wines from his Albany (Berkeley) wine shop.

Joseph Phelps, a Kermit Lynch customer, took advantage of the Rhône curiosity and became the second California Syrah pioneer in 1974 with his Napa plantings for his recently opened Napa Souverain Cellars. Over the next decade issues with appropriate clones, warm climate, and lack of consumer interest resulted in lackluster sales. Despite these problems Rhône plantings grew from eighty acres in 1981 to a 1991 high of over four hundred acres.[50] But in the 1990s increased consumer demand for Syrah outstripped the state's ability to produce enough Rhône wine.

Winemakers and wineries wishing to experiment with Rhône wines faced the immediate problem that new Napa vineyards cost up to $100,000 per planted-acre.[51] This sticker shock was somewhat eased by the new phylloxera and Pierce's disease outbreaks that freed up older vineyard land for planting new varietals and by recent expansions outside of the Bay Area.

At first getting quality rootstock for the new Rhône varietals presented a problem. The state of California did not have a verified plant services program until the late 1980s and this forced early adoptors to use self-importation of "suit-cased" or "Samsonite clones." This resulted in the state facing the 1980s–1990s introduction of over a half-dozen cases of illegal clones. The Plant Protection Act of 2000 stopped this practice but did not alleviate the numbers of poor-quality cones that already existed in the state. Suitcase horror stories of mismarked Roussanne and Marsanne grapes caused problems for Randall Graham's Bonny Doon Le Sophiste blend. Complicating matters was the fact that Rich Kunde of Sonoma Grapevines Nursery had bought cuttings from Graham that he in turn sold to Zaca Mesa and other wineries as Rousanne cuttings. It was later revealed that the cuttings were mismarked, and Zaca Mesa had to relabel its Rousanne wine as Viognier. After numerous lawsuits and a nursery-wide infestation of black goo fungus, Sonoma Grapevines went out of business.

Despite the rush to the old varietal, growers feared a shortage of disease-free and disease-resistant rootstock. To overcome this problem the Paso Robles Perrin family, Tablas Creek Estate Vineyard, began to import disease-free rootstock from ENTAV in Beaucastel, France, for their nursery and vineyard. Deborah Golino, director of the UC Davis Quarantine and Research program, oversaw the project to clone mother vines and set a goal to provide five hundred thousand vines of Syrah, Roussanne, Grenache, Mouvedre, and Counoise Rhône vines. The problem was that the nursery process would take ten to fifteen years to accomplish the task.[52]

Santa Barbara County became one focal point for the resurgence in the 1980s, and over a fifteen-year period (1982–1997) a small group of Santa Barbara winemakers helped usher in the region's Rhône era. In 1982, while doing sales at Zaca Mesa Winery, Bob Lindquist had gotten hooked on Rhône wines after visiting Berkeley wine merchant Kermit Lynch. In his words, "He was preaching the Rhône gospel back then, and he always said California should be doing more with Syrah."[53] Zaca Mesa winemaker Ken Brown also caught the Rhône fever and Zaca Mesa became the first Santa Barbara winery to plant Syrah vines. The program got off to a slow start as *Wine Spectator* magazine scored their 1985 Syrah at 78 and their 1986 at 79.

In 1982 Lindquist, along with Zaca Mesa colleague Jim Clendenen, joined forces to combat their fear that northern corporate wineries were buying up all of Santa Barbara County's Chardonnay and Pinot Noir grapes leaving few opportunities for small independent wineries. As a result the two came together to build a permanent facility at the Santa Maria Bien Nacido Vineyard and feature Rhône wines. They were joined by Los Angeles lawyer Tom Stolpman who with his wife Marilyn planted Rhône varietals in Santa Ynez Valley and in 1993 opened a new winery in Los Olivos. Slowly other Santa Barbara wineries like Andrew Murray, Bryan Babcock, Craig Jaffurs, and Chuck Carlson joined the Rhône Crusade. The real turn for the wine came in the late 1990s when Qupé and Ojai Syrahs began scoring 89 and 90 and in 1996 Zaca Mesa's Syrah scored a 94 (number six in the year's top ten wines) in *Wine Spectator* magazine.[54] The region had a new red-wine darling.

CHANGE ON THE HORIZON

While many believed that expansion of the Santa Barbara region could be an answer to the domestic wine shortages, the honor fell elsewhere. Market forces had pushed commercial wine growth to Monterey and the Central Valley where cheap land, water, and cheap labor still existed. For years Gallo wines had prospered in the Central Valley, and Mondavi gambled that the Central Valley area of Lodi, despite its hot climate, was worth the risk for middle-price-point wines. So much so that he built a $6 million, 72,000 square-foot winery with over $7-million worth of new equipment to produce 3.5 million cases of wine per year. David Lucas, vice president of Mondavi grower relations, believed "Lodi is way out-front in California in terms of vineyard management."[55] This slowdown proved to be good for the Santa Barbara industry as winemakers big and small regrouped and began concentrating on making premium wines from their cool climate region.

Notes

1. Rich Cartiere, "1995: U.S. Vintners 'Worst Best Year Ever,'" *Wine Business Monthly*, March 1996, 1–2.
2. Kim Marcus, "The Wine Boom: Is There No Limit on Prices?" *Wine Spectator*, 15 June 1997.
3. Ibid.
4. "Twenty Years of Wine History: 1990s," *Wine Spectator*, 30 April 1996.
5. M. L. Hilton, Rich Cartiere, and Christian McIntosh, "Capacity and Demand Debate," *Wine Business Monthly*, July 1996, 1,4,6.
6. Kim Marcus, "Grape Prices Rise in California as Demand Surges," *Wine Spectator*, 31 March 1996.
7. Matt Kramer, "Wine in the American Mainstream," *Wine Spectator*, 31 March 1994.
8. Santa Barbara County Agricultural Commissioner, "1999 Santa Barbara County Agricultural Production Report," 17 April 2000.
9. James Laube, "When Ordinary Is Excellent," *Wine Spectator*, 31 July 1995.
10. Data compiled by analyzing all the *Wine Spectator* Buying Guides, 1990 through 1999.
11. Kathleen Sharp, "Big Wineries Head South," *Santa Barbara News-Press*, 19 June 1988.
12. Ibid.
13. Kathleen Sharp, "Northern Operations Expand Southward," *New York Times*, 17 June 1990; Mike Dunn, "Vintners' Great Expectations," *Sacramento Bee*, 22 March 1989.
14. Matt Kramer, *Making Sense of California Wine* (New York: William Morrow and Company, 1992), 7–10.
15. Dan Berger, "Major County Vineyard May Be Sold," *Santa Barbara News-Press*, 14 April 1987, B-1; Dan Berger, "Sale of Vineyards Hits Snag," *Santa Barbara News-Press*, 13 June 1987.
16. Michael Moone, "Management and Marketing at Beringer Vineyards and Wine World, Inc.," an oral history conducted in 1989 by Lisa Jacobson, Oral History Center, The Bancroft Library, University of California, Berkeley, 1990.
17. Barbara Banke and Jess Jackson, oral history conducted by Richard P. Ryba, 11 February 1994, tape recording, Santa Maria, California, Special Collections University of California, Santa Barbara, Santa Barbara, California.
18. Frank J. Prial, "Californian Wins Middle Market and Ruffles His Rivals," *New York Times*, 4 January 1997.
19. Barbara Banke and Jess Jackson, oral history; Mike Raphael, "Winery Hopes for Planners' OK," *Santa Barbara News-Press*, 30 December 1989, B-3; Dan Berger, "Santa Maria Area Vineyards Are Sold," *Santa Barbara News-Press*, 4 May 1987, B-1; Dan Berger, "Tepusquet Vineyard Sold In Joint Deal," *Santa Barbara News-Press*, 3 July 1987.
20. Dan Berger, "Sale of Vineyards Hits Snag," *Santa Barbara News-Press*, 13 June 1987.
21. Jerry Rankin, "Firestone Buys J. Carey Cellars; Owners' Wines Blend, Politics Don't," *Santa Barbara News-Press*, 26 January 1986, A-1, A-6.
22. "Prudential Insurance Sells Sierra Madre Vineyard," *Los Padres Sun*, 17 August 1988; Kathleen Sharp, "Vineyard Sold for $8.5 million," *Santa Barbara News-Press*, 19 August 1988, A-19.
23. Robyn Bullard, "One Part Chuck Ortman, Three Parts Vineyard," *Wine Spectator*, 15 April 1994, 31; James Laube, "Napa Valley's Beringer Vineyards in Play; Investor Group May Pay $300 Million for Wine World," *Wine Spectator*, 15 December 1995, 11; James Laube, "Sonoma's Chateau St. Jean Appears Headed to Wine World," *Wine Spectator*, February 29, 1996, 10; James Laube, "Wine World's New Treasure," *Wine Spectator*, 15 May 1996, 25.
24. Nora K. Wallace, "Santa Maria Valley Touted as Emerging Wine Region," *Santa Barbara News-Press*, 23 August 1990, B-1, B-4.

25. Kathleen Sharp, "Northern Operations Expand Southward," *New York Times,* 17 June 1990; Kathleen Marcks Hardesty, "Byron Winery's Sleek New Home in California," *Wine Spectator,* 15 October 1996.

26. Jeff Morgan, "California's Jed Steele Decides to Put Down Roots," *Wine Spectator,* 15 June 1996.

27. Chelsey Steinmann, "You're the Man, Ken Brown," *Santa Barbara Independent,* 11 September 2010.

28. Dan Berger, "Wine Notes: Collectors Are Now Owners of Benedict," *Los Angeles Times,* 9 August 1990.

29. James Laube, "Richard Sanford Starts Again in Santa Barbara with New Pinot Noir and Chardonnay Vineyards," *Wine Spectator,* 31 March 1996, 14; Bob Thompson, "Sorting Out the Sites," *Decanter,* 1991.

30. Dan Berger, "Winemaker of the Year," *Los Angeles Times,* 31 December 1992, H-18.

31. Frank J. Prial, "Wine Talk," *New York Times,* 30 April 1997.

32. Pat Murphy, "Austin Cellars Serving Fine Art with Its Wine," *Santa Barbara News-Press,* 6 December 1993, B-6.

33. Jay Stuller, "Hollywood and Wine: Making the Most of an Image," *Hemispheres,* January 1995, 89–95.

34. Kim Marcus, Jeff Morgan, Bruce Sanderson, and Daniel Thomases, *Wine Spectator,* 30 April 1996, 11.

35. Tom Garret, "New Santa Barbara Vintner Plans Rhône Varieties," *Wine Spectator,* 30 April 1996.

36. "Mondavi Winery to Buy Byron Vineyard," *Los Angeles Times,* 9 December 1989; Barney Brantingham, "To Our Health," *Santa Barbara News-Press,* 24 December 1989; Nora K. Wallace, "Santa Maria Valley Touted as Emerging Wine Region," *Santa Barbara News-Press,* 23 August 1990, B-1, B-4.

37. Jeff Morgan, "Mondavi Buys Key Santa Barbara Vineyard," *Wine Spectator,* 30 April 1996, 13.

38. Jeff Morgan, "'Mad Rush' to Chile by California and French Vintners," *Wine Spectator,* 31 May 1996, 8–9; Thomas Matthews, "Onward and Upward," *Wine Spectator,* 30 June 1996, 55–56.

39. Rich Cartiere, Teri Shore, and Marshall Farrer, "Calif.'s 'Vineyard Royalty' Doubles Holdings," *Wine Business Monthly,* May 1996, 1–6.

40. Ibid. Between 1993 and 1996 Kendall-Jackson purchased Geoffrey's Cellars, Mission Trails, Battaglia,

41. Ibid.

42. Jeff Newton, telephone interview by Victor W. Geraci on 9 November 1994.

43. Tad Weber, "Area Growers See Green; Vintage Prices Are Toasted," *Santa Barbara News-Press,* 14 October 1988, B-1, B-2.

44. Ibid.

45. Raymond Estrada, "The Grapes of September," *Santa Barbara News-Press,* 17 September 1989, F-1, F-3.

46. Ibid.

47. Mark van de Kamp, "Santa Barbara Land Boom Continues," *Santa Barbara News-Press,* 3 August 1999; Jim Hammett, "Meridian Opens Santa Barbara Tasting Room," *Santa Barbara News-Press,* 7 April 1999.

48. Mark van de Kamp, "Winery Pitches Big New Building," *Santa Barbara News-Press,* 9 December 1999.

49. Frank J. Prial, "Food: Syrah Rediscovered," *New York Times,* 16 January 1994.

50. Frank J. Prial, "Wine Talk: Syrah Takes Root in America," *New York Times,* 2 February 2000.

51. Jeff Morgan, "Napa Valley Vineyards Prices Hit $100,000 an Acre," *Wine Spectator,* 31 August 1999.

52. "Rhone Venture in California May Transform State's Viticulture," *Wine Spectator,* 31 May 1995.

53. Jeff Morgan, "Syrah Arrives in California," *Wine Spectator,* 30 April 1999.

54. James Laube, "A Second Look at the Top 10 Wines of 1995," *Wine Spectator,* 15 December 1996.

55. "Mondavi Opens Huge Barrel Cellar for Fighting Varietals," *Wine Spectator,* 31 May 1995.

Chapter Eight

Booming Business:
Continued Problems

As we have seen, the 1980s and '90s "wine revolution" pushed the wine industry into satellite wine regions like Santa Barbara.[1] In 1976 over 90 percent of premium wines came from France, and by the 1990s California wineries began to reverse this trend. Assisting the American market shift was the fact that French growers tenaciously adhered to traditional terroir restrictions and refused to make changes in the stagnant post–World War II European economy. On the other side of the Atlantic, new California viticultural experiments, with the help of the University of California, sought to utilize modern scientific methods to improve terroir and they were rewarded worldwide by middle-class consumers with disposable incomes.[2]

But all was not perfect for growers and wineries as they faced a new set of challenges that in the end affected both large vintibusiness and small boutique wineries. New environmental concerns, antigrowth factions, lack of availability of cheap vineyard land, anti-alcohol forces, pest and disease outbreaks, marketing issues, globalism, new science and techniques, and a quest for super premium wines placed pressure on large and small wineries alike. Santa Barbara's advantage in this new global wine market emanated from its smaller premium wineries that had benefited from a de-escalation of vineyard expansion by the 2000s.

Environmentalism: Limits and Restrictions for Winery Expansion

Wine consumption increased throughout the nineties and stimulated the continued expansion of the industry. By 2000 Napa had grown to 45,401 acres, Sonoma supported 57,149 acres, Monterey County grew to 42,259 acres,

Santa Barbara had reached 17,566 acres, and the entire state now had over 425,695 acres of wine grapes.[3]

Winery tourism became critical for smaller wineries to market and sell their premium wines. So much so that the Santa Barbara County Vintner's Association placed regular ads in the *Los Angeles Times* to encourage wine tasting at the region's now forty-five wineries.[4] Some, like wine writer Dan Berger, touted numerous accolades about Zaca Mesa, Brander, Firestone, Sanford, and Au Bon Climat and viewed Santa Barbara as a natural Burgundy-like region for premium Chardonnay and Pinot Noir wines.[5] Berger's "Wine Tour" articles even provided tasting maps with a legend describing location, hours of operation, fees, and notable wines.[6] The draw for tourism, in an atmosphere of Old-West, early-California spirit and Santa Maria BBQ, drew many visitors to taste at Gainey, Fess Parker, Mosby, and Foxen and local wineries began to pride themselves in their hospitality.[7]

Wine writers and publications helped fuel the tourist influx with descriptions of beautiful facilities and the region's high-quality premium wines. The *Los Angeles Times* article "The Rest of the Best" named Jim Clendenen's Au Bon Climat Chardonnay as "the real excitement in California wine in the last decade." The article went on to describe Babcock's wines as pushing the envelope and "dramatic proof that good grapes can be bent into all sorts of shapes and still be intriguing."[8] The paper then described Andrew Murray's Rhône collection of Syrah, Roussanne, Mouvedre, Grenache, and Viognier wines as an example of the "Good Life."[9]

As wine tourism increased many Santa Barbara citizens feared that the county would become another tourist trap like Napa and Sonoma. Less than three hours hours from Los Angeles, the small towns of Santa Ynez, Los Olivos, Buelton, and Solvang became crowded with over 3.5 million tourists yearly and locals began to complain that Highway 246 had become impassable. One reason Michael Benedict gave for selling his vineyard in 1990 was that he "wanted to get out of the tourist industry."[10] Bob Lindquist agreed and was "concerned about the potential for us to turn into another Napa Valley."[11]

But, by the mid-1990s wine industry expansion slowed as environmentalists and no-growth citizen groups, empowered by home-rule ideals, fought the invasion of "Grapescape" on the few remaining rural landscapes left in California.[12] Bay Area wineries felt the environmental pinch first as those opposed to the rapid expansion quickly realized that the federal government regulated wine but that local governments controlled land use. With this knowledge local environmental groups began a decades-long battle against urban sprawl, traffic congestion, and water quality issues. Janet Cobb, executive officer of the California Oak Foundation, believed that vineyards were just as destructive as housing or commercial development. In her words, "We're allowing them to go wherever they please, and that should not be the case."[13]

Industry officials believed that these environmental arguments were overblown. In Sonoma County vineyards made up less than 5 percent of the total area yet maintained the highest community profile. They argued that the real enemy was urban sprawl. Throughout the 1960s–1990s people moved from urban areas to be near open space and the fashionable trend of the wine lifestyle and embraced "their surrounding neighbors, in pursuit of their hobby."[14] To stop this neighborhood invasion, locals formed groups like the Watershed Protection Alliance and the Sonoma County Conservation Action. By 1998 these Sonoma groups had become powerful enough to sway local officials into creating ordinances to oversee food service, special events (weddings, corporate parties, banquets, plays, entertainment), and retail sales on agricultural lands. Wineries, of course, feared what this would do to their personal customer relationships and direct winery sales. Tourist-related industries like hotels, restaurants, and boutique shops also became concerned about the effects of restricted tourism on their businesses.[15]

While some Santa Barbara County groups acted to protect thousands of acres of undeveloped agricultural land, others promoted wine industry growth. Local planners at first tried to avoid a Napa/Sonoma land-use fiasco and sought ways to protect the environment and agricultural character of the county while encouraging both vineyard and winery growth. At first this did not anger no-growth proponents because they felt that this type of slow-growth could not happen because much of the local rural acreage was registered under the Williamson Act that restricted development. Developers, on the other hand, saw the Williamson Act as a legal barrier to be circumvented. To push their case developers first elicited the support of Santa Barbara County supervisor Bill Wallace and then attempted to undermine the Williamson Act by proposing a revision of zoning laws that protected large-acreage ranches from "cookie cutting" developers and discouraged reasonable parceling for small- or medium-sized vineyard land.[16] Seeing an all-out land-use battle on the horizon, county planners offered a compromise plan based on clustering (the concept of transfer of development rights) that would allow farmers and ranchers to develop a small portion of their land while leaving the rest in agriculture for perpetuity.

Owners of the three-thousand-acre Rancho Todos Santos, east of Los Alamos, utilized this policy and removed 150 acres from preserve to build thirty-eight residential units and a winery. Actions like this only served to anger anti-growth forces, who responded by organizing for a fight over land use.

As more and more wineries flourished and tourism expanded, many locals worried that the peaceful rural landscape they had escaped to would vanish and this drove many of them into local politics and decades of land-use battles. These anti-growth advocates bombarded Third District supervisor Gail Marshall, member of the Santa Ynez Valley General Plan Advisory Committee, with numerous complaints. Most dealt with the expanding number of winery events that brought hundreds if not thousands of visitors to the local community. The county had no set event policy and the addition of twelve wineries in one year pushed many citizens to call for a policy that would require each winery to apply for a permit for each event. Speaking at a citizens meeting, celebrity columnist Rona Barrett, Santa Ynez resident, told fellow citizens, "We are concerned about what will happen to the future of the valley." Another angry citizen responded: "Grapes do not need amplified music."[17]

Increasing fears of being overrun by the wine industry pushed anti-growth proponents to join forces with environmental groups, and together they called for a complete stop to the county's wine-grape and winery expansion. Since the 1969 Santa Barbara oil spill disaster, the city and county of Santa Barbara had developed a strong environmental community that helped enact some of the strictest land-use laws in California and the United States.[18] Initial beliefs that wineries and vineyards seemed compatible with open space, organic agriculture, and sustainable agriculture had changed. They believed that the wine industry peddled the ideas of the ambiance of small towns, spectacular scenery, and outdoor activities in order to make money. Many Santa Barbara citizens, after carefully studying the effects of tourism and wineries on the northern California environment, vowed to not let this happen to their communities.

Angered by what they saw happening in Napa and Sonoma, extreme Santa Barbara environmentalists took action to stop winery expansion in the county. Some wished to save older trees and conserve habitats for endangered species and fought to change the definition of what constitutes an old tree to include any tree growing before California statehood in 1850.[19] Of course farmers and ranchers reacted negatively to the idea, seeing it as an infringement of their property rights.

In February of 1999 Jess Jackson's Cambria Winery received a fax from the Santa Barbara County Farm Bureau advising local wineries that Earth First, a

Santa Barbara environmental group, was advocating sabotage of vineyards in Napa, Sonoma, and Santa Barbara. The group specifically targeted Jackson because he had cut down over eight hundred oak trees to expand his vineyard operations. The *Earth First Journal* condemned industry officials in an article and militantly stated:

> Perhaps we will join K-J for a little afternoon wine tasting at its Cambria wineries in Santa Maria, and if K-J doesn't remove their newly planted grapevines and irrigation pipes in a prompt and orderly fashion, perhaps some brave midnight warriors will have to do it themselves, the old fashioned way.[20]

The publication also included a map indicating the location of seven other local wineries and the number of oak trees removed. Group members later said that the map and statement were for "the identification and exact locations of these vineyards," and "not intended to encourage the strategic destruction of any equipment on site."[21]

Moderate environmentalists, through the Sierra Club, engaged in more reasonable actions by utilizing the court system. Local groups sued the county planning department, county supervisors, and Jackson for violating county land-use ordinances. Judge James Brown of the Santa Barbara Superior Court struck down the suit as collateral because the Sierra Club had never filed a complaint during the permit process and ordered the environmental group to pay more than $17,000 to cover K-J's court costs.[22]

These heated confrontations taught vintibusinesses statewide that they must proactively regain their image as stewards of the land. Some looked to the Oregon wine region that had already proved that wineries and grape growers could adopt sustainable agriculture techniques.[23] As a first step grape growers and wineries requested that the University of California Cooperative Extension sponsor a January 1998 seminar entitled "How to Work Effectively with Regulatory Agencies." The seminar provided educational and practical advice on how to navigate the various permits required by county and state planners, the U.S. Fish and Wildlife Service, California Fish and Game, the Regional Water Quality Control Board, and the ever-watchful eye of local environmental groups like the Environmental Defense Council and the Community Environmental Commission. The ninety seminar participants simulated the permit processes and various required public sessions.[24]

Some of the stress of Santa Barbara expansion declined as communities developed restrictive land-use policies that inflated prices of Santa Barbara agricultural land and forced wine-grape developers to look elsewhere for unrestricted, cheap vineyard land. A case in point would be the 1995 and 1996 Austin, Texas 360 acres of wine grapes planted by Santa Barbara pioneer Dale Hampton. He became the Lone Star state's number one developer of wine-grape lands and let everyone know how easily and quickly a restriction-free process can work.[25]

Many of those who felt the pinch of county restrictions moved north on the Central Coast to nearby Paso Robles along Highway 101 and Highway 46, on the north, and San Miguel and Templeton, on the south. Paso Robles contained huge parcels of inexpensive ($2,000 per-acre) plantable vineyard lands with minimal land-use restrictions. Local winemaker Gary Eberle, Eberle Winery, likened it to the Oklahoma land rush.[26] The region's production jumped 72 percent in ten years as the county exploded from 6,500 acres of vineyards in 1991 to 15,000 acres in 1999.[27] Bay Area wineries like Gallo of Sonoma, Glen Ellen, Sebastiani, Robert Mondavi, Beringer, J. Lohr, Villa Mt. Eden, and Fetzer, to name a few, utilized Paso Robles grapes and acreage.

Despite restrictions and activism from zero-growth proponents, persistent small wineries continued to appear and by 1999 Santa Barbara County boasted that it had an industry of over fifty wineries and just under 18,000 acres of wine grapes.

PROTECTING NATIVE OAK TREES

By the late 1990s environmental groups in Santa Barbara County, and throughout the state of California, began to lobby to protect the state's native ancient oak trees. Much of their angst had begun in 1997 when Kendall-Jackson winery cut down 843 oak trees in Los Alamos to make room for a 540-acre vineyard. In a short time environmentalists and members of the general public joined together to support two November 1998 state initiatives (Propositions K and O) to preserve native oak trees. The state initiatives failed at the polls and left county governments to address the issue.

With the defeat of the propositions, Santa Barbara County supervisors, by a three to two vote, moved to require farmers to get permits to remove oak trees. Supervisors Gail Marshall, Susan Rose, and Naomi Schwartz led the charge, along with support from Greg Helms of the Environmental Defense Center and Selma Rubin a Proposition K supporter. In the words of Santa

Barbara Earth First member John Calvert, "It's time to do what Mother Nature needs."[28] Agricultural opposition to the permitting process came from the County Farm Bureau, County Cattleman's Association, Coalition of Labor, and agricultural and business leaders, who feared that it would interfere with conducting business and their property rights. Victor Tognazzini, farmer and chair of the County Agricultural Advisory Committee believed: "This is not just about oaks—it's about control over and discretionary review of agriculture."[29] In the end it became a struggle between urban supervisors Marshall, Rose, and Schwartz versus agricultural north county supervisors Joni Gray and Tom Urbanske who both supported the agricultural cause.

Tensions somewhat eased in 1999 as grape growers began offering compromises in order to get development permits. Sunmet, a Fresno County viticultural firm, while in the permitting process, promised to cut down no oak trees for its new 530-acre vineyard on its recently purchased 1,500-acre Rancho Alamo property off Highway 135. The deal required them to sacrifice over seventy-five acres of land to protect oak trees.[30] The biggest victory for the environmentalists and wine industry came when Kendall-Jackson set forth a plan to maintain over eight thousand mature oak trees on 760 acres, utilized seeds from these oak trees to grow replacement trees, set up a fourteen-acre vernal pond to protect Tiger Salamanders, and set aside $100,000 for scientific studies and attorney fees. Further support for oak tree protection came when the Santa Barbara County Vintner's Association developed a volunteer oak tree protection guideline that included a pledge to plant ten oak trees for each one removed.[31]

COMPETITIVE DOMESTIC AND GLOBAL MARKETS

In the early 1990s a European monetary crisis saw the English pound drop 10 percent in value, France lobby for European economic unity, and Germany cut prime lending rates. This European economic chaos resulted in a reduction in the price of most American goods on the world market, including wine. On the upside, these factors increased the value of the dollar and many nations purchased more secure American dollars. The downside was that consumers balked at high prices for California wine, and the decrease in sales resulted in warehouse overstocks and further discounted prices. Continued pressure on wine prices came with a 1991 increase of the Federal Excise Tax from twenty-seven cents per gallon to $1.17 for wineries producing over forty thousand cases per year.[32] To handle the economic downturn many California wineries created a second, lower-priced label, ended grape contracts, and stopped buying expensive premium grapes from upscale wineries and vineyards. This led corporate wineries to buy up smaller vineyards and look for shortcuts to control their costs.[33]

Global markets were not the only economic concern for grape growers and wineries. The continuing need for quality grapes created a 1990s movement to increase production with new marketing plans and efficiency schemes. A group of wine businessmen put together Vintech as a management company to supply assistance in financing, marketing, outsourcing services, and vineyard management. In the early 1990s the corporation's general manager Mike Rowan announced their intentions to attempt to dominate San Luis Obispo and Santa Barbara Counties with their new business model. Months later the company went bankrupt.[34] These pressures for efficiency to raise profit margins pushed Fred T. Franzia's Bronco Wine Company to mislabel nearly $5-million-dollars'-worth of wine. The United States Justice Department's investigation resulted in Franzia pleading guilty and paying a $2.5-million-dollar fine.[35]

Some northern producers feared that the new satellite regions would grow to outshine the Napa and Sonoma brands. By this time Monterey County almost equaled the size of Napa and Sonoma and 80 percent of their grapes went to northern wineries. Ken Shyvers, Robert Mondavi winemaker, believed that Monterey would "emerge as California's Burgundy."[36] Since the 1960s the Monterey "Sleeping Giant" evolved through trial and error to become what Monterey winemaker Rick Smith considered to be dominated by industrial viticulture. Smith also believed that there would still be a small role for boutique wineries because of cheap land prices.[37]

Other California wineries met increased wine demand by buying foreign wine, grapes, and vineyards for lower-price-point wines under their personal labels. Fetzer winery bought four hundred thousand gallons of wine from Chile, and Robert Monday formed a $12-million-dollar Chilean partnership with Villa Errazuriz for a joint Viña Calima label. Agustine Huneeus, president of Franciscan Estates, bought 400 acres in his native home of Chile hoping that his $10-million-dollar investment would provide two hundred fifty thousand cases per year.[38]

The California international search for grapes, vineyards, and wine went beyond Chile. Foreign wine regions were also interested in American partnerships, and some purchased wine operations as a means to get their products into the American distribution system. To this end, Central Coast Paragon Vineyard

Company entered a partnership agreement with Australian-based Southcorp (Penfolds, Lindeman) that country's largest winemaker. Jose Fernandez, president of Southcorp, had been "looking for an area in the United States to make the kind of Shiraz and Cabernet that Penfold's and Lindeman are known for." The Australians also purchased a six-hundred-acre vineyard in Cresto near Paso Robles to grow Shiraz and Cabernet.[39] Southcorp's attempt to purchase Zaca Mesa in 1999 was rejected by owner John C. Cushman III.[40]

PESTS, DISEASES, AND CLIMATE CHANGE

In 1873 California grape growers first found phylloxera in their vineyards and by the 1880s the disease had nearly destroyed the French and California industries. Scientists and growers never found a cure, and in the end, solved the problem by grafting native American rootstock with European varietals. Over a century later the louse returned for a new attempt to destroy California viticulture.

A new strain of phylloxera, called Biostrain B, hit northern grape growers hard as vineyards planted on old UC Davis AxR No1 resistant rootstock succumbed to the new strain. Bad news came to Santa Barbara County when Firestone Vineyards in Santa Ynez, which had taken a risk and planted on non-resistant rootstock, announced that they had an outbreak. This meant that at least 9,500 acres of the region's vineyards were susceptible to contracting the disease. The crux of the problem was the fact that California had no plant quarantine procedures for importing disease-free plants or ensuring healthy plants. To address the problem Deborah Golino, director of the UC Davis Foundation Plant Materials Services (FPMS), with funding by Robert Mondavi, Louis M. Martini, and the California Association of Winegrape Growers started a new statewide program to ensure healthy nursery stock for expanding vineyards.[41] None too soon as economists predicted that by the year 2000 the industry would have to spend $1 billion to replace thousands of acres infested with the new strain of phylloxera.[42]

Just as growers battled phylloxera another old pest returned to threaten California's vineyards. In the late 1800s Pierce's disease had devastated the Southern California industry and the bacteria that keeps vines from drawing water returned a century later. This time the bacteria was spread by a blue-green sharpshooter insect that had already destroyed over $6 million in vines in Southern California's Temecula Valley. It seems to have started in plant nurseries in the southern part of the state and it quickly destroyed $33 million in vines in Napa, Sonoma, and Mendocino. Making matters worse was the fact that two of the state's and Santa Barbara's most popular varieties, Chardonnay and Pinot Noir, seemed to be most susceptible. Concerns over the pest grew when UC Riverside entomologist Dr. Richard Redak predicted that it could take ten or more years to develop a disease-resistant plant.[43] A new quest to replant, treat, and look for genetic-resistant stock began. Thankfully, in Santa Barbara diseased plants had only been spotted in Goleta and downtown Santa Barbara and had not reached the region's vineyards, yet.

THE MARKETING PROBLEM OF NEO-PROHIBITION

As Santa Barbara County developed its premium wine industry, competitive wineries sought ways to expand their market share. Premium wine prices held steady at 10 percent growth per year; but there was a dark side to this growth. Many American and Santa Barbara artisan wineries relied on tourists, local retail, and direct wine shipments to customers for up to 75 percent of their sales. As we have seen, direct marketing became an issue for these wineries as fifty different sets of state laws regulated interstate shipments of wine.

Over the last decade the anti-alcohol community had quietly continued their attacks; but they became reinvigorated in 1998 when the Treasury Department's BATF moved to approve favorable wine statements on labels that instructed consumers on where to find information about the potential health benefits of moderate wine consumption. The policy met quick resistance from neo-Prohibitionist groups. In South Carolina, Senator Strom Thurmond's two-decade campaign against alcohol now focused on the Wine Institute as conspirators promoting alcohol. The ninety-six-year-old Thurmond had a negative view of alcohol as a member of the First Baptist Church, hardened by the fact that his estranged second wife was an alcoholic and his twenty-two-year-old daughter had been killed by a drunk driver.

As part of his anti-alcohol campaign Thurmond introduced three bills to attack wine. He wanted to triple the federal excise tax on wine and use the estimated $7.9 billion to help fund the National Institute of Alcohol Abuse and Alcoholism. The other two bills would ban all health claims on labels and move alcohol from the BATF to the Department of Health and Human Services.[44] To Thurmond's dismay, in February of 1999 BATF sided with the Wine Institute suggestion of label verbiage stating, "To learn the health effects of wine consumption send for the Federal Government's Dietary Guidelines for Americans." BATF officials also approved the Coalition for Truth and

Balance (ad hoc group of twelve wineries) statement, "The proud people who made this wine encourage you to consult your family doctor about the health effects of wine consumption."[45] Thurmond fought the addition of these statements on labels and intimidated Treasury Department Secretary Robert Rubin into holding hearings about labeling issues. Bowing to Thurmond's concerns the BATF instead approved negative label additions.[46]

This series of events made Thurmond the lightning rod for pro-alcohol forces and resulted in his picture on the July 31, 1999 cover of *Wine Spectator* magazine, declaring, "Strom Thurmond, Wine's Public Enemy #1."[47] Marvin Shanken, owner of *Wine Spectator,* believed that Thurmond was trying to get payback for governmental and societal attacks of his state's tobacco industry.[48]

Labeling issues in Santa Barbara County were more proprietary as Foxen and Fess Parker entered a dispute over the use of the Foxen name on wine labels. The disagreement started when Fess Parker winery used the words "Foxen Cuvée" and "Fleur de Foxen" on two of its labels. Foxen winery decided to file a trademark infringement suit against the larger Parker winery claiming that the Foxen name on the label would confuse consumers. To help pay the $90,000 in legal costs, Foxen held a fundraising event named "Foxen is Foxen." All worked out in the end as Parker winemaker Eli Parker decided to relabel all the wine in question.[49]

Of the fifty states, thirty-eight had restrictive alcohol policies that punished wineries, consumers, and distributors with varying degrees of fines and imprisonment for direct buying of California wines. Neo-Prohibitionists now wanted to step up the game by having a restrictive federal alcohol distribution policy, thereby eliminating the laws of the twelve states that were wine friendly. The wine industry fought the federal policy idea because they felt that it blocked small California wineries out of direct trade with consumers. Large wineries were somewhat insulated from these policies because their large production capacity made it possible for distributors to legally deliver their wines to retailers in all states through the three-tier system of certified wholesalers. Small wineries on the other hand, with their limited capacity, lacked access to the distribution system and feared bankruptcy if they could not sell directly to consumers in all states.

In response, groups like the Family Winemakers of California, American Vintners Association, Coalition for Free Trade in Licensed Beverages, and the Wine Institute formed the Direct Shipping Coalition. The issue became more convoluted in 1999 when Senator Orin Hatch (R-UT) and Senator Mike

DeWine (R-OH), with lobbyist support by Wine and Spirits Wholesalers of America, proposed federal legislation that would make it illegal for wineries, retailers, and wholesalers to offer internet-based sales and the bill provided for enforcement through the federal courts.[50] Representative Joe Scarborough, (R-FL) sponsored the Twenty-First Amendment Enforcement Act (HR2031) that passed in the House of Representatives by a 310 to 122 vote.[51]

California senator Dianne Feinstein (D-CA), along with California governor Pete Wilson, wrote to Hatch, arguing the case for direct shipments.[52] In the Senate version of the bill, Feinstein sponsored an amendment to require checks of shippers with power to revoke winery licenses if illegal sales were made. As both the House and Senate worked on federal regulation (HR2031 and S557) to stop internet and interstate sales, many congressman like Richard W. Pombo (R-Stockton, CA) argued that "teenagers are not going to order a $25 bottle of wine over the internet and then patiently wait for its arrival in the mail."[53] Robert Koch, senior vice president of the Washington, D.C., Wine Institute office, argued that "the whole underage-access complaint is being driven by wholesalers."[54] The legal stakes increased when eight states (Florida, Georgia, Indiana, Kentucky, North Carolina, Oklahoma, Tennessee, and pending legislation in Texas) made it a felony to order out-of-state wine. Resistance to the growing number of restrictive states came from the Napa-based consumer group "Free the Grapes" that urged consumers and vintners to mail corks to members of congress to "uncork consumer access to fine wine."[55]

But all was not lost. In New York State the legislature voted for reciprocal trade status for the country's second-largest wine market. State senator John Kuhl and Assembly-person Herman Ferrell pushed to allow out-of-state wineries to be able to ship two cases per month to New York consumers.[56] In return California would reciprocate by allowing California consumers to purchase New York wines.

Marketing attacks on small wineries did not stop with direct and internet sales. Governor George Ryan of Illinois signed into law the Illinois Wine and Spirits Industry Fair Dealing Act of 1999. Sponsored by liquor distributors, the bill restricted a winery's right to fire its distributors without "good cause," and allowed the state Liquor Control Commission to continue their relationship. Distributors claimed the law was needed to protect them against foreign suppliers that arbitrarily dumped wines in the American market. The first test of the law came in April of 1999 when the Kendall-Jackson winery ended its distribution agreement with Judge & Dolph and was ordered, under the new law, to continue doing business with the firm. Jess Jackson responded with a lawsuit.[57] Three years later a U.S. District Court judge overturned the law on the grounds that it violated the Commerce Clause of the U.S. Constitution.

In 1999 the Wine Institute responded to the direct shipment legal issues with their voluntary "Wine Industry Code For Direct Shipping." Modeled from principles suggested by the Coalition for Free Trade, Family Winemakers of California, American Vintners Association (later WineAmerica), and recommended by the National Conference of State Legislatures, the document addressed the major issues by promoting sales verified with an adult signature in states or counties that permitted alcohol sales. Despite the large array of neo-Prohibitionist attacks on wine, the California and Santa Barbara industries continued to flourish. If one can judge by a June 1999 *Wine Spectator*'s lavish eight-page photographic description of restaurants, wineries, and hotels of Santa Barbara, the city had become a major player in regional vintibusiness and a first-class tourist wine destination.[58]

As the millennium ended, wine consumption and sales continued to grow. In the end the Bay Area grape shortages of the '80s and '90s eased as additional plantings in Monterey, San Luis Obispo, Santa Barbara, and the Central Coast came into full production. This new supply freed up a limited amount of premium wine grapes for small independent labels and it allowed many small independent vineyards and wineries to move toward sustainable, organic, and biodynamic wine making. Thus, the next two decades became an era of expansion for garagisti, artisan, and boutique wineries.

Notes

1. Jim Gordon, "Between the Headlines," *Wine Spectator,* 30 April 1996; Ted Loos, "As They Saw It," *Wine Spectator,* 30 April 1996; Jeff Morgan, "Boom Time for California Vintners Means Higher Prices and Grape Shortages," *Wine Spectator,* 15 May 1996.
2. Gordon, "Between the Headlines," *Wine Spectator,* 30 April 1996.
3. Grape acreage statistics are from the USDA and CDA yearly reports, 1980–2000.
4. "Mid-Coast Wineries Welcome Visitors," *Los Angeles Times*, 26 August 1999, 263.
5. Dan Berger, "Wine Tour: Santa Barbara: Fulfillment of a Mission," *Los Angeles Times*, 26 September 1991, H25.
6. Dan Berger, "Wine Tour: Happy Trails to You," *Los Angeles Times*, 26 September 1991.
7. Barbara Hansen, "Wine Tour: Wine's New Frontier," *Los Angeles Times*, 26 September 1991.
8. "The Rest of the Best," *Los Angeles Times*, 2 January 1992, H32.
9. "Murray: The Good Life," *Los Angeles Times*, 18 July 1996, H6.

10. Kathleen Sharp, "Sour Grapes over Tourist Boom," *Los Angeles Times*, 3 December 1992, A3.

11. "Wineries: Santa Ynez Valley Is Booming," *Los Angeles Times*, 3 December 1992, A-34 and B-3.

12. Art Pine, "Grapes," *Los Angeles Times*, 18 February 1999, A8.

13. Ibid.

14. Judy Kimsey, "Regulation: Growers and Environments Strive for Harmony in the Hills," *Wine Business Monthly*, January 1999, 61.

15. Chris Finlay, "Wineries and Tourism: A Symbiotic Relationship," *Wine Business Monthly*, May 1999, 8–9.

16. Mike Chase, "More Homes on the Range?" *Santa Barbara Independent*, 8 August 1996, 23–25.

17. Mark van de Kamp, "A Double-Edged Sword in Santa Ynez Valley," *Santa Barbara News-Press*, 11 November 1998.

18. Otis L. Graham, Robert Bauman, Douglas W. Dodd, Victor W. Geraci, and Fermina Brel Murray, *Stearns Wharf: Surviving Change on the California Coast* (Santa Barbara: Graduate Program in Public History, University of California, Santa Barbara, 1994).

19. James Sterngold, "Davis Seeks Rule to Protect Older Trees in California," *New York Times*, 10 September 2001.

20. Cassandra Larson, "Vineyard Development Turns Environmentalist Heads: The Best Defense against Possible Offense," *Wine Business Monthly*, May 1999, 50 (48–53); Tim Tesconi and Randi Rossman, "Threat against Vineyards Reported: Environmental Groups May Retaliate for Cutting Oak Trees," *The Press Democrat* (Fresno, CA), 24 February 1999; and B. W. Rose, "Threat against Vineyards a Mix-Up," *The Press Democrat* (Fresno, CA), 25 February 1999.

21. Ibid.

22. "Sierra Club to Pay K-J's Legal Costs," *Wine Business Monthly*, July 1999, 10.

23. Mark Neal, "Agriculture Must Be in Front of Environmental Movement," *Wine Business Monthly*, October 1998, 8-10; Lisa Shara Hall, "Oregon Takes a Leadership Role with Sustainable Agriculture," *Wine Business Monthly*, August 1999, 43–47.

24. Renee Cashmere, "Current Issues: Central Coast Growers Strive to Stay One Step Ahead of Regulations," *Wine Business Monthly*, December 1997, 41–43.

25. Mark Stuertz, "Texas Looks into 21st Century, California's Hampton Farming Helps Lead the Way into the Future," *Wine Business Monthly*, July 1996, 10.

26. Dan Berger, "Paso Robles Finds Its Place in the Wine World," WineToday.com, 3 February 1999.

27. Ibid.

28. Mark van de Kamp, "County Pursues Permit Process for Cutting Oaks," *Santa Barbara New-Press*, 15 September 1999.

29. Ibid.

30. Melinda Burns, "New vineyard to respect land, oaks," *Santa Barbara News-Press*, 17 May 1999.

31. Mark van de Kamp, "A New Leaf," *Santa Barbara News-Press*, 3 November 1999.

32. "Twenty years of Wine History," *Wine Spectator*, 30 April 1996.

33. Dan Berger, "Doing the Discount Shuffle," *Los Angeles Times*, 16 April 1992, H-39.

34. Frank J. Prial, "Wine Talk," *New York Times*, 13 February 1991.

35. "Winery Admits Falsifying Varietal labels," *Wine Spectator*, 31 January 1994.

36. William Grimes, "A Taste of 1999: Monterey: The Next Napa (or Is it Burgundy)," *New York Times*, 30 December 1998. In 2000 the three largest wine regions in California were Sonoma with 57,149 acres, Napa with 45,401 acres, and Monterey with 42,259 acres.

37. Monterey land averaged $5,000 per acre compared to $40,000 plus in Napa. Jeff Morgan, "California's Sleeping Giant: Monterey County Awakens to the Challenge of Making Great Wine," *Wine Spectator*, 15 June 1997.

38. Jeff Morgan, "Mad Rush to Chile by California and French Vintners," *Wine Spectator*, 31 May 1996.

39. Jeff Morgan and Harvey Steiman, "Huge Aussie Winery's California Future," *Wine Spectator,* 15 September 1997.

40. Mark van de Kamp, "Southcorp's Purchase Offer for Zaca Mesa Dies on the Vine," *Santa Barbara News-Press,* 28 May 1999.

41. Kim Marcus, "New Davis Facility to Help California Clean Up Vineyards," *Wine Spectator,* 15, April 1995.

42. "Twenty Years of Wine History," *Wine Spectator,* 30 April 1996.

43. Jeff Morgan, "Vineyards under Siege: An Old Pest Poses a New threat to California," *Wine Spectator,* 15 June 1998; Stephanie Finucane, "Grape Growers Fear Blight of Winged Insect," *Santa Barbara News-Press,* 24 November 1999; Lynn Alley, "Southern Californias Vineyards Hit by Pierce's Disease," *Wine Spectator,* 15 November 1999.

44. "Thurmond Calls for Wine Institute Investigation," *Wine Business Monthly,* April 1999, 8; Kim Marcus, "Strom Thurmond's Crusade against Wine," *Wine Spectator,* 31 July 1999.

45. Kim Marcus and Dana Nigro, "Vintners Win Approval for Health Statements on Labels," *Wine Spectator,* 30 April 1999.

46. Kim Marcus, "Strom Thurmond Wins Concession in Wine Label Battle," *Wine Spectator,* 30 June 1999.

47. Kim Marcus, "Strom Thurmond's Crusade against Wine," *Wine Spectator,* 31 July 1999, cover, 38–44.

48. Marvin Shanken, "Our Worst Enemy in Washington," *Wine Spectator,* 31 July 1999.

49. Jeff Morgan, "Foxen and Fess Parker Wineries Resolve Labeling Feud," *Wine Spectator,* 23 July 1999.

50. Cyril Penn, "Direct Shipping Issue Gains Increasing Visibility," *Wine Business Monthly* 6, May 1999, 43–44; "Key Senator Supports States in Crackdown on Home Delivery of Wine," *Wine Spectator,* 15 May 1999.

51. Dana Nigro, "Home Delivery Crackdown Approved by Wide Margin," *Wine Spectator,* 15 September 1999.

52. "Feinstein and Wilson Get Involved in Direct Shipping Debate," *Wine Business Monthly,* November 1998, 9.

53. Nigro, "Home Delivery Crackdown," 12.

54. "Key Senator Supports States in Crackdown."

55. Dana Nigro, "Home Delivery Battle," *Wine Spectator,* 31 August 1999.

56. Dana Nigro, "Proposed New York Law Would Legalize Direct Shipments," *Wine Spectator,* 31 July 1999.

57. Ted Appel, "K-J Suit Takes on Illinois Law," *Press Democrat,* 10 June 1999.

58. Jean T. Barrett, "Santa Barbara: This City Promises a Wealth of Winery Day Trips, Along with Near-Permanent Sunshine and Warmth," *Wine Spectator,* 15 June 1999, 79–86.

Chapter Nine

Wine Is Here to Stay

A Successful California and American Wine Industry

In the second half of the twentieth century American vintibusiness became a major player in international wine trade and California wineries successfully recreated an American wine tradition based upon the new California wine style. Success came as vintners aimed aggressive marketing programs at consumers with disposable incomes while at the same time educating a new generation in the health and lifestyle benefits of premium wine. The only downside to the massive growth of this market was the inability of wineries to match supply with increased demand. Thus, growers and producers spent three decades expanding acreage and production. This increased production lead to successful regional wine industries that quickly fell prey to a modern vintibusiness structure whereby larger wine corporations stabilized supplies of quality wine grapes through mergers and buyouts and smaller artisan wineries became dependent on agritourism and a healthy American economy that promoted luxury spending. So much so that agricultural economic scholar James Harold Curry III believed that the "internal systemic logic" of concentrating businesses in the American wine industry became the driving force.[1] Thus, regional wine industries played a major role in the development and continued success of the modern American and world wine industry.

Throughout the 1990s, wine become a major agricultural contributor to the American economy and by 1999 the American wine industry contributed about 207,000 jobs, payed $3.2 billion in wages, and directly contributed over $12 billion to the Gross Domestic Product. Average ATF taxes collected fell just under $500 million and the industry grew from 579 wineries in 1975 to a 1999 high of 2,081. At that time only the states of North Dakota and Alaska produced no wine and California led the pack with 1,056 wineries with New York in second place with 136 wineries.[2] Santa Barbara had similar impressive statistics as local sales had increased by 35 percent since 1996.[3] That same year 54 percent of the county's 39,200 tons of wine grapes found their way to wineries outside Santa Barbara County.[4] The county now boasted of 16,500 acres of vineyards, fifty-plus wineries, produced seventy-one thousand cases of wine, employed 589 people full-time, paid out a total gross payroll of $22 million, and spent $41 million in the county (taxes, goods, and services).[5]

Despite these impressive figures, American wineries during the 1970s, '80s, and '90s failed to meet increased consumer demands. Wine wholesalers and vintibusinesses responded to the shortages by importing increasing amounts of New Zealand, Australian, Chilean, Argentinean, South African, French, Spanish, and Italian wines.[6] Wineries then moved to counter this unfavorable balance of trade by expanding wine exports to an all-time high of 10 percent of all their total wines produced.[7] Additional governmental support came with the 1989 Canadian/American Free Trade agreement (CAFTA) and the 1994 North American Free Trade Agreement (NAFTA).[8]

This expansion of exports continued against tough odds due to differences in U.S. and EU laws on production practices, labeling, and the fact that EU nations exported 12 percent of their product to America.[9] This did not slow down the American export movement as large vintibusinesses successfully expanded exports as they practiced what David Scott Shaw, agricultural economist, identified as success by market persistence over a long period of time.[10] A short time later fellow agricultural economist Juan Solana Rosillo agreed that persistence is key but added the caveat that the marketing power of vintibusiness structures gave them the advantage of a "marketing subsidiary."[11] In other words large American wineries benefited from purchasing small foreign wineries, enabling them to take advantage of their distribution networks and vice versa. Over the long haul these moves solidified the American vintibusiness industry as part of the global wine industry. The major roadblock for American vintner's was convincing consumers to pay five to ten dollars more for premium American regional wines.[12]

Yet, throughout the 1990s, long-term projections for continued growth never dimmed. John Love, World Agricultural Outlook Board (USDA), predicted that "a robust economy—providing more discretionary income—is the key to continued growth in consumption." Love also envisaged continued growth through 2010 at a rate of 2.5 percent down slightly from 3 percent over the last half of the 1990s.[13] Confident Wall Street investors viewed this reduced growth as still promising and continued to invest in vintibusinesses like Beringer Wine Estates, Brown-Foreman Corporation, Canandaigua Brands, Chalone Wine Group, Golden State Vintners, Ravenswood Winery, Robert Mondavi Corporation, and Willamette Valley Vineyards, to name a few.[14]

SANTA BARBARA'S REGIONAL SUCCESS

As we have seen, increased consumption drove California wineries to expand in the latter half of the twentieth century and Santa Barbara County bene-fited from this growth. Between 1960 and 1980 U.S. table wine consumption increased from 22 million cases to 151 million cases.[15] This rebirth of the mod-ern California wine industry resulted from northern vintibusiness dependence on satellite regions' inexpensive wine grapes supplied by the expertise of local grape growers and vintners. As California premium wine sales continued to soar by more than five-fold to over 34 million cases, the role of Central Coast vineyards and wineries continued to play an important role in meeting this demand.[16] During this period most Santa Barbara wine grapes were shipped north, leaving a limited amount of fruit for use in the region.

The crucial shift for Santa Barbara viniculture and viticulture came when American wine consumers developed a taste for the region's premium dry varietal wines. To measure this success the Santa Barbara County Vintners Association commissioned Gomberg, Fredrikson, and Associates, Wine Industry Consultants from San Francisco, to compile economic reports for the industry in 1992, 1996, and 1998. These surveys statistically demonstrated the explosive growth pattern for the county and confirmed that the local industry had made a transition from grape growers, to wineries, to vintibusinesses. The Santa Barbara wine industry moved from a 1972 grape-growing region with 1,840 acres of wine grapes and no commercial wineries to a 1990 regional wine industry with 9,542 acres and thirty-plus wineries. The evolution to vin-tibusiness completed itself between 1992 and 1998 as wine industry invest-ment in the county tripled to approximately $433 million; planted vineyard acreage grew to 16,500 acres, and the number of wineries jumped to fifty-six.[17] In 1998 local wineries passed the one-million-case production mark and industry revenues reached $136 million up from $59 million in 1992 (a 130 percent gain).[18]

The Santa Barbara county industry had truly benefited from ample capi-tal provided by wine entrepreneurs and its local class of gentrified farmers (doctors, lawyers, dentists, retired CEOs, and businesses wishing to diversify). Together the two groups produced a lucrative industry whereby vintibusinesses owned just over 50 percent of the vineyard land and 78 percent of local grapes were used by county wineries or by wineries outside the county that owned local vineyards—including Beringer Wine Estates, Kendall-Jackson Vineyards, Robert Mondavi Winery, and Sutter Home Winery.[19] Two-thirds of the wineries were smaller independent wine businesses with annual productions of fifteen thousand cases or less, and the ten largest wineries produced about 80 percent of the county's six-hundred-thousand-case annual production.[20] In a 1999 economic update, Gomberg and Fredrikson projected that "if all reported planting plans go forward as expected in 1999, county vineyards will exceed 20,000 acres by the year 2000."[21] The predicted expectations for the year 2000 fell short of the 1999 overly optimistic Gomberg and Fredrikson prediction as the local industry peaked at around 18,000 acres.

Gomberg and Fredrikson were not the only financial wine industry experts to predict a bright future for Santa Barbara wines. The 2000 Economic Report by Motto Kryla Fisher, LLP (MKF), a Napa-based winery tax consultant, market researcher, accounting, and strategic planning firm, while reporting less acreage growth touted the region for its extraordinary growth. Vic Motto, partner in MKF, emphasized the substantial increase in wine-related revenues from $136 million in 1998 to $360 million in 2000. Motto called Santa Barbara County "one of the special, unique places in the world where world-class wines can be grown."[22]

Continued Success for Santa Barbara Artisan Wineries

The Santa Barbara County wine industry ended the twentieth century as a well-established and successful wine enterprise. But there were some underlying issues that needed resolution if the growth were to continue. As we have seen, vintners faced increased land prices (up between $5,000 and $10,000 per acre) and a barrage of land-use restrictions by planners and environmentalists. Fears over access to land incentivized corporate wineries to buy up existing local vineyards in an attempt to secure their production needs for premium wine grapes and in turn created wine-grape shortages for small independent winemakers.

Some argued that the county still remained a place where wine avocations could be realized. Gerry Moro, retired Santa Barbara contractor, decided to invest all his time and capital into starting a winery. In 1989 he gave up luxuries, rented out his home and moved into a trailer and began production of his Morovino label. The former Olympian (Canadian Decathlon entrant in the 1964 Tokyo and 1972 Munich Games) got advice from Bill Wathen and Dick Dore while working a crush at Foxen Vineyard. His biggest concern was the county's shortage of quality wine grapes.[23]

A less confident view of the county's ability to nurture a new generation of wine-makers came from veterans Lindquist and Clendenen. Lindquist believed that:

> there's going to be a saturation point because the wine market isn't really growing. Every case of extra wine that's produced in Santa Barbara County pretty much has to take a case of wine sale away from somebody else. Santa Barbara is on a growth curve, but there is going to be a saturation point, I think. You know, we all keep hoping that some miracle will occur and that Americans will stop drinking Coca-Cola with their meals, and start drinking a couple glasses of wine. And if that happens, then wine sales could boom. But I'm not holding my breath for it.[24]

When asked if he could start the same type of operation in the 1990s, Clendenen answered with a resounding no. In fact he believed that young people out of college could not raise enough startup capital unless they had personal contacts. For himself, he felt that if he were starting now he would opt to be "the winemaker for some 50,000 case producer or 100,000 case producer," and then start his wine "on the side and let it grow to the point that I could live off it completely."[25]

As the first generation of Santa Barbara winemakers aged, many wondered who would be the county's second-generation leaders. Napa lessons had taught that second-generation California winemakers faced more complex challenges than many of their pioneering parents.[26] Robert Smiley, UC Davis Graduate School of Management, warned that American family businesses too often fall victim to failure when the second generation cannot deliver when they only use what they learned from their parents.[27]

Survival of small independent wineries proved to be dependent upon their ability to recapitalize the winery on a generational basis. Because of this factor many owners choose to sell due to health, estate problems, divorce, lack of capital, partner disputes, or simply retirement. Others choose to sell because of the squeeze and competitiveness of large corporations, government regulations, and labor problems. To avoid inheritance taxes of up to 50 percent of the estate over $600,000, many owners placed their wineries in a trust to protect the business for their heirs.[28] Some took advantage of a 1978 congressional decision that allowed inherited family businesses to amortize payment of the estate taxes over a ten-year period. This circumvented selling of the company's stock to pay for taxes.[29] In Santa Barbara wineries like Firestone, Fess Parker, and Gainey faced this future challenge.[30]

Problems aside, investment in the Santa Barbara region continued. Dave Yates and Craig Jaffurs left the aerospace industry in 1994 to start Jaffurs Wine Cellar and quickly became known for their Rhône wines.[31] In 1995 Curtis Winery became part of the Firestone family and winemaker Chuck Carlson put his twenty-plus years of Rhône experience to good use. Steve Clifton, USC graduate and rock singer, after working at Rancho Sisquoc and Beckman, partnered with Greg Brewer to create Brewer-Clifton, devoted to single-vineyard wines. By 2001 Robert Parker, *Wine Enthusiast,* declared that their wine was "the single greatest revelation of my 2001 tastings."[32] That same year Neil and Francine Afronsky planted eighty-five acres of Bordeaux and Rhône grapes in their Westerly Vineyard. The Afronskys sold the vineyard in 2006 to Chicago financier Jack McKinley but kept rights to their label.

The growth continued as electronic keyboard designer Tom Beckman bought the Houtz Vineyard in 1994 and in 1996 planted his 125-acre Purisima Canyon Vineyard. Over the next decade Beckman's son Steve converted the vineyard to Rhône varietals grown with biodynamic practices. That same year Peter Cargasacchi planted sixteen acres of Pinot Noir on his Santa Rita Hills farm and within a few years began selling grapes to Ken Brown, Brewer-Clifton, Siduro, and Hitching Post. Au Bon Climat winemaker Jim Clendenen's wife, Morgan, founded Cold Haven Cellars and specialized in Viognier grapes.[33]

Growth continued in 1997 when Barry Henley planted his 77-acre Syrah and Chardonnay White Hawk Vineyard in Cat Canyon and sold grapes to Adam Tolmach. Hollywood cinematographer Steve Larner and wife Christine established a 133-acre vineyard and sold grapes to Gainey, Jaffurs, and Kunen wineries.[34] In 1999 Qupé winemaker Bob Lindquist's wife, Louisa, founded the Verdadf label, which she devoted to Spanish-style wines.[35]

Despite the threat of a winery oligopoly, the influx of new, smaller wineries continued throughout the 1990s. Although large northern corporate vintibuisnesses controlled two-thirds of the vineyard land, they did not totally control grape production or keep new entrants from the field. By 1996 local vintners, large and small, crushed 45 percent of locally grown grapes for regional labels.[36]

Most local industry leaders anticipated continued growth as long as consumer demand for quality wines stayed strong and government policy did not restrict growth.[37] In a short period of thirty years, Santa Barbara wine entrepreneurs had reestablished the county's wine industry by adapting Bay Area wine-by-design agricultural and business techniques.

Agritourism became a way of life for artisan wineries and remains the largest factor for success of these small wineries in the United States, particularly Santa Barbara County. Over 75 percent of the county's premium wineries were small family-owned businesses producing less than fifteen thousand cases annually.[38] The destination allure of wineries, when coupled with a strong economy that provided ample disposable income, had made niche or artisan wineries successful. For continued success these wineries depended upon American hyper-consumption of expensive snob appeal wines, in what Cornell University professor Robert H. Frank labeled as "Luxury Fever."[39]

Santa Barbara County had learned to entice agritourists from its roughly midway position between the megalopolises of San Francisco and Los Angeles. Due to this geographic position, winery reports estimated that in 1998 almost 500,000 visitors flocked to tasting rooms along the industry's two "wine road" destinations and Santa Barbara County tourist surveys reported that visitors spent 60 percent of their time in wine country. Agrotourism increased winery direct sales to a new high of seventy-one thousand cases and winery event ticket sales reached the $2-million mark. Winery events and the Santa Barbara County Vintners Association's two festivals helped produce "induced tourist" spending in hotels and restaurants that reached $11 million in 1998.[40] These figures were proportional to the Napa Valley's 4.9 million and Sonoma Valley's 2.5 million visitors.[41]

As jug wine, under three dollars per bottle, dipped to an all-time low of 47 percent of total wine sales, wineries began producing more premium wines.[42] Jug wine sales had dropped dramatically in the past thirty years and modern consumers had shown that they were willing to spend a little more on better-quality wines like those found in Santa Barbara County.

Santa Barbara County wineries produced the majority of their wine for the premium wine market and by 1997 the average Santa Barbara premium wine retailed at fourteen to fifteen dollars per bottle compared to a national average of $7 per bottle. Local wineries now enjoyed a 4 percent share of the total California premium wine market, and the majority of the county's wine revenue was driven by Pinot Noir and Chardonnay wines.[43] In *Wine Spectator's*

1999 review of Pinot Noir wines, 23 percent (forty-two out of a total of 182 wines tasted) were from Santa Barbara and averaged a score of 87 out of a 100 (low of 79 to high of 92) with an average price of $26 dollars per bottle.[44] Chardonnay wines showed similar results with 10 percent of the wines from Santa Barbara (21 out of 216 wines tasted) with an average score of 89 points at a $23-per-bottle average price.[45]

For many wineries the real worry was their ability to provide investors with a continued favorable rate of return. *Baron's Dow Jones Business and Financial Weekly* predicted in the summer of 1998 that a wine glut of historic proportions was on the horizon.[46] The magazine cited the facts that over half of American twenty-one- to twenty-four-year-olds never drank wine and that over the next few years over 100,000 new acres (23 percent gain) of vineyards would come into full production. Newcomers to the industry worried that escalated prices paid for land and wineries would fail to achieve profits over the long haul.[47] Lewis Perdue, editor and publisher of *Wine Investment News* predicted that:

> a lot of wineries that have become used to easily selling all they could make and raising prices whenever they wanted to are suddenly going to find they no longer have those luxuries. A lot of people who think they are immune to the coming glut will find they are not.[48]

Prohibition and the Great Depression had taught the industry that lower-level consumers would buy alcoholic beverages with lower prices and more punch for the dollar. If this pattern holds true for future economic down cycles, cheaper jug wines made by Gallo, Sebastiani, Almaden, Inglenook, and Franzia would suffer the least. However, super-premium wineries would survive because in bad times the rich still purchase high-end wines. But middle-class consumers faced with pinched pocketbooks tend to move down to the under $10 bottles of wine. Thus, threats of depression or recession like phylloxera gnawed at the roots of the Santa Barbara niche industry and its predominately premium wines. Many worried that this could possibly drive many of its wineries from the rural landscape.

Optimistic members of the wine community refused to believe the doomsayers and their tales of woe. Rick Beard, Groezinger Wine Merchants, believed that, "Unless there's a serious market turnaround, something comparable to the 1987 crash, I don't think we'll see prices go back down." Beard went on to say, "I don't think we will ever see a glut of high-end, premium wines."[49] Many in the industry felt that wine pricing was more than a means to figure a return on investment. They believed that recent price ascension equated with quality in the minds of consumers. If consumers spend less in an upcoming glut, healthy wine businesses will lessen their profit margins and survive just fine until the next boom.

For Santa Barbara county fears of a Napa-like urban and vintibusiness encroachment on the rural landscape continued to loom into the next millennium. But, on the bright side, Napazation of Santa Barbara County had created a successful vintibusiness industry that was well positioned to withstand future challenges.

Notes

1. James Harold Curry III, *Agriculture under Late Capitalism: The Structure and Operation of the California Wine Industry* (PhD dissertation, Cornell University, 1994), abstract.
2. Kim Marcus, "U.S. Winery Total Grows at Fast Pace," *Wine Spectator,* 15 September 1999, 21.
3. Ibid.
4. Gomberg, Fredrikson, and Associates, "The Wine Industry's Economic Contribution to Santa Barbara County: 1998 Survey Update," prepared for the Santa Barbara County Vintners Association in June 1999.
5. Ibid.
6. Steve Barsby and Associates for Vinifera Wine Growers Association, "The Economic Contribution of the Wine Industry to the U.S. Economy, 1997," *Wine Business Monthly,* August 1999, 29.
7. Judy Kimsey, "Globalizing the Wine Industry: Shipping to the European Union," *Wine Business Monthly,* November 1998, 1, 13. American wine exports reached a 1998 high of $262.5 million up from a 1997 high of $188.6 million.
8. Eric N. Sims, *A Study of the California Wine Industry and an Analysis of the Effects of the Canadian-United States Free Trade Agreement on the Wine Sector,* with a Note on the Impact of the North American Free Trade Agreement on California Wine Exports (PhD dissertation, University of Arkansas, 1995), passim.
9. Ibid.
10. David Scott Shaw, *Firm Export Strategies and Firm Export Performance in the United States Wine Industry: A Longitudinal Study* (PhD dissertation, Purdue University, 1996), passim.
11. Juan B. Solana Rosillo, *Firm Strategies in International Markets: The Case of International Entry into the United States Wine Industry* (PhD dissertation, Purdue University, 1997), passim.
12. "Wine: A Mix of Old and New Techniques to Improve Quality," *Los Angeles Times,* 30 September 1996, D-10.
13. ohn Love, "The Long Future of U.S. Wine Value," *Wine Business Monthly,* August 1999, 34–37.
14. Abby Sawyer, "The Wine Industry on Wall Street: As Business Booms an Increasing Number of Wineries Consider Public Stock Offerings," *Wine Business Monthly,* December 1997, 1, 10–14; "Wine Market News," *Wine Business Monthly,* July 1999, 41–47.
15. Ibid.
16. Ibid.

17. Ibid.

18. Ibid, 2.

19. Gomberg, Fredrikson, *The Wine Industry's Economic Contribution to Santa Barbara County: 1998 Survey Update*, 3.

20. Gomberg, Fredrikson, and Associates, *Santa Barbara Report*, 1994.

21. Ibid., 3.

22. Business Wire, "Santa Barbara County's Wine Industry Experiences Tremendous Growth." Document ID: FC20011115540000031, 15 November 2001.

23. Kathleen Marcks, "Former Olympian Takes on Winemaking Challenge," *Wine Spectator*, 31 August 1996, 15.

24. Robert Lindquist, oral history conducted by Sarah Case, 24 February 1994, Santa Ynez, tape recording, Special Collections University of California, Santa Barbara, Santa Barbara, California.

25. Jim Clendenen, oral history conducted by Richard P. Ryba, 10 February 1994, Santa Ynez, tape recording, Special Collections University of California, Santa Barbara, Santa Barbara, California.

26. Robyn Bullard, "Sons and Daughters," *Wine Spectator*, 30 September 1993, 29–35.

27. Ibid.

28. Louis S. Freeman, "Combining the Use of Corporation, Partnerships, and Trusts to Minimize the Income and Transfer Tax Impact on Family Businesses and Investments," Taxes 62 (December 1979): 857–80.

29. Robert F. Schnier, "A Study of the Will to Survive of the Family-Owned Wineries of California," (master's thesis, Pepperdine University, 1982), passim.

30. Mark van de Kamp, "Tax Cut Boosts Family Farms," *Santa Barbara News-Press*, 2 August 1997, B-1, B-2.

31. Gabe Saglie, "Cheers! Jaffurs Celebrates 20 Years," *Santa Barbara News-Press*, 6 November 2014; Gage Saglie, "Gabe Saglie: Jaffurs Tastes through 15 Vintages of Syrah," *Santa Barbara News-Press*, 11 August 2016.

32. Corie Brown, "It'll Take More than Amore to Shine," *Los Angeles Times*, 29 November 2006.

33. Patrick Comiskey, "When Life Dealt Them Grapes They Made Wine," *Los Angeles Times*, 29 March 2006.

34. Corie Brown, "The Exciting Up-and-Comers," *Los Angeles Times*, 5 September 2007; Dennis Schaefer, "Beckman Wines: Quality across the Board," *Santa Barbara News-Press*, 13 November 2003; Dennis Schaefer, "Curtis Winery: In the Rhône Zone," *Santa Barbara News-Press*, 26 June 2003.

35. Comiskey, "When Life Dealt Them Grapes."

36. Mark van de Kamp, "Report Predicts Boost for Economy," *Santa Barbara News-Press*, 31 July 1997, B-1; Gomberg, Fredrikson, and Associates, *The Wine Industry's Economic Contribution to Santa Barbara County Based on the Santa Barbara County Vintners Association 1996 Economic Survey* (San Francisco: Gomberg, Fredrikson, and Associates, 1997), passim.

37. Anthony Gene White, *State Policy and Public Administration Impacts on an Emerging Industry: The Wine Industry in Oregon and Washington* (PhD dissertation, Portland State University, 1993), 97–104.

38. Gomberg, Fredrikson, *The Wine Industry's Economic Contribution to Santa Barbara County* (1997), passim; M. L. Hilton, "Out of the Garage and into Haute Cuisine: Boutiques Wines Find Their Place at the Table," *Wine Business Monthly*, January 1999, 34–38.

39. Michael J. Okoniewski, "Robert H. Frank: Resisting a Society's Rage to Spend," *New York Times*, 14 August 1999; Robert H. Frank, *Luxury Fever: Why Money Fails to Satisfy in an Era of Excess* (New York; Free Press, 1999).

40. Gomberg, Fredrikson, *The Wine Industry's Economic Contribution to Santa Barbara County* (1997), 7. The report also stated that in 1998 winery tourists spent 10,700,000 dollars on wine and two million dollars on other sales.

41. Laura Madonna, "Making the Consumer Connection: The Importance of Tourism to the Wine Business," *Wine Business Monthly,* May 1999, 1.

42. "Jug Wine Sales Down: Revenues Up," *Wine Business Monthly,* May 1999, 10.

43. Gomberg, Fredrikson, *The Wine Industry's Economic Contribution to Santa Barbara County* (1997), 5.

44. Statistical information compiled by the author from the "Wine Spectator Buying Guide: Special Report California Pinot Noir," *Wine Spectator,* 15 September 1999, 158–64.

45. Statistical information compiled by the author from the "Wine Spectator Buying Guide: Special Report Chardonnay Review," *Wine Spectator,* 30 April 1999, 142–51.

46. Jay Palmer, "The Coming Glut: Why the Wine Industry's Long String of Price Hikes Is About to End," *Baron's Dow Jones Business and Financial Weekly,* 3 August 1998, 25–29.

47. Ibid., 25.

48. Ibid., 25–26.

49. Abigail Sawyer, "Premium Wine Prices Soar with Economy: No Glut at High End of Market," *Wine Business Monthly,* January 1999, 14–18.

Chapter Ten

The New Millennium Brings New Challenges

The new millennium brought hopes for continued growth and success for California and the Santa Barbara wine industry. In 2000 California's 1,450 wineries produced 238.9 million cases valued at $26.3 billion on 568,000 acres of vineyards (up from 335,200 acres in 1990).[1] Santa Barbara County's three AVAs grew to just under 18,000 acres of wine grapes—an increase of over 9,000 acres over the last decade.[2] Domestic wine sales increased but just as important were California wine exports that had grown to over thirty-two million cases with a value of over $560 million up from 12.2 million cases with a value of $137 million in 1990.[3] Adding to the growth was the fact that U.S. wine consumption increased 1 percent in 2001 to 231 million cases with forty-four brands accounting for more than 60 percent of all sales.[4] Consumers were also excited about the new California Rhône varietals and Santa Barbara County had twenty-five winemakers producing their California version of the classic French wine. Investors still viewed Santa Barbara County as a good place for expansion into the premium wine industry and Jon Fredrikson of the Gomberg Fredrikson Group called Santa Barbara County the California wine industry equivalent of Silicon Valley.[5]

Over the past four decades, the California wine industry had attempted to keep up with demand by planting more grapes and shifting from the centuries old trial-and-error system to a wine-by-design model dependent upon science and technology to achieve both vineyard and winery production goals.[6] A new era of vintners studied their consumers and utilized sales statistics to fill market needs. But these pluses created an untenable obstacle for those wishing to enter the California wine industry. In the 2000s, increased land prices exacerbated the problem and drove wine prices even higher. Would-be vintners in 2002 could pay $180,000 per acre for quality Napa and Sonoma vineyard land and by 2016 Santa Barbara vineyard land prices hovered around $80,000 per acre up from a 1995 per acre cost of $33,500.[7] The California Chapter of the American Society of Farm Managers and Rural Appraisers predicted a slowdown in vineyard planting and Solvang Real Estate broker T. Hayer confirmed this prediction for Santa Barbara County.[8]

Wilfred Wong, Beverages and More buyer, threw a wet blanket on the idea of California wine greatness by stating that, "California wines have been the darlings of the wine industry, and they've become snotty and think they can charge whatever they want."[9] Some even believed that these premium wines had become a "signifier" of social class.[10] Wine connoisseurs who use to glorify the wine-making paradigm of Old World (terroir-based delicate and refined fruit taste) now spoke about the marvelous characteristics of New World (fruity, scientific) wines. Matt Kramer believed that American wine drinkers do not identify any real differences and that "to see wine through the Old World / New World paradigm is to blind yourself to today's borderless wine reality."[11] No matter how one felt about wine snobbery, the fact remained that for fifteen consecutive years wine consumption had increased and Americans drank more wine than Italians and some predicted they would soon surpass the French.[12]

Yet, as good as these figures look on paper, there were still many challenges to overcome. California growers, statewide, worried about a wine glut as over one hundred thousand acres came online. The scare of a glut drove many to expand exports into places like China where an economic revival over the last few decades had left many of its citizens with disposable incomes. Marketers predicted that Asia could add over 250 million drinkers to the world market. Archaeological evidence showed that China had made wine since 212 BC, but today most of the state-run wineries only produced cheap red wines and blended many of them with lesser imported foreign wines. To satisfy consumer demands the short-term Chinese government plan was to allow foreign imports while government owned wineries expanded their one hundred thousand acres and four hundred wineries.[13]

Problematic for the California industry was the fact that both domestic and international competition increased. At home domestic competition increased as all fifty states now boasted of having bonded wineries and many individual state legislatures moved to protect their local wine industry.[14] Global competition also loomed heavily on California wineries, who only produced 7 percent of the world's wine and Santa Barbara produced a meager 2 percent of that figure. Tom Beckman, SBCVA president, believed the county would be okay because of their ties to the premium market. Not all agreed with Beckman's observation. Lewis Perdue, *Wine Industry Insight* news editor, believed that no grower would be safe in a glut and Joe Carrari, Los Alamos vintner, believed that the only way to survive was through long-term winery contracts. Dale Hampton agreed, "I've told everyone who's called me that if you go into the grape market without a contract in your hand then you're not a very smart individual."[15] Having high-quality grapes and wines was not enough and *Wine Spectator*'s James Laube believed that success stories like California Chardonnay had become a "victim of its own success."[16] The fact remained that in a wine-glut corporate wineries purchase fewer grapes, leaving farmers and small estate wineries to deal with the majority of the financial losses.

NEVER-ENDING PEST AND DISEASE BATTLES

The recurrence of the glassy-winged sharpshooter and Pierce's disease in the late 1990s began to reach a critical point as vine damage continued to threaten vineyards statewide. Between 1997 and 1998 the disease had killed 150,000 acres of grapes (the 1892 outbreak killed only 40,000 acres) and caused over $6 million in damage to the industry.[17] The problem became so widespread that California Governor Gray Davis instructed the California Department of Agriculture to declare a state of emergency so that Vice President Al Gore and Agriculture Secretary Dan Glickman could declare the pest a federal agricultural emergency. With congressional support and President Bill Clinton's signature, the federal government pledged $22.3 million for research to develop resistant vines and Governor Davis signed a bill to add another $13.8 million. Assemblywoman Patricia Wiggins (D-Santa Rosa) called for an assessment of $3.00 for every $1,000 of farm gate value (what grapes are worth when they leave the vineyard) to try to raise an additional $5 million to combat the disease.[18] In 1993 inspectors found sharpshooters in Goleta and Carpenteria and the state quickly allocated $175,000 for early detection and inspection programs in Santa Barbara County.[19]

Concerns over the spread of the disease intensified as eleven counties reported outbreaks and the pest got within a dozen miles of Napa and Sonoma. Initially grape growers treated the sharpshooter like any other pest and pressured county agricultural commissioners to approve intensified pesticide spray programs. This approach to solving the problem met immediate roadblocks from environmentalists, forcing the Sonoma County Board of Supervisors to reject John Westby's, Sonoma Agricultural Commissioner, attempts to approve spray programs. Lucy Kenyon, Sonoma Sierra Club, believed, "While the wine industry is important to a lot of people, including members of the Sierra Club, the health of human beings and the environment must take precedence."[20]

After initial research scientists found the new evolved sharpshooter to be bigger, more mobile, and able to feed on a wider range of plants. The pest had already destroyed 2,500 acres of wine grapes in Temecula and regional leader Callaway Winery had to go north to Santa Barbara County for grapes to meet its wine production needs. At the nearby UC Riverside, entomologist Matthew Blua warned, "I've studied plant diseases throughout my career and if I were to describe a worse-case scenario, it would be what we are seeing."[21] Further disheartening news came when Russ Mizel, University of Florida, warned that, "There's not a whole lot of data suggesting that [the glassy-winged sharp-shooter] will do anything but spread throughout the entire state of California." He continued, "It is just a question of when is it going to happen, how long it takes, and can you slow it down."[22] Statewide, the industry braced itself for the long-haul battle with the insect. In Santa Barbara County Foxen Vineyards helped raise money for the fight by giving up contract rights to three tons of Bien Nacido Pinot Noir grapes valued at $3,000 per ton. The auction sold the grapes for $4,500 dollars per ton with profits going for research.[23]

Pierce's disease was not the only disease to strike California. Eutypa, a fungal disease, hit the state's vineyards causing $260 million in crop losses. The disease reduces crop production by 90 percent and usually takes two to three years to express itself as it shrivels shoot growth. The only known solution is removal of infected shoots and even then the vine usually dies within ten years. The voluntary nonprofit American Vineyard Association financed a $1,750,000 grant to help researchers study the disease and treatment solutions.[24] Making matters worse was the fact that the oak tree preservation concerns were far from over. Nurseries with oak trees in San Diego and Los Angeles reported an outbreak of the fungal disease *Phytophthora armorm* more commonly called "Sudden Oak Death." Spread by airborne spores, the disease has no cure and could possibly harm vines in wine country areas with oaks, such as Santa Barbara.[25]

NEO-PROHIBITION CONTINUES

Over the past century American battles between the anti-alcohol and the pro-alcohol forces had not been resolved, and the wine industry trend toward higher-alcohol premium wines played into the hands of anti-alcohol forces. Up to the 1990s winemakers and enthusiasts had attempted to distance themselves from higher-alcohol distilled spirits under the guise that wine was lower alcohol and a cultural and religious beverage. This argument held up at the time because most California table wines registered between 12 and 13 percent. But, as growers and winemakers sought a distinct California style these alcohol levels gradually rose. University scientists had given the industry new super-clones that reduced viruses, allowed leaves to stay green longer, and extended photosynthesis, resulting in higher sugar (brix) levels. Add to that new yeasts that were more efficient in converting sugar to alcohol or what Santa Barbara winemaker Bruno Di Afonso referred to as the "Schwarzenegger kinds of yeasts. They would ferment a building if given a chance."[26] Wine alcohol averages rose to the 14 to 16 percent level and required that some wines be processed to remove excess alcohol. In reality a 15 percent wine has 25 percent more alcohol than a wine at 12 percent. This increase made it harder for winemakers to separate themselves from other alcohol products.

After years of lobbying for inclusion of the mention of the health benefits of moderate alcohol consumption in government dietary suggestions, the Wine Institute finally made some headway. The 1995 USDA "Dietary Guidelines" suggested that wine in moderation was an acceptable part of the Mediterranean Diet. Needless to say many neo-Prohibitionists found this claim unacceptable. The new statement prompted Republican senator Strom Thurmond to pressure the USDA to include a warning about the potential for alcohol abuse in the 2000 guidelines. John DeLuca, fearing the adverse interpretation of the new statement, lamented that Thurmond's addition to the label did not acknowledge the extensive research on the positive health benefits of moderate wine consumption.[27] The issue somewhat resolved itself in 2005 when the guidelines conveyed the compromised message of, "The consumption of alcohol can have beneficial or harmful effects" and it went on to suggest that one glass of wine for women and two glasses of wine for men could be part of a healthy diet.[28] This was a limited success for the wine industry as alcohol consumers continued to receive mixed messages about alcohol and the role of wine in one's daily diet.

By the end of 2000 the neo-Prohibitionist pressure on alcohol intensified as President Bill Clinton signed a law redefining legal alcohol blood levels while driving to be 0.08 down from the 0.10 level found in thirty-two states. In order to continue to receive federal highway funds, states were required to comply with the new levels. This carrot/stick approach of tying federal transportation funds to a state's acceptance of new lower limits worried restaurants and wineries with tasting rooms.[29]

Neo-Prohibitionists continued to make wine part of what many saw as the nation's alcohol problem and in 1988 Congress passed its first alcohol labeling requirements. Introduced in the House of Representatives as H.R. 5210, the Alcoholic Beverage Labeling Act required that the labels of alcoholic beverages carry a government warning for pregnant women and people who operate cars. In 2000 West Virginia Democratic senator Robert Byrd unsuccessfully sponsored a new bill to enlarge the size of warning labels on wine and include the words "May Cause Health Problems." Supporters wanted a wider label with large red or black letters on a white background with an exclamation point inside of a triangle.[30] Further labeling threats came in 2007 when the Alcohol and Tobacco Tax and Trade Bureau (TTB) proposed that all alcoholic beverages carry a serving facts panel, like foods, on their labels, complete with calorie counts for carbohydrates, fats, and proteins.[31] While the idea did not gain immediate traction wine-maker Randall Graham, in a sarcastic move, labeled his Bonny Doon wines listing the ingredients as grapes, sulfur, yeast used, and any filtering agents.[32]

DIRECT MARKETING FIASCO

Fears of increased restrictions on direct marketing and mail-order purchases scared small premium wineries throughout California and Santa Barbara. With only twenty-three states permitting winery direct shipping, small wineries were at a disadvantage to large commercial operations that dominated the three-tier system. Because small wineries were left out of this traditional distribution chain, they depended heavily upon being able to ship directly to past visitors, collectors, and enthusiasts. These direct marketing concerns directly affected the daily business of all Santa Barbara small wineries and tasting rooms.

Their fears materialized as wine consumers in twenty-six states found that buying wine directly from wineries could lead to fines and jail time. This led to a rebellion by some consumers who argued that this violated free trade under the constitution's commerce clause. In response alcohol wholesale distributors pressured state and federal governments to protect the traditional three-tier system where wineries sold wine to distributors, who collected taxes and then resold to retailers, who in turn sold to consumers. Wholesalers argued that the Twenty-First Amendment (Repeal of Prohibition) had given states broad rights to regulate the sale, distribution, and importation of alcoholic beverages. As a result, by the year 2000 the United States had fifty varied sets of state alcohol laws, hundreds of county laws, and no consistent federal regulation. The system was further burdened by internet sales that permitted buying across state lines. These fears were heightened by the fact that small wineries could not get the dwindling number of distributors to carry their brands. To protect their dominance of the wine market's distribution channels, Juanita Duggan, CEO Wine and Spirits Wholesalers of America, vowed that her organization would vigorously oppose direct sales.[33] The wine industry again turned to the Wine Institute for assistance. In a short time, the newly appointed Wine Institute CEO Robert Koch advocated for more open trade in both interstate and global markets.[34]

Sides were drawn up and the battle over direct shipment of wine heated up. Wholesalers attempted to convince Americans that kids would be able to purchase alcohol illegally and states would lose tax revenues if direct shipping were made legal. Religious neo-Prohibitionists, fighting for the souls of the drunken nation, joined forces with Mothers Against Drunk Drivers (MADD), Students Against Drunk Drivers (SADD), and the Wine and Spirits Wholesalers of America to keep the three-tier system as a means to regulate alcohol distribution. Wine drinkers countered the attacks by forming the Coalition for Free Trade and Free the Grapes to fight for legal direct shipments. Craig Addis, Santa Barbara Winery Marketing Director, believed that all the fury over underage phone and internet orders was a scare tactic designed by wholesalers attempting to keep complete control of the distribution chain. In his words, "In reality I've never heard of underage drinkers ordering a bottle of wine and having it delivered to their house." Worried about losing market share, Louis Lucas lamented that he thought these restrictions would cost him 10 percent of his sales.[35]

By 2002 the federal courts entered the fracas over direct-shipping bans. Over the past few years, courts had overturned shipping bans in Virginia and North Carolina that both states had designed to protect their own vintners. As expected, the two states immediately appealed the decisions. In the meantime wine industry leaders waited anxiously for the hopeful overturn of New York State bans.[36] The state of Texas also went through a series of court challenges, and in 2000 Texas judge Melinda Harmon declared that the state's direct shipping ban was illegal because it violated the United States Constitution's free-trade guarantees. In response to being challenged by the federal court, the

Texas Legislature passed a 2001 law allowing Texans to ship wine from Texas wineries to their own homes but not wine from out of state. Lone Star wine lovers challenged the law in 2002 and a Third District Federal Judge overturned the new law.[37]

In a direct attack on small wineries, California State assemblyman Marco Firebaugh introduced Assembly Bill 1922 in an attempt to eliminate the so-called gray or parallel market that allowed small wine importers to import and resell wine. The proposal aimed to set a California precedent for the direct marketing battle. Proponents of the bill fought to shore-up the traditional system that designated official U.S. importers who then could sell to retailers. Small-scale importer Michael Opdahl, Joshua Tree Imports of Pasadena, believed that, "This bill is designed to do one thing: consolidate more of the power that the large distributers already have and drive away competitors." Those opposed to the bill feared that it was anti-consumer and would make rare and small-production wines harder to purchase. In response over fifty retailers joined with the Family Winemakers of California in opposition of the bill and warned that retailers would lose $100 to 200 million in sales and that the state would lose $5–10 million in tax revenue.[38] After a one-month political firestorm, Firebaugh pulled the bill from the docket. This did little to resolve the mass confusion over direct buying of wine, and federal courts continued to slowly resolve the problem state by state.

In 2003 a Florida federal court ruled that the state's ban on interstate shipments was unconstitutional, but Judge Richard Berman stayed his decision, knowing that his ruling would be challenged. A short time later a federal court in Michigan ruled that their state's wine shipping bans were illegal.[39]

Both sides of the direct-shipping controversy began to expect that the final decision would lie with the United States Supreme Court. Planning for this outcome the Coalition for Free Trade hired Kenneth Starr, of Whitewater and Monica Lewinsky fame, to prepare for the eventual high-court case. Starr believed, "These are laws that are designed to handicap and hinder out-of-state wineries," and therefore violate the Constitution.[40] The preparation proved prudent as the Supreme Court agreed to hear the direct-to-consumer case in 2004 based on the Michigan and New York appeals. The highest court in the land would have to decide the outcome of the conflict based upon the Twenty-First Amendment's assigning the power to control alcohol sales and distribution to states versus the Commerce Clause that allowed free trade between states.[41]

In the meantime, many states continued to enforce their alcohol laws. In Massachusetts state attorney general Tom Riley with the State Alcohol Beverages Control Commission set up a sting operation. In the operation five underage volunteers made eight purchases online using their own credit cards and addresses. Ten retailers were named in the warrant and UPS, DHL, and Fedex faced pressure for not verifying the ages of the receivers. Wine and Spirits Wholesalers of America said the operation proved the need for the three-tier system over direct-buying online.[42]

While waiting for the Supreme Court decision, Costco attempted a work-around for the hodgepodge of fifty different state laws. The giant retailer had recently become the largest wine retailer in America, and they battled their home state of Washington over restrictions on wine sales. Costco sought legal relief from the Washington State Liquor Board that required the use of the three-tier system, mandated at least a 10 percent retail profit, and prohibited volume discounts to retailers. In December of 2005 U.S. district judge Marsha Pechmann backed Costco but again everyone expected the decision to be appealed.[43] The appeal landed in the Ninth Circuit Court of Appeals in 2008 and the judges denied Costco's claims.[44]

In 2005 the United States Supreme Court ruled five to four in the *Granholm v. Heald*, 544 U.S. 460 (2005) case against the states of Michigan and New York because their direct shipment laws had discriminated against out-of-state wineries, violating the U.S. Constitution's Commerce Clause.[45] Justices Anthony Kennedy, Antonin Scalia, David Souter, Ruth Bader Ginsburg, and Stephen Breyer struck down the Michigan and New York laws. Justice Kennedy wrote that "States have broad power to regulate liquor under the Twenty-First Amendment," but that "this power, however, does not allow states to ban, or severely limit, the direct shipping of wine while simultaneously authorizing direct shipment by in-state producers."[46] Their decision clearly allowed direct shipment of wine as long as state and out-of-state wineries were treated equally.

Regretfully, the decision did not set a clear path for the future of national direct sales. The states of Florida, Connecticut, Indiana, Massachusetts, Ohio, and Vermont still had discriminatory laws on the books, and state legislatures had to create new policies and laws. Thirteen states, including California had "reciprocity" laws allowing wine shipments only from other states that allow out-of-state wineries to ship to their residents. Many believed this system discriminated against nonreciprocal states. Some states considered laws requiring wineries to register and pay taxes in order to sell within their state. Complicating the mix were the fifteen states that banned wine shipments altogether.[47] In a way Prohibition still ruled the day, and a cohesive wine direct-buying system would have to be resolved at a later date.

Dark Clouds on the Horizon

The decade of the '90s was the longest sustained period of economic growth in the nation's history and more citizens than ever had disposable incomes to purchase premium wines. Plans to meet consumer demands were off to a great start in 2000 as California wineries crushed a record-setting 3.3 million tons of wine grapes, up 27 percent from 1999. But the mood of the country darkened in 2001 after the 9/11 attack on New York City and the bust of the technology sector in the "Dot-com Bubble." American consumers had less money to spend on wine and often filled their cellars with more competitive imported foreign wines and dined out less in restaurants. As a result many economists predicted a slowdown in the entire U.S. economy, and in late 2001 Robert Smiley, Dean of the University of California, Davis Graduate School of Management, agreed and warned that the wine industry would be affected.[48] International fears, a grape glut, and a slow economy hung over the wine industry like a late fall rain cloud as ripe grapes waited to be harvested.

The wine industry is a cash-flow business dependent upon a continual flow of money through the pipeline of farm to production to sales. If any point along the flow is upset, the rest of the process faces problems. Unlike industrial widget production grape farmers cannot easily adjust production numbers. If grapes are scarce it can take farmers upward of a decade to get new vineyards online, and on the opposite side, grape-gluts could force farmers to pull up vines or dump grapes. The recession of 2009 presented such a problem as consumers had less disposable income for the purchase of premium wines, forcing price slashes for wine. Throughout the state grape prices dropped as wine prices fell and Santa Barbara growers and wineries suffered. Before the recession Brewer-Clifton single-vineyard wines sold for $60 to $80 per bottle. With reduced sales the winery moved one-half of its production to a $40 regional blend aided by grower Peter Cargasacchi, reducing his grape prices by 10 percent.[49]

Everyday Concerns and Distractions

As the industry shifted into full production, growers began to worry about the availability of a dependable supply of cheap labor. Many Americans believed that American workers needed strict immigration policies and laws to keep undocumented workers from taking their jobs. In a move to keep agricultural concerns from hiring nonresident workers, Homeland Security began to enforce $10,000 fines to businesses that hired illegal workers. This worried strawberry and grape growers that had depended on these workers over the last half-century. Further pressure on the numbers of field workers increased as the service industries, like hotels, restaurants, and residential gardeners, drew additional workers from the fields.[50]

Another unexpected distraction came as those with physical disabilities won the right to have equal access to public buildings. The 1990 Americans with Disabilities Act ensured that Americans with disabilities could enjoy "major life activities." The act gave businesses, government buildings, public facilities, and schools time to remediate their facilities to serve all citizens. But many of those affected felt that the change was happening too slowly. In the late 1990s through early 2000s, Jarek Molski sued over five hundred California businesses for ADA violations. As a result, Santa Barbara, San Luis Obispo, Monterey, and Santa Clara Counties had eighty-one wineries facing legal actions for violations of the Disability Act. To avoid legal problems local wineries like Fess Parker, Firestone, Sanford, and Zaca Mesa scrambled to update their facilities. The process toward conversion slowed down in 2005 when U.S. district judge Edward Rafeedie ruled that Molski was "running a systematic scheme of extortion" and barred him from filing further cases without permission.[51]

Everyday distractions also tempered how vintners viewed the industry. Byron Babcock remembered when he borrowed a neighbor's tractor and the steering failed while going down a hillside. Luckily, they both survived. Karen Steinwachs recalled getting attacked by killer bees, and Larry Schaffer almost lost his entire first batch of Tercer wine.[52] Overall, both new and old challenges tempered and directed future growth of California and Santa Barbara wineries.

Notes

1. Wine Institute figures derived from Gomberg-Fredrikson and U.S.D.A. reports.
2. California Grape Acreage Statistics from the California Crop and Livestock Reporting Service, 1990–2000.
3. Wine Institute, "U.S. Wine Exports 1986–1999," The source for these figures came from the U.S.D.A. Trade Data and Analysis reports.
4. "U.S. Wine Consumption Up 1 Percent," *Wine Spectator,* 15 October 2002.

5. Mark van de Kamp, "Curbs on Wine Retailing Hinted," *Santa Barbara News-Press*, 28 June 2000; Eric Asimov, "Lush Wine from a Pacific Breeze," *New York Times*, 3 May 2000.

6. Bruce Sanderson, "Wine by Design," *Wine Spectator*, 15 November 2001.

7. Paul Sullivan, "Owning a Vineyard: The Days of Wine Are Not All Rosy," *New York Times*, 9 September 2016; Mark van de Kamp, "Grape Glut Corks Vineyard Demand; Ranch Land Grows Pricier," *Santa Barbara News-Press*, 5 June 2002.

8. Van de Kamp, "Grape Glut Corks Vineyard Demand."

9. Kim Marcus, "California Takes on the World," *Wine Spectator*, 15 December 2002.

10. Matt Kramer, "Wine's Emerging Class Divide," *Wine Spectator*, 28 February 2007.

11. Matt Kramer, "Buddy, Can You Spare a Paradigm," *Wine Spectator*, 31 May 2008.

12. "U.S. to Drink More Wine Than Italy," *Wine Spectator*, 30 November 2007.

13. Mark Graham, "China's Wine revolution," *Wine Spectator*, 30 November 2005.

14. "Wine across America," *Wine Spectator*, 30 November 2002.

15. Mark van de Kamp, "Santa Barbara County's Booming Wine Industry," *Santa Barbara News-Press*, 3 September 2000.

16. James Laube, "California Chardonnay," *Wine Spectator*, 31 May 2002.

17. Frank J. Prial, "Wine Talk: Feasting Lethally on California Vineyards," *New York Times*, 12 July 2000.

18. Kim Marcus, "Agricultural Emergency Declared in California Due to Deadly Vine Pest," *Wine Spectator*, 31 August 2000; Daniel Sogg and Lynn Alley, "Deadly Vine Pest Reaches Northern California Wine Regions," *Wine Spectator*, 15 December 2000; Mark van de Kamp, "Officials Target Vineyard Disease," *Santa Barbara News-Press*, 24 March 2000; Mark van de Kamp, "Vintners Support Sharpshooter Bill," *Santa Barbara News-Press*, 25 January 2001; "U.S. Targets Sharpshooter with $7 Million," *Santa Barbara News-Press*, 26 May 2000.

19. Mark van de Kamp, "Millions on Tap to Find, Fight Pest," *Santa Barbara News-Press*, 20 May 2000.

20. Daniel Sogg, "Sonoma Wineries and Environmentalists Battle over Pesticides," *Wine Spectator*, 15 December 2000.

21. Kim Marcus, "Agricultural Emergency Declared in California Due to Deadly Vine Pest," *Wine Spectator*, 31 August 2000; "Surviving the Sharpshooter: Southern California Vineyards Hang On," *Wine Spectator*, 15 September 2001.

22. Daniel Sogg, "California Vineyard Apocalypse," *Wine Spectator*, 15 October 2000.

23. "Auctioned Grapes Fetch Heady Price," *Santa Barbara News-Press*, 9 September 2000.

24. Daniel Sogg, "California Growers Attempt to Head Off Another Vine Threat," *Wine Spectator*, 30 April 2001.

25. Thomas Schultz, "Spread of Oak Tree Disease Alarms County Land Holders," *Santa Barbara News-Press*, 30 March 2004.

26. Eric Asimov, "The Hard Stuff Now Includes Wine," *New York Times*, 13 April 2005.

27. Dana Nigro, "Stronger Wording Sought for Alcohol Message," *Wine Spectator*, 30 April 2000.

28. Jacob Gaffney, "New U.S. Dietary Guidelines Keep Stance on Drinking," *Wine Spectator*, 31 March 2005.

29. Jacob Gaffney, "Congress Sets Tough Federal Drunken-Driving Standard," *Wine Spectator*, 15 December 2000.

30. "Feds May Enlarge Warning labels on Wine Bottles," *Wine Spectator*, 31 July 2001.

31. Laurie Woolever, "U.S. Government Mulls Wine Nutrition Labels," *Wine Spectator*, 15 October 2007.

32. Daniel Sogg, "California Winery to List Ingredients on Labels," *Wine Spectator*, 29 February 2008.

33. Dana Nigro, "The Wine Wars: Tide Turns in Direct Shipping," *Wine Spectator*, 15 October 2002.

34. Dana Nigro, "California Wine's Chief Advocate," *Wine Spectator*, 15 October 2003.

35. Frank Nelson, "Restrictions Affect Sales by Local Wineries," *Santa Barbara News-Press,* 8 December 2004.

36. Tim Fish and Dana Nigro, "Wine-Shipping Battle Heats Up in Federal Courts," *Wine Spectator,* 15 June 2002.

37. Dana Nigro, "Federal Judge Overturns Texas Shipping Laws," *Wine Spectator,* 15 September 2002.

38. "California Debates Restricting Wine Imports," *Wine Spectator,* 30 June 2002; "California Bill to Restrict Wine Imports Stalls," *Wine Spectator,* 31 July 2002.

39. Dana Nigro, "Courts Favor Consumers in New York and Florida Wine-Shipping Lawsuits," *Wine Spectator,* 31 January 2003; Dana Nigro, "Federal Appeals Court Nixes Michigan's Wine-Shipping Ban," *Wine Spectator,* 30 November 2003.

40. Dana Nigro, "From Whitewater to Wine: Kenneth Starr Joins Shipping Fight," *Wine Spectator,* 15 May 2003.

41. Dana Nigro, "High Court to Hear Wine Shipping Case," *Wine Spectator,* 31 July 2004.

42. Nick Fauchald and Dana Nigro, "Online Wine Sellers Caught in a Sting," *Wine Spectator,* 31 August 2004.

43. Eric Arnold, "Costco Talks about a Revolution," *Wine Spectator,* 31 March 2006; Eric Arnold, "Costco's Court Win Could Cut Prices," *Wine Spectator,* 30 June 2006; Carol Robertson, "Case 10: We Can't Get It for You Wholesale—Costco Takes On the Three-Tier System," *The Little Red Book of Wine Law: A Case of Legal Issues* (Chicago: ABA Publishing, 2008), 120–27.

44. Eric Arnold, "Costco Loses Long Fight to Reform Wine Distribution Laws," *Wine Spectator,* 30 April 2008.

45. A legal case study of the Supreme Court decision can be found in Carol Robertson, "Case 9: You Can't Take It with You, or Have It Shipped Either—Direct Shipment: The Supreme Court Weighs In," *The Little Red Book of Wine Law: A Case of Legal Issues* (Chicago: ABA Publishing, 2008), 104–19.

46. Dana Nigro, "U.S. Supreme Court Overturns Wine-Shipping Bans," *Wine Spectator,* 16 May 2005; "Justices Lift Ban on Wine Shipments," *Santa Barbara News-Press,* 17 May 2005; Marvin R. Shanken, "A Supreme Decision," *Wine Spectator,* 31 July 2005.

47. Dana Nigro, "U.S. Supreme Court Overturns Wine-Shipping Bans," *Wine Spectator,* 16 May 2005.

48. Jacob Gaffney, "California's 2000 Vintage Sets Record for Size," *Wine Spectator,* 15 May 2001; Daniel Sogg, "California Wine Prices May Drop Due to Grape Glut," *Wine Spectator,* 30 November 2001; Tim Fish, "California Under Pressure," *Wine Spectator,* 15 December 2002.

49. Eric Asimov, "Where Anxiety Is All That's Flowing," *New York Times,* 28 July 2009.

50. "Economy Is Dependent on Work Force of Illegal Immigrants," *Santa Barbara News-Press,* 8 April 2006; Daniel Sogg, "Immigration Rules May Cause Higher Wine Prices," *Wine Spectator,* 31 October 2007.

51. Lynn Alley, "Lawsuits Force California Wineries to Address Accessibility Issues," *Wine Spectator,* 30 April 2005.

52. Gabe Saglie, "Harvest Horrors: Local Winemakers Recall Chilling Tales," *Santa Barbara News-Press,* 24 October 2013.

Chapter Eleven

New Millennium: New Land-Use and Environmental Challenges

After one hundred years of being told that mono-crop, chemical-intensive methods increased production and profits, most wineries learned to depend upon science to maintain wine quality and had moved far away from producing natural wines. In the winery they utilized university-researched and trial-and-error methods like filtration for murky wines, tartaric acid to boost acidity, backfilling with younger wines, adding oak chips, and utilized spinning cones to remove excessive alcohol. In the vineyard they experimented with new rootstocks, new clones, vine spacing, trellising, and increased hang-time. Use of computerized programs, satellite imagery, and new technology in the field and winery became the norm. Most agreed that business efficiency with large-scale production successfully produced consistent industrial wine and that over time wine quality had improved. This model slowly shifted as the environmental movement demanded more eco-friendly wines and pushed and pulled the industry to reevaluate its use of pesticides, herbicides, tree cutting, and destruction of natural habitats, and most importantly, review what it means to be a steward of the land.

Early in his tenure as CEO of the Wine Institute, John De Luca identified the tension between the wine industry and environmentalists. In his words, "I have said on a number of occasions, people and grapes have one thing in common: they love to live in beautiful places."[1] He realized that as suburban communities grew closer to vineyards, that the industry had to rethink its stand on sustainable stewardship. To this end the Wine Institute helped create the California Council for Environmental and Economic Balance subgroup of the California Environmental Group and attended regular meetings with the Sierra Club, Audubon Society, and American Farmland Trust.

As the sustainability pressure heated up the wine industry began to face an increased number of local, state, and federal regulations and restrictions that many industry insiders felt inhibited the further growth of the industry. To counteract corporate wine-ways, "Not In My Back Yard" (NIMBY) enthusiasts, environmentalists, and anti–big business forces quickly learned to lobby government officials and use the courts to restrict the wine industry's unbridled actions and unregulated growth. By 2000 their work heavily influenced Santa Barbara County winery regulations and in essence set up roadblocks from the 1980s to present that did slow down commercial operations. The downside was that the slow and expensive single-track permitting process tended to stifle opportunities for small wineries, while only slowing down large corporate wineries that had the money, lawyers, and time to endure the process. In an effort to ameliorate the discrepancy, the Central Coast Wine Growers Association offered a solution based on classifying wineries by size (small, up to 20,000 cases—medium, 20,000 to 50,000-cases—large, 50,000-plus cases), thus creating a tiered system that would adjust regulations and restrictions dependent upon winery size.[2]

Most farmers were perplexed by all the new environmental rules since they considered themselves to be stewards of the land that produces their crops and provides them with their livelihood. Yet, decades of environmental battles had left Santa Barbara ranchers, farmers, grape growers, and winemakers with a compromised environmental public image. To overcome this negative image most eventually changed how they conducted business.

During the decades of the 1980s and '90s, Santa Barbara County agriculture, with university and government incentives, experienced a shift from rangeland for cattle to a more industrial agricultural model of high-value irrigated crops. Farmers and ranchers viewed themselves as businesspeople and it made sense that they made the best use of their land to increase profits. In the past they had averaged $50 to $100 per acre and earned a mediocre living after land, labor, water, and crop expenses. Most were eager to increase profits, and in less than a decade (1992 to 2000) county farmers had converted over thirty-nine thousand acres or 49 percent of all the county's agricultural land to irrigated crops. This growth included the regional wine industry that grew from nine thousand acres to around eighteen thousand acres. As a result of the rapid expansion and shift in usage, County agricultural production grew from a yearly 1973 figure of $147 million to a 1998 high of $611 million. By converting land to irrigated crops or grape growing and then utilizing new science, technology, herbicides, and pesticides, land-owners stood to make greater profits from industrial agriculture.

Not all residents of the county saw the shift as beneficial. George Rauh, Lompoc anti-pesticide activist, believed "it's a capitalist imperative to extract more from the land, and these farmers are trying to wring every last coin out of the Earth."[3] Limited water resources, protection of watersheds, endangered species, chemical use for weeds and pests, urban encroachment, and destruc-tion of oak trees drove activists to further lament the loss of the old rangeland habitats. The end result was a battle between environmentalists and landown-ers, ranchers, farmers, and viticulturists over the use of the land. As the struggle intensified both sides utilized the courts and halls of local, state, and federal government agencies to plea their case. Santa Ynez residents like Elizabeth Truesdail represented a growing number of locals that complained about the loss of cattle ranching, truck farming, and ruralness of her community as owners converted to the industrial wine-farm model.[4] The visual and aesthetic rural lifestyle of the past met modern agriculture, and the wine industry was at the heart of the chaos.

For over thirty years county strawberry growers and grape growers used methyl bromide to sterilize the soil before planting. The fumigant gas is highly toxic to humans and animals, and many local residents wanted restrictions on its usage. Lori Schirago, environmentalist with the Santa Barbara Environmental Defense Center, believed that the rules did not go far enough and warned, "They do little to protect the public." She continued, "In the Santa Maria Valley there are children on their way to school that pass fields with methyl bromide."[5] Santa Maria and Oxnard strawberry farmers like Darren Gee, on the other hand, fought the proposed restrictions. Gee believed that "these rules will put us out of business. There is no way in hell we can function under these kind of circumstances."[6]

The fear of herbicide and pesticide use had rattled citizens and farmers for decades. But there were those in the wine industry who saw the handwriting on the wall and pushed for more environmentally friendly practices and they drew inspiration and practical advice from Bay Area experiences. Since the 1970s Bob Cantisano, "Amigo Bob," had acted as a consultant on sustain-able wine-grape growing for high-end clients like Fetzer, Honig, Frog's Leap, Davis Bynum, Staglin, and Turley, who all saw his methods as a good way to avoid environmental battles. Cantisano believed "it's not just about farming. It's about the environment, it's about people's long-term health. It's even about making better wine."[7] Many in the wine industry had grown to believe that the negative public perception of the wine industry would only lead to court cases and loss of sales.

Change was on the way and most growers and wineries believed that industry-wide self-regulation was the best way to counter their public relations and legal nightmares. Their hope was that through self-action they would soften what they considered to be draconian government environmental regulations. Many in the wine industry understood how consumers distrusted businesses after recent events like the Exxon Oil Spill and drawn-out legal cases involving tobacco, breast implants, and asbestos. John De Luca studied and learned from these cases and used the Wine Institute to champion policies designed "to get scientists and the university world to hold off the lawyers."[8] Most agreed the best strategy was a preemptive move to green up their industry and avoid the courts as much as possible.

A first plan of action involved utilizing community involvement and educational programs to lessen resident and consumer angst. The Wine Institute entered the fray in 2001 by sponsoring a voluntary Code of Sustainable Winegrowing based loosely upon the Australian "Vision 2020" program. Their new mission statement proposed growing grapes and producing wine with the least amount of impact on the land and environment while at the same time maximizing winery profits. For public relations purposes De Luca declared that the code "is all about saving the land."[9] The program got off to a great start in its first two years as 25 percent of the state's vineyard owners adapted the code making sustainability the new mantra for the California wine industry. So much so that Vice President Al Gore praised the industry for its environmental efforts at the 2008 Barcelona World Meeting on Climate Change and Wine conference.[10] The industry stepped up its stake in 2010 by creating a Certified California Sustainable Winegrowing (CCSW) certification program.[11]

Santa Barbara wineries and grape growers, facing the same extended court battles and unsympathetic politicians, also took up the mantle of land stewardship by searching for common-ground solutions with environmentalists. Most realized that they were part of the chemical problem and worried that their yearly use of over 1 million pounds of sulfur, along with 1.3 million tons of pesticides and herbicides, was damaging local ecosystems.[12] As early as 1994 these environmental concerns had gained the attention of Central Coast wineries (Monterey, Santa Barbara, and San Luis Obispo) and moved them to create the Central Coast Vineyard Team. Supported by a $250,000 grant, to be matched with 40 percent additional funds from the local wine community, the Central Coast wine industry addressed environmental issues. Their move drew the support of William Lyons Jr., California secretary of agriculture, and he commended the region's wine-grape growers for taking this active role.[13]

Kendall-Jackson, after the oak tree fiasco, had learned the public relations and legal lessons on becoming better neighbors. In response the company vowed to cut no more oak trees on its over 3,800 acres of vineyards in the county. Most importantly, they formed a partnership with the Central Coast Vineyard Team and in a short time promoted a sustainable vineyard practice that eliminated the use of chemicals like methyl bromide, mite killer Omite, and weed killers Simizine and Karmax.[14]

Further assistance for Santa Barbara sustainable practices came in 2001 when farmers and ranchers formed the Stewards of Agriculture through Grants, Education, and Science program. The educational nonprofit was part of the National Heritage Foundation that had over five thousand members nationwide. Their goal was to create a dialogue between farmers, ranchers, and environmentalists to achieve sustainable practices.[15] Further public relations efforts came from the Central Coast Wine Growers Association (CCWGA) as their president Bethany Zepponi hosted "Hear It Through the Grapevines" field tours, created a descriptive website, and offered seminars to tout the wine industry's sustainable practices. The Santa Barbara County Vintners Association joined the venture with a $20,000 award to support educational outreach.[16] Statewide the idea of eco-friendly wines began to catch on, so much so that consumers began to flock to the likes of the Santa Monica EcoWineFest to taste organic wines from around the world.[17]

A few Santa Barbara County wineries joined the initial organic winery movement. Bion Rice, Sunstone Vineyard and Winery, welcomed the extra work required by sustainable practices and by 1999 had his vineyard CCOF (California Certified Organic Farmers) certified. He believed that "the main thing is attention to detail and being present in the vineyard as much as possible." Marge Grace, Sanford Winery and Vineyard, pushed to get her vineyard certified in 1999 and remarked, "We'd rather pay local farm labor than chemical corporations."[18] Yet, by 2000 Peggy Miars, CCOF communications director, believed that only about eight thousand acres of the state's 568,000 acres of vineyard land had been certified organic.[19]

On the bright side, the environmental concerns helped bring about substantial change in the wine industry. By 2007 three major approaches to a more environmentally friendly business model solidified—organic, biodynamic, and sustainable in practice. Many growers and wineries instituted philosophies of no use of synthetic chemicals, water conservation, renewable energy, and soil-building programs to become certified by the National Organic Program (NOP) and CCOF. As organic vineyards grew in number, a few growers adopted the more austere form of organic viticulture by fostering the biodynamic practices of Austrian philosopher Rudolf Steiner. They treated their farms as a living organism in a vineyard ecosystem with a lunar cultivation calendar and special organic additives.[20] The most widely adapted environmental approach involved using the Sustainability in Practice (SIP) model. SIP practitioners got to choose flexible, ecological, and economic sound practices to conserve water and energy, recycle, and reduce the use of chemicals.[21] They produced "wines of conviction" that provided growers with the psychological and emotional sustenance of protecting their terroir.

In a short time, wineries and growers across the state attempted to create vineyard ecosystems complete with cover crops, beehives, olive trees to hold soil, the use of owls for mole and gopher eradication, chickens for pest control, and some even used horses instead of tractors.[22] Places like Ridge Vineyard's Lytton Springs winery went so far as to build a facility out of 3,500 bales of rice-straw.[23] In 2010 Santa Barbara vintners Dick Doré with partner Bill Wathen built a 23,000-square-foot facility that ran totally on solar power. They covered a great deal of the cost with tax incentives and power company rebates.[24] Most importantly, the industry realized the cost savings with SIP's more flexible methods and increased consumer approval meant more profits.[25] The movement caught on and by 2006 over 1,165 wineries, accounting for 33 percent on the state's 527,000 acres of grapes, significantly reduced chemical usage. Slowly the industry was attempting to overcome its 1970s–1990s image as enemies of the environment.

Some connoisseurs and everyday consumers worried that large corporate producers would somehow bastardize the true intentions of the organic movement. Matt Kramer, wine writer, warned, "Technologists talk terroir, but they don't necessarily practice it. Rather their intent is to design wines to their own specifications." He also warned that honest vintners' "efforts will continue to be diminished by those who want your image, but are not willing to pay your price."[26] A few years later Kramer went on to warn, "If we lose sight of what is real in wine, if we wind up with wines that are deconstructed and recon-structed, we find ourselves untethered. We and the wines we drink become grotesque." Kramer pleaded for natural wines in an artificial world.[27]

Sustainable practices aside, new climate change worries also threatened wine-grape production in the Santa Barbara region. The Union of Concerned Scientists released their Climate Change in California report that warned of a four- to six-degree Fahrenheit raise in the annual average temperature. A short time later the National Academy of Sciences used computer projections to show changes in California through 2100. These reports predicted adverse conditions for cool climate wine-grape varieties and a reduction in wine qual-ity for regions like Santa Barbara. Despite the warnings, most in the industry adopted the pragmatic approach of Jim Fiolek, SBCVA executive director, who noted that the Santa Barbara region would just graft over to more heat tolerant varietals.[28] Fiolek's rationale worried others who feared a shift in the region's established terroir brands through new varieties and grafting to better clones would set off a new era of trial and error as winemakers searched for the right grapes and wines for the region. They worried that this shift could set the industry back decades. Further concerns over carbon dioxide emissions drove many wineries to solar and wind power systems and the use of carbon mer-chants who charged wineries based on the levels of carbon dioxide they emitted and then used the money to plant trees.[29]

PROTECTING OAKS AND ENDANGERED SPECIES

In the early 2000s Santa Barbara County supervisors were split as to how to handle the oak tree issue. The two north county rural supervisors favored agri-culture, while three urban south county supervisors backed environmental activists. County Supervisor Gail Marshall, who sided with no-growth environ-mentalists and oak tree protection, proposed a two-year moratorium on new tasting rooms until completion of a Santa Ynez Valley General Plan.[30] This angered wineries and grape growers, forcing the board to propose a series of public hearings on how to handle the issue. Activists cited the fact that between 1996 and 1998 over 2,000 oaks had been cut down, including the 843 cut down by Kendall-Jackson. Farmers, ranchers, and vineyard owners disputed this figure and retorted that between 1998 and 2001 only 340 trees had been cut down. Looking for a compromise the supervisors suggested that each ranch could cut down only one blue or valley oak in perpetuity and that landowners could cut thirty coast live oaks every ten years. As part of the proposal, those cutting down the trees had to plant fifteen blue or valley oaks or they could plant ten coast live oaks for each type of oak tree that they cut down.[31] Neither side was happy with the compromise.

In an effort to end the disagreement, both factions eventually endorsed a limited Oak Protection Policy. Environmentalists backed by south county supervisors Marshall, Schwartz, and Rice wanted the term to be fifty years for the set number of trees that could be cut. After much haggling the environmentalists relented and lowered the term to thirty years. Under the new plan landowners could remove 154 oaks every thirty years if they planted 15 oak trees for each one removed. Like most compromises many walked away from the five-year negotiation dissatisfied. Jon Evarts, Santa Ynez resident and author of *Oaks of California* remarked, "This is essentially clear-cutting on the installment plan."[32] Some called south county supervisors Gail Marshall, Naomi Schwartz, and Susan Rice the enemy of family farms and voiced concern that farmers and ranchers were becoming the endangered species. They viewed the Environmental Defense Center as a political group working to take agricultural flexibility away.[33]

The only thing both sides agreed upon was that the issue was far from dead. Dissatisfied local activists in 2003 reminded state legislators that over California's 250-year history Europeans had cut 90 percent of valley oaks and one-third of all oak species combined. They argued that this deforestation endangered the state's sixteen oak species and habitats of over three hundred species of birds, mammals, reptiles, amphibians, and associated plant species. They increased their demands to include government regulation of overgrazing, intensive agriculture, tree cutting, and urban sprawl. To this end state senator Sheila Kuehl advanced SB 711 that required the California Board of Forestry to regulate the conversion of oak lands.[34]

Ranchers, farmers, and vineyard owners responded by taking the issue to court. Their goal was to get a legal ruling to stop all the plans and make these oak tree plans voluntary. Utilizing their professional organizations—Santa Barbara County Cattleman's Association, Coalition of Labor, Agriculture, and Business (COLAB), and the Center for Environmental Equality—they took their case to the Santa Barbara Superior Court. Their case died on November 16, 2004, when Superior Court judge Zel Canter declared that they had no case.[35]

Habitat Struggles

In northern Santa Barbara county resident Jeanette Sainz's daughter found a six-inch black and ivory salamander on their property. Out of curiosity Sainz and her daughter took the creature to the Santa Barbara Natural History Museum for identification. Little did she know that they were about to set off an environmental quest to save the California Tiger Salamander under the Endangered Species Act of 1973 (ESA). In 2000 the United States Fish and Wildlife Service registered the salamander as endangered and instituted a $50,000 fine with up to one year in jail for interfering with its survival. The irony for the Sainz family was that their discovery halted their long-planned conversion of about five hundred acres of grazing land into vineyards—in painful contrast to her neighbors, who had already completed their plantings. She said, "I feel betrayed," "We were the only ones dumb enough to have tried to do everything right," and "we've had to sit here and watch everyone else put their grapes in." The news angered many landholders like Adam Firestone who believed "the greatest threat to the salamander is cars not vineyards."[36] The environmental politics of chemicals, oaks, and habitats had begun to slow vineyard development down.

NIMBY LAND-USE PLANNING

Despite the ongoing struggles over environmental issues, expansion of the Santa Barbara wine industry continued as the Santa Barbara County supervisors approved Don Smith's thirty-acre Royal Oaks Winery and Fess Parker's Los Olivos Country Garden Hotel.[37] The joy over the projects approval did not last long, and worried environmental activists began a new tactic of attempting to halt any rapid rural expansion. Much of their renewed battle came from actions in Napa and Sonoma where growers, short on available land, had begun to plant vineyards on hillsides, resulting in erosion problems in local streams and flatland areas. Citing soil-erosion concerns the Napa chapter of the Sierra Club filed a lawsuit in 1999 against Napa County and three growers. They believed that the Napa government had failed to apply the California Environmental Quality Act (CEQA) guidelines. This lawsuit frightened landholders statewide because these types of concerns triggered the need for Environmental Impact Reports (EIR) that usually cost up to $100,000 and took years to complete. In Santa Barbara County planting a vineyard without a permit and EIR could result in a $50,000 fine.[38]

Many in Santa Barbara County also began to worry about the effect of increased tourism on the bucolic agricultural lifestyle. Bay Area residents over the last three decades bemoaned how their quiet rural landscapes became overrun with tourists and their local lifestyles were interrupted by traffic jams, excessive noise, and overdevelopment. Concerned citizens in north Amador County pushed their local government to join Napa and Sonoma Counties by instituting strict regulations on winery facilities catering to tourists. The only Bay Area exception was Contra Costa County where county supervisors encouraged more tourism and had no size limits on wineries, allowed food preparation, and addressed special winery events on a need-be basis.[39]

With these northern concerns in mind, many members of the Santa Barbara County Board of Supervisors began to ask the crucial question of how many wineries can Santa Ynez Valley support? So in 2000 the board ordered a study to determine winery retail sales, traffic congestion, noise pollution, and any factors contributing to loss of the rural lifestyle. As expected urban supervisor Naomi Schwartz, along with Supervisors Susan Rose and Gail Marshall, again fought vigorously for maintaining the rural character of the valley. Rose commented, "I don't want Los Olivos to become a wine mall" and "I want to support as much as possible the effort of what we call the small wineries or the boutique wineries." Marshall worried that excessive winery events would turn the valley into another Napa. She supported "agriculture and agriculture related activities" as long as there was not a proliferation of retail winery activities.[40] Marshall also envisioned doing away with unlimited new tasting rooms and winery events. She preferred that tasting rooms be located in established commercial zones and that "all future tasting rooms have to be scrutinized very carefully for compatibility with the neighborhood and traffic circulation." She believed "it is not necessary for successful wine marketing to have a tasting room and entertainment events."[41] This of course scared small wineries dependent upon consumer-direct retail sales.

In order to counter this anti-winery position, the local Cattleman's Association and many members of the wine industry joined together in 2003 by committing $121,000 to study positions that favored farmers, ranchers, and viticulturists. Their timing was also tied to the fact that California governor Arnold Schwarzenegger favored ending the Williamson Act. For Santa Barbara's over two thousand farmers the act provided over $700,000 in tax breaks. They lobbied to instead expand the act to include agrotourism businesses like dude ranches, inns, gun ranges, and wineries while slowing down use of agricultural lands for McMansions and subdivisions.[42] Neither side seemed to be in the mood to compromise.

Their concerns came to a head in 2004 when the proposed Santa Ynez 24,000-square-foot Mission Meadows Vineyard and Winery came up for approval. The winery's petition cited their intention to host up to eight events per year (150 to 200 people each) with a production of forty thousand cases yearly with only one-half of the grapes purchased from off-site vineyards. The project met immediate opposition from the National Park Service, the Santa Barbara Trust for Historic Preservation, and the Mission Santa Ines. They claimed the new facility would stress road capacity, destroy the view of the mission, and threaten numerous endangered species.[43] Since the board had five members, the views of the three pro-environment members served as the majority opinion for this and future permit decisions. This forced the SBCVA to a vote of no confidence for the board of supervisors and they refused to endorse winery guidelines based on the board's recommendations.[44] Critics continued to verbalize that wineries, tasting rooms, and site events were nothing more than "parties for profit."[45]

After years of the County Board of Supervisors being split by north county agricultural businesses members versus south county urban environmental members, the 2005 election cycle brought a more favorable business approach to the Board. The old three-to-two environmental power base, led by what the opposition then labeled as the "Twisted Sisters" (Gail Marshall, Susan Rose, and Naomi Schwartz), had successfully instituted a slow-paced and high-cost planning process for planning and development of wineries to protect the rural environment. North county businesses and farmers saw these regulations as an affront to their property rights and convinced vintner and grape grower A. Brooks Firestone to run for supervisor to shift the power toward agriculture and businesses. As a result three property-rights advocates—Brooks Firestone (Third District), Joni Gray (Fourth District), and Joe Centeno (Fifth District)—won control of the five-member County Board of Supervisors.[46] They viewed tasting rooms as being no different than a farm stand selling fruits and vegetables.[47]

The election also helped those supporting tax incentives and updating of the 1965 Williamson Act. The new board looked at giving breaks for guest ranches, building of additional homes, and winery and vineyard expansion. They hoped to help wineries increase processing and preparation space by one acre for every one hundred acres above five hundred acres. That meant a seven-hundred-acre vineyard could now have a seven-acre winery. They also hoped to allow for the use of more off-site grapes to be used for local wines. The old rules mandated that 50 percent of grapes used had to come from the winery's own vineyards; they hoped to reduce that number to 20 percent.[48] Santa Barbara County wineries were grudgingly embracing sustainability, environmentalism, and land-use issues so as to keep their industry growing.

Notes

1. De Luca oral history.
2. James R. Wilson, "Easing wine industry rules," *Santa Barbara News-Press,* 27 October 2003.
3. Mark Van De Kamp, "Changing Farmland," *Santa Barbara News-Press,* 2 January 2000.
4. "Guest Perspective/Elizabeth Truesdail," *Santa Barbara News-Press,* 9 January 2000.
5. Mark Van De Kamp, "Methyl bromide proposal criticized," *Santa Barbara News-Press,* 21 January 2000.
6. Ibid.
7. Robert F. Howe, "California's Eco-Orale," *Wine Spectator,* 30 November 2005.
8. De Luca oral history, 376.
9. Tim Fish, "California's Wine Industry Looks to Green Day," *Wine Spectator,* 31 December 2002.
10. Jacob Gaffney, "Al Gore Praises Wine Industry's Green Efforts," *Wine Spectator,* 15 May 2008.
11. Dana Nigro, "Giving New Meaning to Green," *Wine Spectator,* 31 May 2010.
12. Mark Van De Kamp, "Vintners schedule community forum on sulfur use," *Santa Barbara News-Press,* 20 January 2003; "Unlikely Alliance," *Santa Barbara News-Press,* 15 June 2001.
13. Mark Van De Kamp, "Project to help keep vineyards green," *Santa Barbara News-Press,* 25 January 2001; Mark Van De camp, "State's top ag official commends local growers for resource efforts," *Santa Barbara News-Press,* 8 August 2002.
14. Mark Van De Kamp, "Vintner to reduce reliance on toxins," *Santa Barbara News-Press,* 14 January 2000; "Here's a toast: Vintners reducing use of some pesticides," *Santa Barbara News-Press,* 17 January 2000.
15. Mark Van De Kamp, "New group to explain farming practices," *Santa Barbara News-Press,* 19 January 2001.
16. Mark Van De Kamp, "Vintners reach out to the public," *Santa Barbara News-Press,* 28 February 2001; "Green grapes," *Santa Barbara News-Press,* 17 December 2005; Frank Nelson, "Area grape growers to host yearly outing," *Santa Barbara News-Press,* 24 June 2003.
17. Lynn Alley, "EcoWineFest Spotlights Organic Wines," *Wine Spectator,* 15 September 2003.
18. "Wine of the times interest is growing in organic approach to vineyard cultivation," *Santa Barbara News-Press,* 18 April 2004.
19. Ibid.
20. Justin Lowe, "Understanding Sustainable Wine Standards," *Santa Barbara Independent,* 14 April 2015.
21. Dana Nigro, "Green Revolutionaries: What It Means to Be Green," *Wine Spectator,* 30 June 2007.
22. Ibid.
23. Ibid.
24. Laura Sanchez, "Sipping from the Sun," *Santa Barbara Independent,* 19 February 2010.
25. Nigro, "Green Revolutionaries."
26. Matt Kramer, "An Open Letter to Natural Winegrowers," *Wine Spectator,* 30 November 2002.
27. Dana Nigro, "Matt Kramer Espouses Natural Wines In An Artificial World," *Wine Spectator,* 31 December 2005.
28. Elisabeth Goodridge, "Climate change challenges local wine industry," *Santa Barbara New-Press,* 27 February 2005; "Local Wineries Feel the Heat," *Santa Barbara Independent,* 13 July 2006.
29. Jacob Gaffney, "Change Is In the Air," *Wine Spectator,* 30 June 2007.
30. "The future of tasting," *Santa Barbara News-Press,* 10 August 2000.
31. "Mighty oaks do fall," *Santa Barbara News-Press,* 17 May 2001.
32. "Supervisors OK limited protection of Oaks," *Santa Barbara News-Press,* 16 October 2002.

33. "Letters to the Editor," *Santa Barbara News-Press*, 29 February 2000.

34. "State can, must act to save dwindling oaks," *Santa Barbara News-Press*, 4 August 2003.

35. Mike Eliason, "Ranching interests seek change in oak plan," *Santa Barbara News-Press*, 11 December 2004.

36. James Sterngold, "California winery region torn by debate over use of land," *New York Times*, 3 April 2000.

37. Mark Van De Kamp, "Planners approve new inn, winery," *Santa Barbara News-Press*, 5 February 2000.

38. Daniel Sogg, "Vineyards vs Environment in California," *Wine Spectator*, 15 June 2000.

39. Tim Fish, "Northern California Grapples With Surging Growth of Wine Tourism," *Wine Spectator*, 15 December 2004.

40. Mark Van De Kamp, "Curbs on wine retailing hinted," *Santa Barbara News-Press*, 28 June 2000.

41. Mark Van De Kamp, "Marshall sides with neighbors on wine events," *Santa Barbara News-Press*, 25 May 2000.

42. "County eyes W Act expansion," *Santa Barbara News-Press*, 6 April 2003.

43. "County to weigh fate of winery," *Santa Barbara News-Press*, 5 November 2002.

44. "Winery permit reform advances," *Santa Barbara News-Press*, 5 March 2003.

45. Matt Kettmann, "A Tale of Two Valleys," *Santa Barbara Independent*, 17 January 2013.

46. "Climate shift on county board," *Santa Barbara News-Press*, 14 August 2005.

47. Kettmann, "A Tale of Two Valleys."

48. "Changes to law could aid farmers, ranchers," *Santa Barbara News-Press*, 11 April 2005. *Wine Spectator*, 16 May 2005; "Justices lift ban on wine shipments," *Santa Barbara News-Press*, 17 May 2005; Marvin R. Shanken, "A Supreme Decision," *Wine Spectator*, 31 July 2005.

Chapter Twelve

A Decade of Successful Expansion: 2000 to 2010

Throughout the nation's history Americans have attempted to develop a wine culture based on the terroir of their geographic region. It has not always been an easy task, given obstacles like climate, geography, anti-alcohol beliefs, war, depression, and Prohibition. In the words of *Wine Spectator* writer James Laube, "We [the United States] have evolved into the world's most sophisticated wine society, though at times the process hasn't been pretty." Yet, by the 2000s, "our tastes set standards all around the world."[1] In many ways the 1990s had been a Golden Era for the California wine industry as the state's red wines became the global price leader after surpassing Bordeaux, France.[2] Despite the numerous problems faced by the industry, the first decade of the new millennium provided additional growth opportunities for both large and small wineries.

Wine industry statistics showed that the number of wineries nationally had doubled between 1994 and 2004 to 3,726, with California leading with over 1,700 wineries. Most importantly, all fifty states had wineries and wine was once again part of the American character.[3] Of equal importance was the fact that the California industry was economically stable. Industry projections predicted that consumer consumption would increase to 300 million cases in 2010, up from a 2002 high of 245 million cases.[4] The state's wineries generated $45 billion from 530,000 acres (up 60 percent from the 1993 figure of 332,000 acres) and provided 207,550 full-time jobs with 7.6 billion dollars paid in wages. Just as impressive were figures showing that wine tourism produced $1.3 billion, the industry paid $5.6 billion in state and federal taxes, and sold $15.2 dollars in retail sales.[5] The predictions made from these optimistic statistics continued, and by 2008 American wine exports rose 8.6 percent to $951 million and the United States now exported 119.7 million gallons, up from a 1998 high of 71.9 million gallons, or 5 percent of the world's total wine exports.[6] Helping matters was the fact that Europe's switch to their new euro currency had little effect on wine prices and over the next year the currency exchange rate continued to favor the United States as the dollar dropped 20 to 30 percent in comparison to the euro.[7] The short-term market for American exported wine looked good.

Still, many investors worried that the state's wine prices had escalated faster than any other major wine-producing region in the world, making California wines overpriced.[8] Dire predictions of industry overextension, worldwide wine-glut, sagging tourism, and the Iraq War tempered predictions. For an industry that seemed to be doing so well, experts struggled to explain a new wave of Napa/Sonoma winery bankruptcies—Sonoma Creek, De Loach, Fife Liparite, and Buchanan Cellars. This prompted bankers like Rob McMillan, Silicon Valley Bank, to predict even further bankruptcies.[9] Even industry giant Robert Mondavi Corporation (RMC) faced having to grow in volume and revenue while trying to maintain their premium image.[10] Despite the dark clouds, large efficient operations and small boutique operations flourished.

More importantly for this story, Santa Barbara County could now proclaim its place in the global marketplace. Robert Parker's 2002 *Wine Advocate* magazine named Santa Barbara winemakers John Alban, Greg Brewer, Steve Clifton, and Brian Talley "wine personalities of the year."[11] In 2003 *Wine Spectator* magazine's Top 100 international wines included Byron Pinot Noir at number 77, Sea Smoke Pinot Noir at number 80, and Ojai Syrah at number 96.[12] The best news came in 2006 when *Wine Enthusiast* nominated Santa Barbara County, along with Medoc (France), Prosecco (Italy), Priora (Spain), and winner Colchaqua (Chile), as the year's top international wine regions.[13]

Santa Barbara Adds New AVAs

One of the main purposes for development and recognition of an AVA stems from the idea that terroir provides value by branding premium wines. In other words it allows buyers to have faith in the quality and consistency of regional wines and provides the basis for higher prices. By 2000 California had over eighty AVAs and Santa Barbara's Santa Maria and Santa Ynez AVAs welcomed the addition of the Sta. Rita Hills and Happy Canyon AVAs.[14]

Once a region established an AVA, the local industry had to protect the region's brand reputation and attempts to co-opt the good name of a region were taken seriously. In 2002, to further protect AVA reputations, the California legislature closed a loophole in wine labeling by requiring that wines must contain at least 75 percent of grapes from the region designated on the label. But the new law provided a grandfather clause that allowed brands established before July 7, 1986, to not follow the newly imposed restriction. Since Fred Franzia, CEO of Central Valley Bronco Wines, had recently purchased the exempt Napa Ridge label for $40 million, he petitioned to allow his recent acquisition of Napa Creek, Napa Ridge, and Rutherford labels to keep their old names and continue the use of Lodi and Stanislaus County grapes. California's Third District Court of Appeals ruled in favor of Bronco, but Napa vintners wanted to protect their terroir and in 2004 continued the fight all the way to the steps of the California Supreme Court. The court upheld the idea that brand names must have at least 75 percent of their grapes from that region.[15] For wineries, large and small, branding by AVA was a vital part of marketing premium wines.[16]

In 2001 a second attack on AVA provenience shook the wine world as large producers Mondavi, Kendall-Jackson, and Wente pushed to create a fourteen-million-acre AVA from San Diego to Mendocino. This would allow them to blend Central Valley cheaper wines with grapes they purchased or owned on the Central Coast. Santa Barbara small vintners feared a loss of identity for their Santa Ynez and Santa Maria AVAs and the Wine Institute's board of directors agreed. In a 32–4 vote, the board came out against the new AVA, fearing that it would devalue the prestige and marketing advantage of "estate-bottled" wines.[17]

As Santa Barbara County gained recognition, local winemakers took steps to improve their marketing by further defining the terroir of their region. In the 1970s Lawrence Balzer, Los Angeles retailer and wine writer, made reference to "American Grand Cru in a Lompoc barn" and gave the Santa Rita Hills its first recognition. Three decades later the Department of Treasury established the Santa Rita Hills AVA.[18] Richard Sanford, Bryan Babcock, Wesley Hagen, fourteen grape growers with over five hundred acres of producing vineyards, and two wineries supported the petition for the forty-eight-square-mile viticultural area. Located in northern Santa Barbara County, east of Highway 1 in Lompoc and west of Highway 101 in Buellton, the new region boasted that its "Maritime throat" was best suited for cool-climate Pinot Noir and Chardonnay grapes. The petitioners made the case that the proposed area's cooler Region I climate differed substantially from the larger Santa Ynez Region 2 climate. Petitioners also made the case that its sand, silt, and sandy loam soils differed from the adjacent Santa Ynez AVA. The only real opposition to the petition came from the Chilean Viña Santa Rita Winery whose owners worried that the name would confuse consumers. Both sides supplied historic arguments and cited international trade accords for their case and in the end the ATF found no conflict of interest.[19] But some local growers and wineries in the new AVA worried about the name factor and in 2006 Richard Sanford helped broker a compromise whereby the Santa Rita Hills would be labeled as Sta. Rita Hills to avoid confusion with Viña Santa Rita in Chile.[20] That same year James Laube called the Sta. Rita Hills "California's New Frontier."[21]

The new AVA sparked excitement for Pinot Noir drinkers. Before the 1990s most Pinot Noir in California came from vineyards using trial and error and old-fashioned Burgundy Cabernet techniques. After twenty-five years the Sanford and Benedict vineyard had proved that premium wines could be produced in the cool-climate region by adopting techniques like small yields, closer vine spacing, better clones, and gentler wine handling. With these lessons learned Santa Barbara wineries like Babcock, Brewer-Clifton, Clos Pepe, Fiddlestix, Foley, Hitching Post, Longoria, Loring, Melville, Ojai, Sanford, Sea Smoke, Siduri, and Taz made award-winning wines. As the region gained notoriety, dozens of other wineries began sourcing grapes from the AVA.[22]

Protection of the Sta. Rita Hills AVA brand became an issue when vintner Blair Pence petitioned to include 2,300 acres on its eastern border near Lompoc. Pence had purchased a two-hundred-acre ranch in 2005 and wanted his vineyard included in the AVA. TTB approved the petition despite the opposition of the Sta. Rita Hills Winegrowers Alliance, who wanted to protect the original boundaries. Rick Longoria believed that it set a bad precedent, arguing that "what stops the ranch adjacent to Pence from applying for an expansion? Where does it stop?"[23]

This rethinking of an established AVA led many others to begin thinking about creating more viticultural areas from the original Santa Ynez and Santa Maria AVAs. Many in the statewide industry believed that many existing AVAs were too large and in need of being broken into more grape-specific geographic locations.[24] Most saw this reorganizing process as a maturing of the local industry as it learned the best locations for varietals. The statewide reorganization movement resulted in a 2007 bureaucratic nightmare for the U.S. Treasury's Alcohol and Tobacco Tax and Trade Bureau. Unable to handle all the new applications, the bureau halted accepting new sub-appellation petitions to allow time to study the integrity of new regions.[25]

A short time later the halt ended, allowing for a 2009 petition to establish Happy Canyon as a sub-appellation of the Santa Ynez AVA. Wes Hagen, vineyard manager and winemaker at Clos Pepe Vineyards, proposed the petition for the 23,941 acres containing six vineyards with 492 acres of wine grapes. Hagen's rationale for the new AVA was based upon the fact that the eastern-most inland position of the area provided for a warmer classification than the rest of the surrounding Santa Ynez AVA.[26] The name for the new AVA seemed appropriate because during Prohibition bootleggers produced a "California Moonshine" in the nearby foothills of the Los Padres mountains. Legend has it that folks would "take a trip up Happy Canyon" to purchase the infamous beverage and the name stuck. Santa Barbara County now had a Happy Canyon wine and could boast of having five AVAs with distinctive terroir properties.[27]

CHARDONNAY REIGNS AS THE QUEEN OF SANTA BARBARA WINES

Vintners statewide produced Chardonnay, and many believed as James Laube that "California Chardonnay is the most consistently excellent white wine made in the world." More importantly, new regions like Monterey, San Luis Obispo, and Santa Barbara "add dimension to the market."[28] Since the 1970s increasing consumer demand made Chardonnay the most planted grape in California and by 2007 Americans consumed sixty-four million cases of domestic and imported Chardonnay.[29] In the early Chardonnay days *Wine Spectator's* James Laube worried about continued consistent quality and believed that as winemakers chased the market most "were not equipped mentally or physically to tackle this newfangled grape." They just utilized the same old processes they used for red grapes. But after decades of trial and error and studying Burgundian winery traditions, they finally understood the need for the cool coastal conditions offered on the Central Coast, where they developed their own Burgundy-California style.[30] The only holdback was that some industry insiders were leery of shifts in consumer tastes and feared that there might be an ABC Movement (Anything But Chardonnay).

During the first decade of the 2000s, consumer demand and confidence in California Chardonnay grew and winery marketers embraced the idea that higher per-bottle prices also improved the image of the wine. In response small premium wineries used upscale bottles, designer labels, advertising, celebrity endorsements, and critical reviews to drive up prices. Growers of premium grapes also adopted the image/price phenomenon, which drove the per-ton price of Chardonnay grapes upward. As a rule of thumb, a bottle of wine should cost about 1/100th of the price of a ton of grapes. Thus, grapes at $4,000 dollars per ton should equal about $40 per bottle. Add to this the cost of upgraded bottles, labels, advertising, and profits for the three-tier distribution system and wines now retailed for up to $100 per bottle.[31] In order to keep prices lower for medium-level wines, large corporate wineries expanded their vineyard holdings, used scale-of-economy processing, and relied heavily on the three-tier distribution system.[32]

Santa Barbara County benefited from its cool-climate growing conditions, and Chardonnay became the workhorse wine for both large and small wineries.[33] Recognition for premium California Chardonnay wine peaked in 2002 when *Wine Spectator* editors tasted 11,616 Chardonnay wines and they scored 2000 of them in the 90 or above category. That year Santa Barbara Testarossa Chardonnay, with grapes from Bien Nacido Vineyard, made the year's top 100 wines list with an impressive 91 points.[34] Over the next decade many again spoke of premium vineyards like Bien Nacido, Nielson, and Sanford and Benedict becoming a California Grand Cru.[35]

Just as important for the region's Chardonnay reputation was the 2004 *Wine Spectator* "Editors' Picks: Smart Buys" that focuses on smaller producers with consumer friendly prices like Qupé Santa Barbara County Chardonnay.[36] Continued positive news for the region's Chardonnay came from Eric Asimov, *New York Times* wine writer, who in 2009 proclaimed that California Chardonnay had grown up and singled out Santa Barbara wineries like Fess Parker, Alma Rosa, La Fenêtre, Taz, Melville, and Brewer-Clifton.[37]

PINOT NOIR'S REIGN AS KING OF SANTA BARBARA WINES

If Chardonnay was the Queen of Santa Barbara wines, then Pinot Noir could claim the title of King. Until the 1980s most Pinot Noir vines in California were clones used in Burgundy to make sparkling wine that produced an indistinctive table wine.[38] To remedy this, growers, vintners, and researchers set out in the 1990s to improve the quality of Pinot vineyards and wines. The shift began when the UC Davis Foundation Plant Services offered over one hundred different clones on about a dozen resistant rootstocks. As a result, over the next decade vintners significantly improved both grape and wine quality.[39]

Regretfully, they also faced lackluster sales and winter El Niño rains, coupled with a cool spring and summer heat that resulted in poor fruit quality.[40] Decades of a steep learning curve, for what many called the "heartbreak wine," allowed winemakers to adapt and produce a spectacular 2002 vintage.[41]

But it would be new plantings in the Santa Lucia Highlands of Monterey, the Sta. Rita Hills of Santa Barbara, and Sonoma that elevated the grape to new heights. In *Wine Spectator* the new Pinot Noir vintages scored more 90-plus ratings than any prior vintage and Santa Barbara's Sta. Rita Hills AVA scored well. The cool spring, low crop yields, and long hang-time provided for dense concentrated flavors and great wines.[42] Global consumers quickly recognized Santa Barbara's Sta. Rita Hills Pinot Noir for its dark and intense mineral qualities and labels like Bonaccorsi, Loring, Clos Pepe, Sanford, and Sea Smoke rose to the top.[43] In 2004 *Wine Spectator*'s list of the top 100 wines in the world included number 63 Sea Smoke Pinot Noir 2002 (Sta. Rita Hills).[44] By 2005 Richard Sanford's single-vineyard Pinot Noir garnished him the title "Pinot King" and *Wine Spectator* listed three Santa Barbara wines as part of their "Hot New Dozen of California Pinot Noir." They included Badger (Bruno D'Alfonso Sta. Rita Hills) and Native 9 (Jaime Ontiveros Santa Maria) that both scored 91, along with Pali Wine Co. (Cargasacchi Vineyard) at 90 points.[45]

In a 2006 *Wine Spectator* Pinot Noir tasting, the magazine named the "Magnificent 30" of Pinot Noir wines tasted and five Santa Barbara wineries made the list. Michael and Jennie Lee Bonaccorsi's 2004 Sta. Rita Hills Pinot scored a 91 and Brian Loring's Sta. Rita Hills, from Cagasacchi vineyard, received a 92. Adam Tolomach's Ojai Vineyard had two wines at 92— Santa Maria Salomon Hills and Sta. Rita Hills Clos Pepe. Further up the list at 93 points were three wines from Kris Curran's Seasmoke Vineyard and Wes Hagen's Clos Pepe Sta. Rita Hills 2004.[46] The real winner was the Sta. Rita Hills AVA whose cool climate vineyards became internationally known for their quality premium Pinot Noir.

The accolades continued in 2007 when a *Los Angeles Times* tasting panel tried twenty-four bottles of Santa Barbara County Pinot Noir (eleven from Santa Maria and thirteen from the Sta. Rita Hills). The reviewers labeled the region's Pinot grapes as "rich, powerful, heavy, inky, and high alcohol versions of the wine." Sta. Rita Hills Siduri (Clos Pepe Vineyard 2004) placed first with Melville 2003 at second. Third to fifth place went to Santa Maria wines Au Bon Climat, Rancho Ontiveros, and Ambullneo.[47] Some began to think that Santa Barbara Pinot Noir seemed to be approaching perfection.[48]

RHÔNE WINES: THE NEW (OLD) KID ON THE BLOCK

As Rhône wines became trendy, consumer demand sparked a worldwide upsurge in production of the tannic Syrah grape. California had grown Rhône varietals for almost two hundred years, but only since the 1960s when Brother Timothy of Christian Brothers gave budwood to Arthur Schmidt had it been a viable wine varietal.[49] For years the interest in Syrah waned until Australia reintroduced modern wine drinkers to Syrah (Shiraz in Australia) where the grape composed 40 percent of all the wine they produced.[50] In 1990 California had only two hundred acres of Syrah grapes and that grew to over seventeen thousand acres in 2004.[51] This growth allowed for an early 2000s breakout for Santa Barbara County Syrah and recognition for the county's Rhône Rangers. Production of premium Rhône wines reached a peak in a 2007 *Wine Spectator* tasting of over three hundred Rhône wines, of which nearly 25 percent scored 90-plus points.[52]

Rhône varietals had been tested in Santa Barbara County since the 1980s when Ken Brown, Zaca Mesa's first winemaker, mentored future stars like Jim Clendenen, Bob Lindquist, Adam Tolmach, Lane Tanner, and Ben Silver. Zaca Mesa continued its Rhône program even after suffering a setback after genetic testing proved that their thirty-six-acre Roussane vineyard, planted in 1993, was actually Viognier.[53] Early pioneers Adam and Helen Tolmach began their six-thousand-case Ojai Vineyard and suffered in the 1990s as Pierce's disease destroyed their vineyard and pushed them to purchase fruit from the disease-free five-acre Roll Ranch at the base of the Topatopa Mountains near Ojai.[54] Ron Melville, Pacific Stock Exchange executive and Calistoga grape grower, began a quest to look for Sta. Rita Hills land for a Syrah and Viognier vineyard. With sons Chad and Brent, they planted a sixty-acre vineyard in Los Alamos.[55]

After twenty-plus years Rhône pioneer wineries like Zaca Mesa, Qupé, and Ojai finally received recognition and awards for their premium Syrah wines.[56] Bien Nacido Vineyard sourced Rhône grapes to Qupé, Kynsi, and Beringer, and the Santa Ynez Valley provided grapes for Stolpman, Beckman, and Andrew Murray.[57] Angela Osborne, New Zealand native and London wine trader, started her Grenache production with her Grace Wine Company in 2006 utilizing Santa Barbara fruit, and the *San Francisco Chronicle* named her as a winemaker to watch. In 2009 Keith Saarloos converted his parents' Ballard Canyon apple orchard to seventeen acres of Syrah and opened the Sarloos and Sons tasting room.[58] Wine enthusiasts touted the likes of

McPrice Myers, Kaena by Mikael Sigorium (Fess Parker assistant wine-maker), Joey Tinsley and Larry Schaffer (Fess Parker winemaker) for their premium Rhône wines.[59]

In 2010 *Wine Spectator* tasted over 425 Rhône wines produced between 2006 and 2007. In the tasting Santa Barbara Rhône wines scoring above 90 included Jaffurs, Zaca Mesa, Sin Qua Non, and Naked Truth. Just as important were highly popular Grenache wines and blends of Syrah, Grenache, and Mouvedre.[60] Santa Barbara Rhône wines had begun to come out of the shadows.[61]

SAUVIGNON BLANC: THE OTHER WHITE WINE

Many early attempts by California wineries to produce French Sancerre and Pouilly-Fumé Sauvignon Blanc wines produced a mediocre wine with off-putting vegetal flavors. Not willing to give up, many continued improving their wines and by the 1990s a few began to find a California Sauvignon Blanc voice with a rounder, more tropical-fruit-flavored wine. Consumers rewarded their persistence over the next two decades with a consistent 9 percent yearly growth in sales.[62]

Traditionally, Sauvignon Blanc standards for California emanated from the grassy and fruity Dry Creek and smoky Mondavi Fumé Blanc. The variety's natural tendency to overcrop resulted in inferior wines; but in Santa Ynez Valley Fred Brander stood out by producing a distinctive fruit-forward version.[63] Sparked by the New Zealand surge of Sauvignon Blanc wines, a new group of hip wine drinkers began to flock to Napa, Sonoma, and Santa Ynez for premium Sauvignon Blanc wines. Also in Santa Barbara, Mary Beth Vogelzang started her 1998 Vogelzang Vineyard as a supplier of high-quality Sauvignon Blanc grapes. In Santa Barbara's Santa Ynez Valley Vogelzang, Fiddlehead, and Brander led the way.[64]

CONSOLIDATION CONTINUES

Consolidation in the wine industry has been an on-again, off-again business practice throughout the industry's history as vintners sought more efficient ways to produce and market their products in boom-and-bust cycles. Starting in 2000 there seemed to be a new transition occurring as fifty major California wineries were bought and sold. Vintibusinesses needing fruit and more control of grape prices bought up vineyards and wineries for their mid-level wines and sold them through the traditional distribution system. This market adjustment was necessitated by the fact that in the 1980s there were eleven thousand wine wholesalers and that had dwindled down to below three thousand in the new century. In the words of Gladys Horiuchi, manager of communications for the Wine Institute, "As those two tiers consolidated the producers had to [consolidate] as well to get distribution and retail clout."[65]

The consolidation flurry began in 2000 when Australian beer maker Foster's purchased California vintner Beringer for $1.4 billion and assumed their $319 million of debt. The purchase included 8,300 acres in Santa Barbara County with over 5,000 acres in vineyards. Part of their plan included shipping grapes from the 2,950-acre White Hills Vineyard to their planned 550,000-square-foot Meridian Vineyard facility in Paso Robles.[66] During this decade Constellation became the world's largest wine company by selling mid-market brands like Almaden and Inglenook and using the proceeds to purchase premium wine labels. Between 2001 and 2007 Constellation purchased Simi, Franciscan, Ravenswood, Australian BRL Hardy, Robert Mondavi, Canadian Vincor International, and Fortune Brands. Their portfolio now included Californian, American, Canadian, Australian, and Italian wine labels.[67]

William "Bill" Foley, chairman of Fidelity National Financial (FNF), left his Jacksonville, Florida, high-power job in 1994 to move to Santa Barbara and restart his life with a new career in the wine industry. Born and raised in Texas, the West Point–trained engineer earned a Master's Degree in business administration and then pursued a law degree from the University of Washington. In 1984 he utilized his collegiate training to lead a group of investors to do a leveraged buyout of Fidelity National Title Insurance. He brought these skills to wine where he believed that the wine industry is "a very emotional business" where the very best wineries "are boutiques that are terribly mismanaged" and "winemakers are great artists, but are not necessarily good at business." Foley developed a plan to put together a consortium of six or seven premium wineries and develop his own distribution and sales company.[68]

In 1996, with this philosophy in mind, he started his LinCourt Vineyards (named after daughters Lindsay and Courtney) and by 1998 purchased the Sta. Rita Hills 460-acre Rancho Santa Rosa as the basis for his Foley Estate Winery. Over the next two decades, Foley leveraged his Santa Barbara business into a multibrand portfolio with a production base of over five hundred thousand cases. He purchased the 220-acre Ashley's Vineyard in the Sta. Rita Hills in 2007 and renamed it Las Hermanas and the push continued in 2008 as he purchased the Santa Barbara Firestone Vineyard, Merus in Napa, Three Rivers Winery in Walla Walla, Washington, and Venge in Napa. The very next year Foley purchased Sebastiani Vineyards in Napa, Wattle Creek Winery in the Alexander Valley, Grove Hill in New Zealand, Vavasaour in New Zealand, Clifford Bay in New Zealand, Goldwater in New Zealand, and the Napa Valley Kuleto Estate. By 2010 Foley controlled seven hundred acres in Santa Barbara County and one thousand acres in Napa and Washington.[69]

Foley's expansion dreams were far from over. In 2010 he purchased Chalk Hill in Sonoma, EOS in Paso Robles, and in 2011 purchased Te Kairanga in New Zealand. The next year he established Foley Johnson in Rutherford, Lancaster in the Alexander Valley, Roth in Sonoma, and Langtry Estates in Lake County. More recent purchases included The Four Graces in Australia, Martinborough in New Zealand, Mt. Difficulty in New Zealand, and Foley Sonoma.[70] Foley's version of wine by design created a modern global wine empire.

William Hill, wine industry veteran, developed over a dozen Napa vineyards and launched William Hill Estate (later purchased by Gallo) and Bighorn Cellars in Napa. The Stanford Business School graduate started the Premier Pacific Vineyards (PPV) in 1998 by consolidating thirty properties in California, Oregon, and Washington mainly dedicated to Pinot Noir and Bordeaux varietals. With $250 million in funding from CalPERS and the Common Fund, he launched his PPV business plan designed to plant, maintain, and then sell the producing vineyards. He hoped to get top prices for his vineyards by selling to small premium wineries and advertising their "Showcase Wines." Seeing Santa Barbara as a premier location for Pinot Noir, Hill purchased Mount Carmel Vineyard (near Seasmoke Vineyard), Salsipuedes with over 3,500 acres, and 132 acres near Foley. Santa Barbara faced a new form of vineyard capitalism.[71]

Kendall-Jackson properties on the Central Coast produced one of the top mass-produced Chardonnay wines in the world. In order to manage their growing operation, in 2000 they hired Lewis Platt, Hewlet Packard CEO, to oversee the winery and study the possibilities of completing an Initial Public Offering (IPO) to help fund further expansion.[72] By mid-March of that year, the operation purchased the Sonoma Matanzas Creek vineyard to increase their expanding Chardonnay capacity.[73] Expansion continued in 2005 as the Robert Mondavi Corporation faced financial woes and agreed to sell the Byron label to Jackson Family Wines.[74] Jackson wines also started an experimental program to build a boutique winery under the umbrella of the larger corporation with its Cambria Winery. Winemaker Fred Holloway oversaw the niche winery and instituted high-end protocols like utilizing the best clones, making single-block wines, and updating barrel programs.[75]

During this time Fess Parker looked for numerous ways to expand his production. In 2000 Parker proposed what he considered a compromise solution to the county's lack of crush-pad facilities while at the same time calming fears of winery intrusion into rural spaces. He investigated transforming the abandoned Lompoc Grefco Mineral Incorporated diatomaceous earth plant into what he envisioned as "the Lompoc Valley Wine Center."[76] It never got off the ground and in 2003 Parker created the Fess Parker Wine Center in an old Chili Factory in the Santa Maria Industrial Park. That same year Parker expanded his Los Olivos winery by 16,300 square feet to include more wine tasting, a kitchen, and underground wine storage.[77] To capitalize these expansions Parker sold three vineyards for $22.8 million—two on Camp 4 and the Ashley Vineyard.[78]

After forty years Richard Sanford found himself caught in the classic business conundrum of needing to expand and move his winery up to the next level. Sanford Winery's fifty thousand cases of premium Pinot Noir and Chardonnay needed more efficient production and lower price-point capacity to maintain a positive cash flow. Many of their single-vineyard La Rinconada Vineyard Barrel Pinot Noirs scored 91 in *Wine Spectator* and sold for fifty dollars per-bottle, but this price range left them out of the profitable middle price-point market. Complicating the expansion idea was the slowdown caused by three successive Pinot Noir short-crops and philosophical differences among partners over sustainability practices. This led Richard and Thekla Sanford to break a decades-long partnership with Robert and Janice Atkin and Bob and Mary Kidder to go off on their own.[79] In 2002, sans Richard Sanford, the Sanford winery took on the Terlato Wine group as partners. The rapidly expanding Terlato group included Paterno Wines International, Rutherford Hill, Chimney Rock, and Alderbrook.[80] Sanford winemaker Bruno D'Alfonso did not fare as well as the Terlato group fired him for insubordination and locked him out from wines he had stored there since 1986.[81] The Sanfords started over with the Alma Rosa Winery and Vineyards.

California wine giant E & J Gallo made the corporate decision to diversify their portfolio by expanding into the premium wine market. In 2002 they purchased Louis M. Martini and Mirassou wineries and added their labels to their product line and began to look for other opportunities. In 1998 Cory Holbrok purchased a 105-acre equestrian center in the Santa Ynez Valley and soon thereafter started the thirty-thousand-case Bridlewood Winery. The new winery first caught the attention of Gallo when they sued Bridlewood for name infringement of their established Modesto based Burlwood Cellars. Gallo lost in court and eventually resolved the issue in 2004 by purchasing the financially strapped winery.[82]

Boutique Labels and Wineries Expand

While larger corporate wineries merged and bought smaller competitors to meet their production needs, Santa Barbara County continued to add smaller wineries, with and without vineyards, to the regional industry. Greg Brewer left his position as a French instructor at UC Santa Barbara for a job at Santa Barbara Winery where he met Steve Clifton. In 1996 the two created the Brewer-Clifton label and utilized only fruit purchased from Sta. Rita Hills vineyards.[83] Other late 1990s wineries to the region included Bob Davis's one-hundred-acre Sea Smoke Vineyard and Kathy Joseph's Fiddlehead Vineyard.[84] John and Helen Falcone purchased Rusack Vineyards from Geoff and Alison Rusack who had purchased it as the Ballad Canyon Winery in the mid-1990s.[85] In 1997 Jim and Mary Dierberg, Hermann, Missouri, grape growers, planted their Dierberg Vineyard in Santa Maria.[86] Rick Longoria planted his eight-acre Sta. Rita Hills Fe Ciega (Blind Faith) Pinot Noir Vineyard in 1998 and the next year Peter and Rebecca Work developed their organic Ampelos Cellars in Lompoc. Charles Banks established his eighty-three-acre Jonata label in 2000 as an organic ecosystem winery in Santa Ynez complete with 120 chickens, 100 sheep and goats, 20 hogs, and 16 turkeys.[87] The next year Chad and Mary Melville launched their *Samsara* (Sanscrit word for eternal cycle of life) to produce wines from specific micro climates within a single vineyard.[88] In 2005 Bill and Roswitha Craig opened their sixty-five-acre Solvang Winery and brothers John and Steve Dragonette, along with partner Brandon Sparks-Gillis, started Dragonette Cellars.[89] A year later Bill (retired Ernst & Young CEO) and Nancy Kimsey planted twenty-two acres of Rhône grapes in Ballard Canyon.[90] In 2009, after a decade working in Napa, John and Helen Falcone started their Falcone Family Vineyards.[91] Michael Roth and Craig Winchester created the Lo-Fi label dedicated to Los Olivos biodynamic grapes and a cellar style utilizing indigenous yeast, little or no sulfur dioxide, and minimal intervention.[92]

As Santa Barbara County expanded, consumers began to equate premium quality with specific AVAs and specific winemakers. As the relationship between consumer and winemaker intensified, local winemakers became very protective of their regional branding. Fred Franzia, in a stretch of marketing etiquette, labeled a $4.99 Bronco Wine Company Chardonnay as Santa Barbara Landing. This did not please local winemaker Craig Addis who was selling $14- to $22-per-bottle Chardonnay from grapes sourced from vineyards within the county. Addis unsuccessfully petitioned the Alcohol and Tobacco Tax and Trade Bureau to force Franzia to remove the label.[93]

State and federal governments provided some assistance for both large and small wineries. In an attempt to make California brands more flexible against international brands, the U.S. Alcohol and Tobacco and Trade Bureau shifted to a more generous and competitive grape requirement. Wines bearing county, multi-county, or state appellations could carry a vintage date if 85 percent of the wine came from grapes picked in the labeled year (down from a 95 percent requirement). This allowed more flexibility for blending wines more on a scale with European practices.[94] Direct assistance for small wineries came in 2003 when California assemblywoman Patricia Wiggins promoted AB15405 that allowed wineries to take orders from consumers at charity events as long as the transaction was completed at the winery and delivered at a later date. At the same time state senator Wesley Chesbro introduced SB 88 to allow permits for wineries to sell unopened bottles at events.[95]

Great Medical News for Wine

Medical news supporting the drinking of wine increased as study after study purported that moderate wine consumption had positive effects on human health. A new study published in the 2004 journal *Nature* described the benefits of resveratrol (3,5,4'-trihydroxy-trans-stilbene) a compound found in wine. Researchers found that worms fed a resveratrol-supplemented diet lived 14 to 24 percent longer according to co author David Sinclair of Harvard Medical School.

Further good news came in 2005 from the National Institutes of Health subgroup National Institute on Alcohol Abuse and Alcoholism (NIAAA) whose findings supported the USDA Dietary Guidelines on alcohol consumption. The group found that 60 percent of Americans drank moderately and 35 percent abstained. Leaving about 5 percent of the population as alcohol dependent.[96] The news helped put neo-Prohibitionists' concerns into perspective.

Over the next few years, the positive medical studies supporting moderate wine consumption piled up. A Stanford study showed that alcohol activates the heart's production of aldehyde dehydratenase 2 to process alcohol consumption. A UCLA study said that it helps prevent the onset of Alzheimer's disease and a Swedish study said it cuts the risk of developing rheumatoid arthritis by 50 percent. More good news came as a Spanish study revealed that moderate wine consumption reduced your chances of getting a cold or the flu. Others found positive results for reducing throat cancer, lowering diabetes risk, solving sleep problems, and reduction of heart disease.[97]

MARKETING

During the latter part of the nineteenth century, consumers could bring their empty jugs to a local winery to purchase refills. This convenience fell into disuse during Prohibition as local wineries disappeared. The practice did not continue after repeal of Prohibition as new commercial wineries abandoned bulk wine and distributed bottles through the three-tier system for retail customers. Instead, wineries looked for new ways to market wine and reeducate Americans about wine culture by improving upon the old idea of visiting a local winery to buy wine. From the 1950s through the 1980s tasting rooms came into being and this time visitors to the winery could purchase bottled wines. As a result winery tasting rooms evolved into a business hub for retail sales, especially for small operations. After a visit to a tasting room, visitors could expect pitches to join wine clubs and expect email and mailer sales pitches. To enhance the experience and brand recognition, wineries began to court customers through barrel tastings, tours, music events, dinners, weddings, crush parties, and private tastings.[98] A further aid to sales for small wineries arrived in 2003 as Assembly Bill 1505, sponsored by Patricia Wiggins (D-Santa Rosa), allowed wineries to sell wine offsite at sponsored charity events.[99]

Industry-wide, wineries looked for novel ways to attract new consumers and expand sales into new markets. A growing number of producers reached out to Hispanic consumers, who at that time made up about 13 percent of the total United States population. Studies found that of the 25.4 million Americans who drank wine at least once a week 2.9 million were Hispanic and that their numbers had increased by 31 percent over the past four years. These figures encouraged Univision star Sábado Kreutzberger, known as "Don Francisco," to launch a wine from his native Chile. Beringer Blass Wine Estates cultivated the market by releasing thirty thousand cases of White Zinfandel with Spanish/English labels and began offering Spanish-language winery tours.[100]

Wine marketers also began to realize the importance of their female market as statistics showed that women bought 77 percent of all wine and consumed over 60 percent of wines purchased. Wine marketers began to speak about "Girlie" wines and how to aim them at American women. Beringer Blass Wine Estates (Foster's group) responded with a promotion by popular author Jennifer Weiner of a low-calorie Chardonnay labeled as "White Lie Early Season Chardonnay." The wine had grapes from Santa Barbara County picked early while they had lower sugar levels and then further de-alcoholized to produce a 9.8 percent wine. Kris Curran, Sta. Rita Hills Curran Wines, took exception with this promotion because she felt that "it's implying that women don't have as sophisticated a palate." She said, "I'd rather have one great glass of wine and a small piece of dark chocolate than a whole box of Snack Wells."[101]

Wine exports had been increasing over the last two decades and hopes for continued growth blossomed. In 2006, after twenty-two years of negotiating with the European Union, the United States signed a historic trade agreement that eliminated many of the barriers to import and export wine. European members agreed to accept all legal winemaking practices and United States members agreed to not use French names like Champagne, Port, Sherry, and Burgundy. This new export market became a game changer for medium-size and larger wineries wishing to increase sales, distribution, and global expansion deals.[102]

Wine became so popular that the state-of-the-art laboratory at the federal government's Ammendale, Maryland, ATF National Laboratory Center earmarked $600,000 to study American wines. This allowed the ATF to become more proactive in certifying wine geographic origin, determining pesticide levels, and verifying that a wine's contents contained the varieties named on the label. Wine purity and authenticity issues now had a watchdog.[103] Further attempts to deliver the perfect wine to consumers consistently seemed to be within reach when New Jersey developer Gene Mulvihill bought the exclusive rights to a prototype wine scanner. The device could detect oxidized or vinegary wine without opening the bottle.[104]

THE POP CULTURE SIDEWAYS EFFECT

When screenwriter Rex Pickett wrote his first novel, *Sideways: The Ultimate Road Trip, The Last Hurrah*, little did he realize how his buddy road-trip fiction would secure the global image of Santa Barbara wines.[105] In 2005 Alexander Payne directed a film based on the novel about the bromance between characters Miles (Paul Giamatti) and Jack (Thomas Hayden Church) set in Santa Barbara. In the movie Pinot Noir wine served as a metaphor for relationships in that both require care and attention. *New York Times* wine writer Eric Asimov believed that, "the movie's novelty is a measure of the awkward and singular relationship that Americans have with wine."[106]

The film dramatically increased Santa Barbara wine tourism and provided a large boost to small labels that depended on direct sales through tasting rooms. By receiving two Golden Globes, five Oscar nominations, and countless good and bad reviews, the movie featured Santa Barbara tasting rooms like Fess Parker, Firestone, Foxen, Kalyra, Andrew Murray, and Sanford. Labels mentioned and shown in the film included Fiddlehead, Sea Smoke, Whitcraft, and Hartly Ostini. Upon reflection James Laube believed that the movie changed the market just like the Paris tasting of 1976 and the *60 Minutes* "French Paradox" episodes.[107] The movie helped brand Santa Barbara wine, and tourists worldwide rushed to get premium wines from the region.

The buddy flick promoted an epicurean image of Santa Barbara and made local Pinot Noir a star, resulting in wines flying off the shelves. The resulting "Sideways Effect" included the production of forty thousand copies of the "Sideways Wine Tour Map" by the Santa Barbara Conference and Visitors Bureau. Fox Spotlight Films assembled a forty-eight-page booklet "The Sideways Guide to Wine and Life," and the Buellton Days Inn room 203, featured in the movie, was consistently booked. Not to be outdone the Hilton Group put together a "Sideways Wine Tasting Survival Package" that included stain remover, aspirin, Alka-Seltzer, a corkscrew, and a bottle of local wine. To allow customers to relive restaurant scenes from the movie, the Hitching Post restaurant served a special menu based on the meals and wines enjoyed by the characters. Over the next few months, the restaurant realized a 20 percent rise in business and tried to accommodate constant requests to sit at the same table as the movie's stars. In downtown Santa Barbara Doug Margerum's Wine Cask wine shop saw a brisk rise in Pinot Noir sales and Jim Clendenen recalled, "I've sold more Pinot Noir in the last year than ever, and all since November, when the movie came out." Frank Ostini, Hitching Post restaurant, celebrated the fact that "sales of Highland (Pinot Noir) are up 400 percent."[108] On the downside, Merlot wine suffered as many consumers heeded the advice in Miles's famous line, "If anyone orders Merlot, I'm leaving. I am not drinking any fucking Merlot."[109]

Notes

1. James Laube, "Our Curious Wine Culture," *Wine Spectator*, 30 April 2009.
2. Kim Marcus, "California Takes On the World," *Wine Spectator*, 15 December 2002.
3. Nick Fauchald, "Roster of American Wineries Booms," *Wine Spectator*, 15 December 2004.
4. "U.S. Wine Consumption Sees Biggest Increase in 10 Years," *Wine Spectator*, 31 December 2003; "Grapevine, *Wine Spectator*, 15 May 2007.
5. Daniel Sogg, "California Wine: A $45 Billion Industry," *Wine Spectator*, 30 September 2004.
6. Eric Arnold, "American Wine Exports Reach $951 Million," *Wine Spectator*, 15 May 2008; Mark Van De camp, "State's exports of wine growing," *Santa Barbara News-Press*, 8 May 2002.

7. "As Dollar Slides, Prices for Imported Wines May Rise," *Wine Spectator*, 30 April 2004; Jacob Gaffen, "Euro Switch Has Little Impact on Wine Prices," *Wine Spectator*, 31 March 2002; Nick Fauchald, "French Wines Still Facing Hard Times in U.S. Market," *Wine Spectator*, 30 November 2003.

8. James Laube, "California," *Wine Spectator*, 31 January 2003.

9. Tim Fish, "California Winery Woes: From Boom to Bankruptcy," *Wine Spectator*, 15 November 2003.

10. James Laube, "Mondavi at the Crossroads," *Wine Spectator*, 15 October 2003.

11. Dennis Schaefer, "Santa Barbara wine—by the numbers," *Santa Barbara News-Press*, 11 July 2002.

12. "Top 100 Profiles," *Wine Spectator*, 31 December 2003.

13. Dennis Schaefer, "Santa Barbara County wines in the spotlight (again), *Santa Barbara News-Press*, 5 September 2002; "Santa Barbara County enjoyed the distinction of being nominated by *Wine Enthusiast* magazine for its annual Wine regions of the World Award," *Santa Barbara News-Press*, 8 January 2006.

14. "Vintners say new label close to home," *Santa Barbara News-Press*, 16 June 2001; Mark Van De Kamp, "Vintners cheer appellation failure: local take," *Santa Barbara News-Press*, 14 August 2002.

15. Daniel Sogg, "Court Rules That California Can Require Napa-named Wines to Come From Napa," *Wine Spectator*, 15 October 2004; Frank Nelson, "Santa Barbara County Vintner's Association pleased with the California Supreme Court," *Santa Barbara News-Press*, 6 August 2004.

16. A legal case study of this label and terroir issue can be found in Carol Robertson, "Case 11: The Taste of Wine—Wine Appellations and the Importance of Terroir," *The Little Red Book of Wine Law: A Case of Legal Issues* (Chicago: ABA Publishing, 2008), 128–145.

17. "Name-calling shaking up wine world," *Santa Barbara News-Press*, 25 April 2001.

18. Matt Kettmann, "Robert Balzer Breaks the Sta. Rita Hills," *Santa Barbara Independent*, 21 August 2014.

19. "Establishment of Santa Rita Hills Viticultural Area (98R-129P)," *Department of Treasury Federal Register*, 27 CFR Part 9 v. 66 n. 105, 31 May 2001.

20. Marc Wortman, "Grapevine," *Wine Spectator*, 15 May 2006.

21. James Laube, "California's New Frontier," *Wine Spectator*, 15 June 2006.

22. James Laube, "Santa Barbara's New Frontier," *Wine Spectator*, 15 September 2003; "America's Best Pinot Noirs," *Wine Enthusiast*, 21 October 2013.

23. Gabe Saglie," Raise a glass? Expansion win in local wine areas leaves some winemakers fermenting," *Santa Barbara News-Press*, 8 September 2016; Mary Ann Worobiec, "A Larger Sta. Rita Hills," *Wine Spectator*, 15 June 2013.

24. James Laube, "Appellations Run Amok," *Wine Spectator*, 31 October 2011.

25. Lynn Alley, "U.S. Government Puts Hold on Approving New Appellations," *Wine Spectator*, 31 October 2007.

26. "Establishment of the Happy Canyon of Santa Barbara Viticultural Area, (2007R-311P)," *Department of Treasury Federal Register*, 27 CFR Part 9 v. 74 n. 194, 8 October 2009.

27. Daniel Sogg, "The Santa Barbara Edge," *Wine Spectator*, 31 October 2008.

28. James Laube, "California Chardonnay's Appealing Diversity," *Wine Spectator*, 31 January 2000; James Laube, "California Chardonnay," *Wine Spectator*, 31 January 2005.

29. Bruce Sanderson, "Great Grapes: Chardonnay America's Favorite Varietal," *Wine Spectator*, 15 May 2008.

30. James Laube, "New World Chardonnay," *Wine Spectator*, 31 July 2001; Matt Kettmann, "California's Coast with the Most," *Wine Enthusiast*, 15 December 2016.

31. Dana Nigro, "What's Behind the Bottle Price," *Wine Spectator*, 15 December 2002.

32. "California's Best for $15 or Less," *Wine Spectator*, 15 October 2002.

33. James Laube, "Santa Barbara," *Wine Spectator,* 15 June 2006; Eric Asimov, "Chardonnay Finds Its Inner Finesse," *New York Times,* 25 April 2001.

34. "The Top 100," *Wine Spectator,* 31 December 2002.

35. Virginia Boone, Jim Gordon, and Matt Kettmann, "California Grand Cru Chardonnays," *Wine Enthusiast,* 17 August 2016.

36. Kim Marcus, "Editor's Picks: Smart Buys," *Wine Spectator,* 31 January 2004.

37. Eric Asimov, "California Chardonnay Grows Up," *New York Times,* 3 March 2009.

38. "Grapevine," *Wine Spectator,* 15 September 2003; John Winthrop Haeger, *North American Pinot Noir* (Berkeley: University of California Press, 2004).

39. Daniel Song, "Inside Wine: In the Vine Gene Pool," *Wine Spectator,* 31 March 2007; Lynn Alley, "Scientists Unravel Grape Genome," *Wine Spectator,* 15 November 2007; "The Origins of the Grape Program at Foundation Plant Materials Service," *American Journal of Enology and Viticulture,* 51:5, 2000.

40. James Laube, "A Tricky Year for Pinot Noir," *Wine Spectator,* 15 September 2000.

41. Eric Asimov, "A Purple Passion for Pinot Noir: Wines of the Times," *New York Times,* 16 May 2007.

42. James Laube, "The 2002 Vintage Is the One We've All Been Waiting For," *Wine Spectator,* 15 September 2004; James Laube, "Heartbreak No More," *Wine Spectator,* 15 October 2005.

43. James Laube, "California Pinot Noir," *Wine Spectator,* 15 December 2006.

44. "Wine Spectator Top 100," *Wine Spectator,* 31 December 2004.

45. Ross Parsons, "Pinot king's ouster shocks wine realm," *Los Angeles Times,* 19 October 2005; Mary Ann Worobiec, "The Hot New Dozen of California Pinot Noir," *Wine Spectator,* 30 September 2007

46. "The Magnificent 30," *Wine Spectator,* 15 December 2006.

47. Eric Asimov, "A Purple passion for Pinot Noir: Wines of the Times," *New York Times,* 16 May 2007.

48. James Laube, "Approaching Perfection," *Wine Spectator,* 15 October 2011.

49. Patrick J. Comiskey, *American Rhône: How Maverick Winemakers Changed the Way Americans Drink,* (Berkeley: University of California Press, 2016), passim.

50. Frank J. Prial, "Wine Talk; Time to Pucker Up and Say Syrah," *New York Times,* 3 April 2002.

51. Eric Asimov, "California Syrahs, On Such a Winter;'s Day," *New York Times,* 30 January 2014.

52. James Laube, "California Syrah Comes on Strong," *Wine Spectator,* 31 March 2007; James Laube, "Syrah's Rising Tide," *Wine Spectator,* 31 January 2004. The name Rhône Ranger was first used by Oakland wineshop owner Mike Higgins in the 1980s.

53. Ron Trujillo, "DNA test resolves paternity—of vines," *Santa Barbara News-Press,* 25 August 2000.

54. James Laube, "Ojai," *Wine Spectator,* 31 January 2003.

55. "Melville Vineyards leads the small—winery charge," *Santa Barbara News-Press,* 2 September 2004.

56. Tim Fish, "Rhône Quest in California," *Wine Spectator,* 30 November 2007.

57. Joe Czerwinski, "Betting on Syrah," *Wine Enthusiast,* 16 August 2005.

58. Laurie Jervis, "Wine Country: Wine is truly a family affair," *Santa Ynez Valley News,* 2 June 2009.

59. Mary Ann Worobiec, "10 Emerging California Rhône Producers," *Wine Spectator,* 31 March 2009; "California Syrah's Big Push: Promising New Producers," *Wine Spectator,* 31 March 2008.

60. James Laube, "California Rhônes Rise to the Top," *Wine Spectator,* 31 March 2010.

61. Steve Heimoff, "Syrah in the Shadows," *Wine Enthusiast,* 12 October 2011.

62. Eric Asimov, "A Worldly Grape, Home In California," *New York Times,* 18 May 2005; Matt Kettmann, "Sauvignon Blanc Gets Serious," *Wine Enthusiast,* 16 July 2015.

63. James Laube, "California: Value-Priced Wines Power the Appeal of the Golden State's Many Styles," *Wine Spectator,* 31 June 2000.

64. Mary Ann Worobiec, "California Sauvignon Blanc," *Wine Spectator,* 31 August 2009; Matt

Kettmann, "California's Awesome Alternative White wines," *Wine Enthusiast*, 224 June 2015; Mary Ann Worobiec, "Sauvignon Blanc's Expanding Horizons," *Wine Spectator*, 31 August 2011.

65. James Laube and Daniel Song, "Napa Winemakers Cash Out," *Wine Spectator*, 15 October 2007.

66. Mark Van De Kamp, "Australia's Foster's will buy California Vintner Beringer," *Santa Barbara News-Press*, 30 August 2000.

67. Tim Fish, "Constellation Refocuses in Recession," *Wine Spectator*, 30 September 2009.

68. Corin Brown, "Winery shopping spree," *Los Angeles Times*, 5 September 2007.

69. Mary Ann Worobiec, "Growth and Acquisition," *Wine Spectator*, 15 November 2009; Harvey Steiman, "Foley Buys A Stake in Walla Walla's Three Rivers Winery," *Wine Spectator*, 30 April 2008; Eric Arnold, Jo Cooke, Daniel Sogg, and Robert Taylor, "Grapevine," *Wine Spectator*, 31 October 2007; James Laube, "The End of an Era at Sebastiani," *Wine Spectator*, 15 November 2009; "Conversation with William Foley," *Santa Barbara News-Press*, 11 August 2002; Dennis Schaefer, "Vines on ranch yield promise of more good things to come," *Santa Barbara News-Press*, 30 September 2004; Steve Heimoff, "Foley Buys Chalk Hill," *Wine Enthusiast*, 17 August 2016.

70. Augustus Weed, "Bill Foley's Wine Empire," *Wine Spectator*, 30 September 2018, 79-81.

71. Daniel Sogg, "Vineyard Capitalism," *Wine Spectator*, 15 June 2008.

72. Dana Nigro, "Kendal-Jackson Hires Hewlett-Packard Chairman as CEO," *Wine Spectator*, 31 January 2000.

73. Daniel Sogg, "Two Wine Empires Expand in California," *Wine Spectator*, 15 May 2000.

74. Jo Cooke and Daniel Sogg, "The Fallout From Mondavi," *Wine Spectator*, 15 May 2005; Eric Arnold, "Grapevine," *Wine Spectator*, 31 October 2006.

75. Dennis Schaefer, "Cambria has their Mojo workin (overtime)," *Santa Barbara News-Press*, 17 October 2002.

76. Mark Van De Kamp, "Fess Parker woos Lompoc for winery," *Santa Barbara News-Press*, 24 October 2000.

77. Mark Van De Kamp, "Fess Parker expanding his winery operations," *Santa Barbara News-Press*, 8 April 2003.

78. Mark Van De Kamp, "Parker family seeks buyers for three vineyards," *Santa Barbara News-Press*, 26 August 2003.

79. Frank Nelson, "Sanford winemaking partnership fractures," *Santa Barbara News-Press*, 25 September 2005; Gabe Saglie, "Celebrating Sanford & Benedict: 40th anniversary of landmark vineyard," *Santa Barbara News-Press*, 25 August 2016; A history of the Terlato Family and Business can be found in Anthony Terlato, *Taste: A Life In Wine* (Chicago: Agate, 2008).

80. James Laube, "Slim Pickings for California Pinot Noir," *Wine Spectator*, 15 September 2002; "Grapevine," *Wine Spectator*, 30 September 2002; Tim Fish, "A Life In Wine," *Wine Spectator*, 15 November 2004.

81. Frank Nelson, "Sanford," *Santa Barbara News-Press*, 17 December 2005.

82. Frank Nelson, "E&J Gallo Buying Bridlewood Winery," *Santa Barbara News-Press*, 25 March 2004; Lynn Alley, "Gallo Buys Winery in California's Central Coast," *Wine Spectator*, 31 May 2004; "Rideau latest winery put on the block," *Santa Barbara News-Press*, 30 June 2002.

83. James Laube, "Greg Brewer," *Wine Spectator*, 31 July 2003.

84. Kathy Joseph had Beringer as a financial partner and named Seasmoke after the billowing white fog that came off the ocean. James Laube, "Santa Barbara's New Frontier," *Wine Spectator*, 15 September 2003; Harvey Steiman, "Profiles in Pinot Noir: Today," *Wine Spectator*, 15 September 2003.

85. Dennis Schaefer, "Rusack Vineyards sets a new quality course," *Santa Barbara News-Press*, 29 May 2003; Chelsey Steinman, "Husband and Wife Winemakers," *Santa Barbara Independent*, 21 November 2010.

86. Dennis Schaefer, "Schaefer on Wine: Dierberg Vineyard on a roll," *Santa Barbara News-Press,* 31 March 2016.

87. Evan Dawson, "Parallel Universe," *Wine Spectator,* 15 November 2013.

88. Dennis Schaefer, "Schaefer on Wine: Samsara captures cycle of life in wine," *Santa Barbara News-Press,* 14 May 2015.

89. Wendy Van Hom, "Rick Longoria's Fe Ciega," *Santa Barbara Independent,* 17 July 2008; Michael Cervin, "Shoestring Winery," *Santa Barbara Independent,* 16 March 2006; Dennis Schaefer, "Schaefer on Wine; Ampelos amps it up," *Santa Barbara News-Press,* 8 January 2015; Dennis Schaefer, "Schaefer on Wine: Dragonette : Minimal but mindful," *Santa Barbara News-Press,* 29 October 2015.

90. Gabe Saglie, "From barren to beautiful: Kimsey transforms lot into quality vineyard," *Santa Barbara New-Press,* 2 June 2016.

91. Dennis Schaefer, "Schaefer on Wine: Falcone family spreads its wings," *Santa Barbara News-Press,* 7 August 2014.

92. Dennis Schaefer, "Schaefer on Wine: Lo-Fi on the wine turn table," *Santa Barbara News-Press,* 13 July 2017.

93. Eric Arnold and James Laube, "Grapevine," *Wine Spectator,* 31 March 2007.

94. "Grapevine," *Wine Spectator,* 31 August 2006.

95. "Grapevine," *Wine Spectator,* 15 November 2003.

96. Jacob Gaffney, "Mapping Wine's Benefits," *Wine Spectator,* 15 October 2004.

97. Kim Marcus, "Research and Findings: A User's Guide To Wine Science," *Wine Spectator,* 31 May 2009.

98. Tim Fish, "The New California Tasting Room," *Wine Spectator,* 15 November 2008.

99. Frank Nelson, "New law benefits charity wine tastings," *Santa Barbara News-Press,* 6 September 2003.

100. Tim Fish and David Sax, "Wineries Reach Out to Hispanics," *Wine Spectator,* 15 October 2004.

101. Patricia Leigh Brown, "Luring Women With the Chick Lit of Wine," *New York Times,* 27 April 2005.

102. Eric Arnold and Mitch Frank," Grapevine," *Wine Spectator,* 31 May 2006.

103. Lynn Alley, "Your Tax Dollars at Work," *Wine Spectator,* 31 December 2004.

104. James Molesworth, "New Wine Scanner Detects Off Flavors," *Wine Spectator,* 31 August 2005.

105. Rex Pickett, *Sideways: The Ultimate Road Trip, The Last Hurrah* (New York; St. Martin's Press, 2004); "The 10 Greatest Wine Movies of All Time," *Wine Enthusiast,* 31 March 2015.

106 Eric Asimov, "Wine, Women and A Pair of Buddies," *New York Times,* 6 October 2004.

107. James Laube, "Sideways Double Whammy," *Wine Spectator,* 15 May 2005.

108. Eric Asimov, "Best Supporting Grape," *New York Times,* 23 February 2005.

109. Nick Fauchald, "The Sideways Effect," *Wine Spectator,* 30 April 2005; James Laube, "Sideways Double Whammy," *Wine Spectator,* 15 May 2005; Stuart Elliott, "Best Product in a leading role," *New York Times,* 31 January 2005.

Chapter Thirteen

Old Problems, New Challenges

Continued problems with global competition and fluctuating markets, direct marketing laws and policies, land-use battles, attacks from environmentalists, pests and diseases, and borderline business practices persisted. Despite these challenges the Santa Barbara wine industry had evolved into a viable wine region by retaining established commercial wineries and incentivizing a growing number of boutique premium operations. Overall, there was a slowdown in vineyard planting and large commercial wineries retained use of the majority of the county's grapes.

Starting on 9/11 of 2001 and lasting through the recession of 2007–2009, the decades-long trend of rising wine prices slowed down and vintners faced the worst wine recession since the Great Depression. This downturn forced consumers, with less disposable incomes, to either buy less wine or search out cheaper wine. The wine recession fears deepened when some experts declared that California's "Wine Golden Age" had ended. Making matters even worse were the threats by French vintners to exceed their past American export sales numbers to over twenty billion bottles ($169 million in value) to the United States.[1] As American vintners faced this increased competition, they fought back by reducing prices. To the benefit of the American wine industry, the French dreams proved overly optimistic as consumers reduced Bordeaux imports by 3 percent, Champagne fell 21 percent, and Australian imports plummeted by 26 percent. The big exception was a 43 percent increase of cheap Argentinian wine.[2] Essentially, the market was flooded with wine and the laws of supply and demand drove prices downward. Vintners responded by holding back inventory for future sales, reducing short-term production, cutting back on operations, canceling grape contracts, and putting off much-needed modernization projects. This pressure on the supply chain then forced some growers to pull out grapevines, sell vineyards, or stop planting projects. Overall, global competition decreased as American consumers switched to value-priced premium California wines.

To stay competitive, wineries, both large and small, reduced prices and created a buyer's market. Small-sized wineries (up to fifty thousand cases) discounted their inventory for direct-to-consumer programs while large corporate wineries reduced prices to national distributors. Medium-sized wineries (fifty thousand to one hundred thousand cases) suffered the most because they could not depend entirely on consumer direct sales and faced a dwindling number of distributors willing to represent their brand because their smaller production numbers could not meet the quantity needs of large national distributors. The upside to the harsh wine market was the fact that consumers were drinking more premium wines as producers marketed consistently better wines at lower prices.[3] This also spurred a new period of winery consolidation to achieve the cost-effectiveness needed to reduce prices and still make profits.[4] Despite the negative factors it was not the end of times for American wine.[5]

NEO-PROHIBITION

The national saga over federal regulations for alcohol sales continued in a seemingly never-ending battle. Neither side had been satisfied with the 2005 Supreme Court decision that called for enforcement of the Commerce Clause to ensure that states treated both in-state and out-of-state sellers equally. Between 2005 and 2010 the National Beer Wholesaler Association (NBWA) and Wine and Spirits Wholesalers of America (WSWA) funneled over $11.5 million into lobbying and campaign funds to influence passage of a bill supporting the three-tier system, regulating internet sales, and protecting youth from internet and phone alcohol sales. Obviously, this angered the wine industry and the California Association of Grape Growers, Allied Grape Growers, Wine Institute, and Wine America joined forces and poured over $745,000 into lobbying efforts to oppose the bill. Jim Fiolek, SBCVA executive director, called the bill a joke and commented, "How many kids are going to steal their parents credit card and spend 300 to 400 bucks on a case of wine and have to sign for it?"[6]

In 2010 the House of Representatives responded to aggressive lobbying and 119 members sponsored HR 5034, the Comprehensive Alcohol Regulatory Effectiveness Act (CARE). The bill failed to get out of the House Judiciary Committee and proponents unsuccessfully tried again in 2012 with HR 1161. Dry versus wet battles continued.

Despite decades of neo-Prohibition battles, most in the industry stayed optimistic that wine would always be part of American food culture. De Luca spoke for many, "I foresee wine at home on nearly every dinner table as the preferred mealtime beverage to aid in digestion, and in the absorption of vital nutrients. I see wine adding more than nutrition, adding the graciousness provided by it civilized use which distinguishes human dining from animal feeding."[7] Santa Barbara winery owner Brooks Firestone tempered this idealistic view as he believed that "some of the people that go into the wine business lose sight of the practical aspects, because they are so much in love with wine."[8]

SUSTAINABLE LAND-USE ISSUES CHANGE THE SANTA BARBARA INDUSTRY

Decades of struggles between farmers, ranchers, winemakers, environmentalists, and citizens had slowly shifted the development of wineries and vineyards in the region. In the long run these contentious vineyard and winery battles with NIMBY residents and environmentalists slowed down the growth of the Santa Barbara wine industry. Both sides eventually compromised in favor of sustainable agricultural practices in the vineyards, more regulated winery growth, regulated events, and development of urban wine tasting centers. But, a tension still existed, and both sides continued to monitor county supervisor decisions. To this end environmentalists reminded wineries that a 2013 French study had discovered pesticide residues in most wines and they promised future vigilance for their cause. The real change came after a 2013 UCLA study revealed that consumers were willing to pay more for sustainable wines.[9] This made many wineries more willing to commit to a sustainable business model.

New growth and expansion slowly continued throughout the decade of the 2010s. In 2016, after six years of consideration, the Santa Barbara County Board of Supervisors finally approved the Mattei's Tavern project, along with its sixty-four luxury cottages, pool, spa, retail boutique, gym, and a three-thousand-square-foot meeting area.[10] At the same time Ashley Parker Snider and Eli Parker announced the opening of the Bear and Star restaurant in Los Olivos at the Fess Parker Wine Country Inn. The new foodie eatery featured the sourcing of vegetables, beef, fowl, and wine from the seven-hundred-acre Parker family estate.[11]

Despite rigorous restrictions new wineries and vineyards slowly continued to appear. In 2007 ex–Fess Parker employee Larry Schaffer launched his Rhône varietal Tercero label.[12] That same year Madison, Suzanne, and Matt Murphy left their Louisiana corn, soy, and rice farm after its destruction in Hurricane

Katrina for viticulture in Santa Barbara County. They moved to Santa Maria and purchased a two-hundred-acre ranch and immediately drew permits to establish a vineyard and winery. Over the next few years, the Murphys planted seventy-three acres in Pinot Noir, Chardonnay, Sauvignon Blanc, and Syrah vines on their sustainable Presqu'ile (Creole for "almost an island") vineyard. They then used a Napa-based contractor to create a 2,800-square-foot tasting room, a gourmet kitchen, meeting room, and a glass-enclosed blending laboratory for visitor viewing.[13] During this same time period, Matt Dees, Jonata and the Hilt winemaker, purchased the 3,600-acre Rancho Salsipuedes and began planting vineyards.[14] James and Brandon Sparks left Idaho in 2009 and launched their Kings Carey label, sourcing grapes from Sta. Rita Hills vineyards.[15]

After a laborious three years of the permitting process, the County Board of Supervisors, by a 3–2 vote, approved Anthony Vincent's winery proposal. This had been a contentious process because the proposed winery on State Route 154 had drawn numerous complaints about the possibility of noise, traffic, and degradation of the community's rural character.[16] To get the project passed, Vincent negotiated to cut back from eight yearly events to four (all under eighty people), reduced the tasting room size by 1,100 square-feet, and lowered the wineries production to seven thousand cases yearly from a 7,343 square-foot production facility.

Despite these minor victories anti-growth opponents continued their battle to save the county's agricultural heritage. The momentum seemed to be back on their side as recent elections had again shifted the loyalties on the Santa Barbara Board of Supervisors. Because many of the anti-growth proponents were new-comers who had moved to Santa Ynez for the country lifestyle, pro-growth supporters labeled them "ranchette vigilantes." They had no problem with new vineyards; they just wanted no new wineries, events, or tasting rooms. As can be imagined these ranchette vigilantes angered the agricultural community as can be seen by Andy Caldwell, executive director of the Coalition of Labor Agriculture and Business (COLAB) in a *Santa Barbara News-Press* editorial piece where he wrote, "We must allow our farmers and ranchers to make a living off the land." He continued, "The fact is that any farmer, regardless of the crop grown, whose operations are not vertically integrated, makes pennies on the dollar while taking on all the risks associated with farming."[17]

As the battle for winery expansion heated up, the county supervisors in a three to two vote rejected Tom and Debi Stull's Tommy Town Thoroughbreds

(TTT) winery project in Santa Ynez. The opposition referred to the project as another "party-house" and vowed to fight any winery tasting room on Ballard Canyon Road. Opponents believed that the old, narrow seven-mile road, with blind curves and no shoulder, could not handle winery traffic. They vowed to not let their community become another Napa or Sonoma and feared that by okaying this permit it would allow fourteen other wineries to apply for a tasting room.[18] This, of course, angered and energized wine industry allies to rally behind minority supervisors Bob Field and Bruce Porter, whose approach was to punish bad actors and support tourism and wine events.[19]

Andy Caldwell, in a *Santa Barbara News-Press* Guest Opinion, described the fears of small vintners throughout Santa Barbara. He condensed the problem down to the fact that farming alone is a losing proposition and that "Farming operations must be vertically integrated in order to survive." He believed that "California farmers and ranchers face enormous obstacles in the form of water rationing, labor shortages, pesticide prohibitions, land costs, land-use regulations, as well as exorbitant taxes and fees." The problem became exacerbated by the reduction in wine brokers that forced small operations to market up to 60 percent of their wines from their tasting rooms. Caldwell proposed new zoning laws that "allow for landholders to plant, harvest, package, and market the products they sell."[20] The struggle for continued wine industry growth was far from over.

More level heads attempted to find ways to again compromise and keep both pro- and no-growth advocates happy. In 2013 Santa Barbara county planners held a meeting in Los Olivos to find a balance in county agricultural policies and seventy-five members of the wine community attended. The meeting quickly resulted in a loud and heated debate over a new proposal to block winery events for any operation under twenty acres. Local vintner Michael Dobrotin from Lavender Oaks Vineyard accused the board of "stifling competition between a small person and the big guys." Vintner Tom Elsaesser added, "You've taken away the entrepreneurship, the flavor of the Santa Ynez Valley."[21] At least the two sides were still talking, albeit in loud and angry voices.

After years of collecting data and meeting with various stakeholders, the Santa Barbara County Board of Supervisors finally moved in 2013 to attempt a draft winery proposal. The wine industry immediately pushed back against the one-size fits-all approach and no-growth opponents again enumerated their fears of drunk drivers, traffic, noise, and loss of the agricultural lifestyle.[22]

Wine writer Gabe Saglie reminded everyone that in Santa Barbara County a taster could, for ten to fifteen dollars, taste in clusters of tasting rooms and town centers like Buellton and Los Olivos or specialized old industrial areas in Lompoc and downtown Santa Barbara. When compared to Sonoma where tasting rooms were spread over sixteen regions across fifty miles with over four hundred wineries. In this context Santa Barbara County seemed tame.[23] Wine industry studies supported Saglie's claim and cited the fact that Santa Barbara County had 64 wineries and 127 boutique urban wineries, compared to 467 wineries in Napa. Projections predicted that by 2035 Santa Barbara County would only grow to 104 wineries. The study also presented statistics to show that roads were not overcrowded and that most DUIs occurred between 10:00 p.m. and 3:00 a.m. when wineries were closed.[24] The battle continued for another three years.

In September of 2016, after years of waiting, wine lovers, farmers, ranchers, and wineries received the Santa Barbara Planning Commission's proposal to the Santa Barbara County Board of Supervisors as it pertained to the local wine industry. Almost immediately wineries complained that the proposals were draconian in nature and would likely kill the agricultural viability of the region. The board was ridiculed for the four year, $1.25-million anti-winery proposed regulations and many saw restrictions on tourism and winery events as anti–free market capitalism. Dan and Ellen Kessler, Kessler-Haak Vineyard and Wines, believed that it would be "the most restrictive winery ordinance in the United States."[25] Wineries complained that it was not a collaborative process and Third District Supervisor Doreen Farr reminded them that the county had hosted twenty-seven meetings and heard from over eight hundred people before acting.[26] In a letter to the *Santa Barbara News-Press,* Terri Strickland fired back that the "draft winery ordinance got this far because South County (urban Santa Barbara) supervisors form the majority and their liberal mind-set is an anti-business agenda."[27]

On November 23, 2016 the wine ordinances came before the board of supervisors for a final vote. During public comments fifty-five people from the wine industry told the board why they feared the new ordinances. Morgen McLaughlin, Executive Director of the SBCVA, commented, "We, as an agricultural industry and community fundamentally believe that grape growing, wine production, retail wine sales and wine marketing activities are all primary agricultural uses that should be allowed to thrive in Santa Barbara County under a fair and balanced set of regulations." She continued, "The ordinance in front of you as written will go on record as the most restrictive winery

ordinance in the state of California and in the United States." After five years
of heated arguments, many believed that large winery events were the central
issue. Tim Snyder, president of Fess Parker Winery, still believed that: "balance
can be achieved."[28] This time around winery and pro-growth proponents won
by a 4–1 vote. For the time being the industry had some breathing room; but,
anti-growth forces were far from giving up.

More pressure on Santa Barbara ordinances started in 2018 when Napa
environmentalists adopted Santa Barbara type arguments, regulation, and
restriction ideas to update the 1968 Napa Valley Agricultural Preserve dictate.
Environmentalists ensured that Measure C, the Watershed and Oak Woodland
Protection Initiative, would be on the June 5, 2018, mail-in ballot. The measure proposed amending the Napa County General Plan and zoning code by
"creating water quality buffer zones within the Agricultural Watershed zoning
district and restricting tree removal within those zones; strengthening oak
removal remediation standards and establishing a permit program for oak tree
removal once 795 acres of oak woodland have been removed."[29] Arguments
for and against were the same as those used in Santa Barbara. Measure C supporters Mike Hackett and Jim Wilson believed that fifty years of wine industry
exploitation of the landscape for profit must end.

Wine industry supporters argued that it would undermine agriculture—the
one thing that has kept Napa Valley beautiful and made it prosperous. "I get upset
knowing that we, as growers and vintners, are being cast as offenders," said Chuck
Wagner, owner of Caymus Vineyards. "We are the essence of why the valley is
beautiful, and why it's been kept and improved over the years." The County Farm
Bureau and the Napa Valley Grapegrowers called the measure "anti-ag." Ryan
Klobas, Farm Bureau policy director, lamented that, "Already Napa County has
some of the strictest environmental regulations in the country, if not the world."
He continued, "We're concerned about the costs to small family farms."[30] They
further argued that Napa's forty-five thousand acres of vineyards were only about 9
percent of the county's total landscape. Even if the County Planning Commission's
projection of five thousand more acres by 2030 proved correct only 10 percent
would be vineyards, compared to the 80 percent occupied by parks, open space,
and rural lands. The vote was so close that it took three weeks for recounts to determine that citizens had voted Proposition C down by 641 votes out of 35,707 votes
cast.[31] The environmental battle against the wine industry continued statewide.

Fears of vineyard damage due to global warming exacerbated environmental
concerns. In 2007 a Stanford University Woods Institute for the Environment

publication warned that global warming would change California agriculture. The study predicted a 20 to 50 percent reduction in wine-grape production by 2040 for Napa and Santa Ynez vineyards.[32] The dire news continued in 2013 with a National Academy of Sciences of California report predicting that 70 percent of Santa Barbara's wine-growing area would heat up by midcentury, making present varieties and processes obsolete.[33] Many also feared water shortages due to climate change. These fears seemed well founded as records from the 2014 drought revealed a 24,190-ton drop in grape production.[34] Adding to the water fears was the 2011 Los Alamos Vineyard illegal oil fracking incident that in 2014 had sparked the Santa Maria County Supervisors to consider implementing the "Healthy Air and Water Initiative to ban fracking, acidizing, and stream injection."[35] Fearing air quality issues Santa Barbara supervisors also considered keeping track of winery CO_2 release figures from the fermentation process.[36]

Tensions over land use and the environment eventually led to the 2017 resignation of SBCVA executive director Morgen McLaughlin. In her short term she had expanded regional and international outreach, improved the yearly festivals, and commissioned an economic study. The study found that the wine industry provided $1.7 billion to the county's economy, employed 5,700 people, and drew 900,000 tourists yearly. Yet, county politicians and aggressive land-use restrictions held back the local wine industry. In her words, "We are trying to build the DTC (Direct-to-Consumer) side of the business and the tourism side. But we're being hammered extensively with the land-use regulations. That's one of the main reasons why I'm leaving." McLaughlin firmly believed that tourists wanted to visit wineries and attend their events. She also blamed Santa Barbara for not having a County Office of Tourism that could work with wineries and the tourist industry.[37]

The key for the Santa Barbara wine industry was that the land-use struggles forever changed how the wine industry would develop over the next few decades. SBCVA executive director McLaughlin summed it up best in her statement: "What's unusual about Santa Barbara County is that because of existing land-use restrictions, it's disincentivized the estate winery model and encouraged producers to open up stand-alone tasting rooms in urbanized areas."[38] In the long run agricultural vineyards survived, established estate wineries remained, and city and suburban boutique wineries rapidly expanded by utilizing excess grapes and wine from existing vertically integrated commercial wineries and independent vineyards.

MINOR DISTRACTIONS

Starting in 2012 the FDA took a new interest in winery safety and began ramping up winery inspections under the 2011 Food Safety Modernization Act. Over the past twenty years, most wineries had not been inspected and Wendell Lee, general council of the Wine institute, could not recall any inspections of wineries in California. Anxiety rose as vintners did not know what to expect.[39]

As organic farming and winemaking became a serious trend, consumers, activist groups, and winemakers struggled to define what exactly is organic wine and how its processing is different from nonorganic wine. Many organic wineries maintained that certified organic wines could only contain organic grapes, but allowed for the addition of 100 parts per million of sulfite for preservation against oxidation. Just as many organic wineries felt this practice was wrong. Others cited the fact that sulfur dioxide, as a fungicide, was legal in organic vineyards and felt distractors missed the point that organic wines must contain at least 95 percent organic grapes. They also cited the fact that natural fermentation of organic grapes produced 10 parts per million of sulfite well below the FDA standard of 350 parts-per-million.[40] In the end the rules allowed for the addition of sulfite.

In 2014 the SBCVA joined numerous other wine organizations to stop ICANN (Internet Corporation for Assigned Names and Numbers) that planned to sell domain names ending in ".wine" and ".vin" to the highest bidders. Opponents claimed that insufficient safeguards would not stop illegitimate companies from hijacking their names and histories. Worse yet, it could destroy consumer confidence in the local terroir.[41] In another dispute Turn Key Wine Brands LLC took Custom Vine to federal court. Turn Key took possession of special-labeled Santa Barbara and San Luis Obispo surplus wines and for a fee sold them to restaurants and other clients for reduced prices. Turn Key accused Custom Vines, Walnut Creek Broker, for not paying for consigned wines.[42]

Many Santa Maria growers and winemakers often felt neglected by the SBCVA, so they formed the Santa Maria Valley Wine Country (SMVWC) association in 2007 to more directly advertise and market their AVA. One of their major accomplishments was to organize the 2010 Chardonnay Symposium that drew participants from around the world to taste over fifty Chardonnays. But keeping an organization funded and going proved difficult, and in 2014 the organization folded as members became convinced that SBCVA could look after their needs. After disbanding many former members established the voluntary Santa Maria Valley Wine Think Tank.[43]

Growers and wineries continued their diligent lookout for Pierce's disease and phylloxera. But another old pest inconvenienced growers when a resurgence of meal bugs hit the county. Meal bugs secrete a sticky substance that covers vines with a black fungus or "sooty mold" that eventually stresses vines and reduces the quality of the grapes. In 2003 vineyards in Santa Maria and Los Alamos reported some infected vines that were eventually traced to a 1998 planting of infected nursery stock. Treatment was fast and site specific.[44]

Although the Santa Barbara wine industry appeared stable, there were those who pushed the boundaries of business ethics. Past Fess Parker employee Christian Gavin had by the age of forty-one founded Avelina Wine Company and cofounded Oreana Winery as an urban winery. The up-and-coming vintner's career ended in 2015 as the courts found him guilty of embezzling $1.2 million from his partners.[45] In 2017 Charles Augustus Banks IV, past owner of Qupé and Sandhi wines and Mattei's Tavern, pleaded guilty to a single count of wine fraud and received a four-year jail sentence with $7.5 million in restitution to be paid to San Antonio Spurs player Tim Duncan.[46]

The new century presented sizable problems for the wine industry. To survive wineries statewide reduced inventories, shrank acreage, reduced prices, and consolidated.[47] They quickly adapted and recovered, and by the late 2010s Santa Barbara County and the California wine industry reached new highs in the global wine community.[48]

Notes

1. Suzanne Mustacich, "America's Thirst for French Wine," *Wine Spectator,* 15 June 2012.
2. Mitch Frank, "Hard Times for Overseas Wineries," *Wine Spectator,* 15 June 2009.
3. Tim Fish and Mitch Frank, "A Buyer's Market," *Wine Spectator,* 28 February 2010; Matt Kramer, "Is The Golden Age Over?" *Wine Spectator,* 31 October 2010.
4. Tim Fish and Augustus Weed, "California Dealing," *Wine Spectator,* 31 July 2011.
5. Matt Kraemer, "It's Getting Better All the Time," *Wine Spectator,* 31 May 2013.
6. Chelsey Steinman, "Stopping the Direct-to-Consumer Flow," *Santa Barbara Independent,* 1 August 2010; Robert Taylor, "Bill Threatens Wine Direct Shipping," *Wine Spectator,* 30 June 2010; Robert Taylor and Ben O'Donnell. "Battle Over Direct Shipping Heats Up," *Wine Spectator,* 31 August 2010; Rob eat Taylor, "Bill Threatening Direct Shipping Gains New Life," *Wine Spectator,* 30 November 2010.

7. De Luca, 393.

8. Brooks Firestone Oral History.

9. Suzanne Mustacich, "French Pesticides Study Raises Concerns," *Wine Spectator,* 15 December 2013; Liz Thach, "Wineries Believe Sustainability Pays," *Wine Spectator,* 15 November 2014.

10. Gabe Saglie, "Full steam ahead; Inn at Mattei's Tavern sets sights on opening day," *Santa Barbara News-Press,* 21 November 2015.

11. Gabe Saglie, "New Fess Parker venture is a Santa Barbara first," *Santa Barbara News-Press,* 28 June 2016; Gabe Saglie, "Gabe Saglie: Vineyard Lunch: Fess Parker adds Culinary Angle to wine-tasting," *Santa Barbara News-Press,* 5 May 2016; Gabe Saglie, "Parker family announces opening a new restaurant," *Santa Barbara News-Press,* 7 March 2017.

12. Gabe Saglie, "Gabe Saglie: Rhône rising: Local wineries aim to educate through tasting," *Santa Barbara News-Press,* 30 March 2017; Dennis Schaefer, "Schaefer on Wine: Tercero champions underdog varieties," *Santa Barbara News-Press,* 12 May 2016.

13. Dennis Schaefer, "Elevated experience: New deluxe winery carved on a hillside," *Santa Barbara News-Press,* 15 June 2013; Dennis Schaefer, "Schaefer on Wine: Presq'ile: From the ground up," *Santa Barbara News-Press,* 4 August 2016.

14. "In Brief: SB Vineyard Sold," *Santa Barbara News-Press,* 31 July 2014.

15. Gabe Saglie, "Gabe Saglie: Liquid Farm winemaker launches own Kings Carey label," *Santa Barbara News-Press,* 25 May 2017.

16. Nora K. Wallace, "Santa Ynez winery gets board okay," *Santa Barbara News-Press,* 20 February 2013.

17. Andy Caldwell, "Editorials: Guest Opinion: Attack of the ranchette vigilantes," *Santa Barbara News-Press,* 10 March 2016.

18. Angela Slater, "Letters: Preserving Ballard Canyon Road," *Santa Barbara News-Press,* 3 May 2016.

19. Ken O'Keefe, "Letters: Opinion: Vote against more 'party house' tourism" *Santa Barbara News-Press,* 17 April 2016; "Winery rejected after three years of work," *Santa Barbara News-Press,* 7 March 2013.

20. Andy Caldwell, "Editorials: Guest Opinion: Miracles follow the plow," *Santa Barbara News-Press,* 18 August 2016.

21. Zach Noble, "Winery ordinance update discussed," *Santa Barbara News-Press,* 21 November 2013; Matt Kittmann, "As Wine Harvest Ends County Talks Ramp Up," *Santa Barbara Independent,* 29 November 2012.

22. Catherine Shen, "County set to draft new winery ordinances," *Santa Barbara News-Press,* 22 February 2013; Michael Larner, "Letters: Opinion: Fear driving valley's winery controversy," *Santa Barbara News-Press,* 7 February 2013.

23. Gabe Saglie, "Gabe Saglie; Sonoma snapshot: How tasting wine is different here," *Santa Barbara News-Press,* 8 June 2017.

24. Matt Kettmann, "Winery Ordinance Reality Check," *Santa Barbara Independent,* 27 October 2016.

25. Emily Parker, "Wineries battle proposed county regulations," *Santa Barbara News-Press,* 30 October 2016; Lee Rosenberg, "Letters: Opinion: Winery ordinance: Taxation with incompetent representation," *Santa Barbara News-Press,* 13 November 2016.

26. Emily Parker, "Wine ordinance vote set for today," *Santa Barbara News-Press,* 22 November 2016.

27. Terri Strickland, "Letters: Critical meeting on winery ordinance," *Santa Barbara News-Press,* 22 November 2016.

28. Emily Parker, "Half million dollar wine ordinance voted down by supervisors," *Santa Barbara News-Press,* 23 November 2016; Matt Kettmann, "New Winery Rules Still in Limbo," *Santa Barbara Independent,* 2 November 2016.

29. Napa County registrar of Voters actual ballot wording.

30. Esther Mobley, "Battle for Napa Valley's future/Proposed Curbs on Vineyards Divides the County," *San Francisco Chronicle*, 8 April 2018.

31. Aaron Romano, "Napa's Measure C Is dead; the War over Hillside Vineyards Has Just Begun," *Wine Spectator*, 26 June 2018.

32. Ethan Stewart, "Climate Change Threatens Fine Wine production," *Santa Barbara Independent*, 7 July 2007.

33. "Letters: Opinion: Local farms and vineyards under threat," *Santa Barbara New-Press*, 18 August 2013.

34. Jamie Guista, "Drought slows county agriculture; 2015 production down in value from previous year," *Santa Barbara News-Press*, 22 June 2016.

35. Katie Davis, "Letters: Opinion: Fracking ban initiative igniting a movement," *Santa Barbara News-Press*, 22 June 2014; Matt Kettmann, "California Wineries Debate Fracking," *Wine Spectator*, 31 March 2013.

36. "Outgoing vintners exec uncorked," *Santa Barbara News-Press*, 21 June 2017.

37. Gabe Saglie, "Wine Industry shake-up; Leader of Santa Barbara largest vintners group steps down," *Santa Barbara News-Press*, 22 June 2017; Matt Kettmann, "Santa Barbara Wine Country Leader Leaving for Oregon," *Santa Barbara Independent*, 22 June 2017; Matt Kettmann, "From Fingerlakes to Santa Ynez," *Santa Barbara Independent*, 17 April 2013.

38. Matt Kettmann, "Winery Ordinance Reality Check," *Santa Barbara Independent*, 27 October 2016.

39. Harris Meyer, "FDA Takes a Growing Interest in Winery Safety," *Wine Spectator*, 15 December 2012.

40. Dana Nigro, "Fight Over Organic Labeling Leaves Sulfites Rule As Is," *Wine Spectator*, 30 April 2012.

41. "U.S. wine groups put squeeze on wine plan," *Santa Barbara News-Press*, 31 July 2014.

42. Paul Gonzalez, "Santa Barbara winemaker takes contract dispute to federal court," *Santa Barbara News-Press*, 12 December 2016.

43. Gabe Saglie, "Chardonnay goes under the spot light at annual fete," *Santa Barbara News-Press*, 20 June 2013: Sao Anash, "Santa Maria Valley Wine Country," *Santa Barbara Independent*, 7 June 2007; Gabe Saglie, "Santa Maria Wine Association folds," *Santa Barbara News-Press*, 12 February 2014.

44. "Wine growers on the lookout for new pest," *Santa Barbara News-Press*, 18 April 2003.

45. Scott Steepleton, "Cops say winemaker took partners for $1.23M," *Santa Barbara News-Press*, 7 November 2015.

46. Mary Ann Norbom, "Qupé wines and Mattei's Tavern owner sentenced to four years in prison," *Santa Ynez Valley News*, 30 May 2017; Steve Heimoff, "Charles Banks Acquires Qupé Winery," *Wine Enthusiast*, 10 October 2013.

47. Mitch Frank, "The Year in Wine: 2012 in Review," *Wine Spectator*, 28 February 2013.

48. Steve Heimoff, "California Grape Acreage at All Time High," *Wine Enthusiast*, 23 April 2010.

Chapter Fourteen

The Era of Boutique Wineries

After fifty years the Santa Barbara wine industry had become an integral part of the California and global wine community. Continued awards and recognition from wine writers, experts, and most importantly consumers established that the region was here to stay. Overall, Santa Barbara County ranked number thirteen out of the fifty-eight California counties in agricultural production and the county's wine production was number three (behind strawberries and broccoli) at $901 million.[1]

Despite many roadblocks Santa Barbara wineries continued to ferment premium wines and a new era of boutique labels exploded onto the scene. Domestic consumers recognized the region's terroir, and Santa Barbara County branded wines had earned the right to be called premium. While Chardonnay and Pinot Noir continued as the top sellers, numerous other small and large vintners experimented with new grapes and techniques to chase the market. Regretfully, many small wineries found that survival sometimes meant having to sell their winery to keep their label alive.[2]

Business as Usual

Local growers continued their scientific and trial-and-error evolution to define the region's terroir. Bryan Babcock, after five years of experimentation, had used new techniques and gadgets to streamline and make his operation more efficient. Because of the 2007 economic slowdown, Babcock had cut production to ten thousand cases by terminating contacts with other growers. He then sought ways to further lower his farming costs through a process he called "vertical shoot positioning" (VSP) that reduced pruning costs through a trellis system that kept grapes about two-and-one-half feet above the ground. His next growing experiment included what he called "canopy pivoting," whereby he forced grapevines into an upside-down growing position that doubled the elevation of the vines to five feet. To achieve this he invented a rebar pedestal with a helix shaped hook at the top to maneuver a cane to grow in a curtain shape. This "pedestular cane suspension" reduced pruning costs by 30 percent and made for easier access to grapes at harvest time. As an added benefit, during the growing season the pedestal positions could be moved to provide more shade or sunlight as needed.[3] He was so happy with the results of his inventions that he patented his design.

Some wineries looked to expand sales through the growing Chinese export market that serviced 1.3 billion people. Jim and Mary Dierberg, Starlane and Dierberg Vineyards, chose their daughter-in-law, Jia Min Liang Dierberg, to represent their wines in her homeland and by 2012 Dierberg shipped 20 percent of its annual thirty-thousand-case production to Asia. Christian Garvin had a similar plan and shipped 15 percent of his Oreana and Mission Point wines to China and he was joined by Santa Barbara Winery and Melville Winery.[4]

Another way to entice consumers to make brand purchases came in the form of blending Old and New World wines. Morgan Clendenen, Cold Heaven Cellars, teamed up with French winemaker Yves Cuilleron to blend Clendenen's Viognier with Cuilleron's Condrieu wine under the Domaine des Deux Mondes label. Manfred Krankl, Sine Qua Non, partnered with Clos Saint Jean brothers Pascal and Vincent Maurel to blend their Mouvedre and Grenache wines for their California-style Chimère, a Rhône wine. The husband and wife team of Joey and Jennifer Tensley each made a blended Old and New World Wine. Joey partnered with Cecile Dusserre to make a Rhône wine with 50 percent Tensley Colson Canyon Syrah and 50 percent Domaine de Montvac Grenache from eighty-year-old vines. Jennifer partnered with Roger Belland, Domaine Roger Belland, to make Deux Terres blend of Sta. Rita Hills Pinot Noir and Commes Premier Cru in Satenay. The label read: "Red Wine 50% France, 50% America."[5]

New ways to draw customers and build brand loyalty beyond tasting rooms and winery events also expanded during this period. Louis Lucas lamented the slump in Merlot sales after the movie *Sideways,* and he decided to resurrect the wine's tarnished image. To do so he released his 2014 Judge's Reserve Merlot and advertised it as being premium Merlot from a cool growing region.[6] To further their brand recognition, Lucas & Lewellen Wines partnered with Holland America's San Diego to Fort Lauderdale cruise by sponsoring onboard wine tastings, food matches, and tastings of future releases.[7] In order to attract more tasting room traffic, Rick Longoria added an electric vehicle charging station to his newly opened Lompoc wine-tasting room. The facility became part of the Tesla Destination Charging network and more importantly was listed in their GPS website. Longoria believed "Tesla owners are well-heeled, so they're the key demographic for wines in our price range."[8]

Competition from vintibusiness wineries and cash flow continued to be a problem for small wineries, and many actively sought assistance to level the playing field. One means was to capitalize on marketing strategies that relied on the symbiotic relationship between food and wine. They applauded California governor Jerry Brown in 2014 when he signed AB2488 that authorized family wineries, producing under twelve thousand cases of their own wine, to offer "instructional tastings" at certified farmer's markets. Tasters had to be over twenty-one, receive under a three-ounce tasting, could not leave with an open container, and only one winery per day could serve.[9] Another approach for the local industry included the establishment of auxiliary wine businesses. Mike Brown, comanager of the Solvang Corque restaurant, used his BA in culinary management from the Hyde Park, New York, Culinary Institute of America to start Alchemy Vinegar Works in Buellton. The Los Olivos native bought local wines and created quirky vinegars for foodies.[10] The symbiotic relationship between food and wine also influenced a study by Lisa Wise Consulting Inc. that recommend that Lompoc City officials consider a development model based on food, wine, and art.[11]

Adventurous wine enthusiasts continued to try start-up wine businesses and expand older operations. Lebanese octogenarian Tony Vincent planted fifteen acres in Santa Ynez and by 2010 rented crush pad facilities to produce his Vincent Vineyards Wines.[12] The next year Steve Clifton created Palmina Wines, dedicated to Italian varietals, in Lompoc.[13] David de Laski, electric music producer, along with his wife Anna planted two and one-half acres of Gruner and Blaufrankisch grapes to make Austrian wines for their Solminer label.[14] Rick Longoria built his four-thousand-square-foot facility, Justin Willett started Tyler winery, and Bret Urness started Levo wines.[15] After ten years of planning, Dick Doré and Bill Wathen of Foxen Vineyards secured a Rabobank loan and built a twenty-three thousand square-foot facility.[16]

But all was not easy for small operations, and sometimes consolidation was the only answer for cash-flow issues.[17] In 2011 the Napa Culinary Institute of America installed Richard Sanford in their Wine Hall of Fame.[18] Regretfully, the very next year Sanford and wife Thekla hit hard times and declared Chapter 11 bankruptcy to save their Alma Rosa winery. Happily, Bob Zorich, Houston investor and 1971 UCSB graduate, bought Alma Rosa and paid off the $2.5 million debt and allowed the Sanfords to remain as the face of the brand.[19]

After thirty-one years Bob Lindquist sold his Qupé Winery to Charles Banks, a Santa Barbara–based investor. The deal put Banks in charge of the business decisions and left Lindquist as the winemaker.[20] That same year Craig Jaffurs sold his downtown Santa Barbara winery to winemaker Daniel Green and Jaffurs agreed to stay on for one year.[21]

In an odd twist, even celebrities wanted to get in on the premium boutique craze. Cassandra Peterson, science fiction's Elvira, Mistress of the Dark, in consultation produced five hundred cases of Macabrenet–a tart Cabernet in Solvang, although she used grapes sourced from Temecula.[22]

Terroir Recognition: Redefining Old AVAs and Winemaker Associations

Many began to realize that the original AVA boundaries may have been too broad and included smaller microclimate areas capable of success for different varieties. In 2013 vintner Michael Larner proposed taking about 7,800 acres from the Santa Ynez AVA to create the Ballard Canyon AVA. The new area contained ten commercial wineries with 565 acres of grapevines. He described the area as not as warm as the Santa Ynez designation and not as cool as the adjoining Sta. Rita Hills. Petitioners Steve Gerbac, Wes Hagen, and Jeff Newton pushed for federal recognition of the reimagined area and won approval in 2013.[23]

A few years later in 2016 thirteen bonded wineries, including Gainey, Brander, and Buttonwood, received ATF permission to create the Los Olivos District AVA from parts of the old Santa Ynez AVA. Fred Brander had submitted the petition in 2013 after eight years of gathering data to support his claim. This sixth Santa Barbara AVA included over 1,120 acres of vineyards on 23,000 acres with twelve bonded wineries and forty-seven commercially producing vineyards. The vineyards were mainly dedicated to Bordeaux varietals like Merlot, Cabernet Sauvignon, and Sauvignon Blanc.[24]

Good news in the form of increasing wine consumption fueled the continued growth of the entire California wine industry. Newly released consumption statistics revealed that every year since 1994 there had been a rise in the amount of wine American adults consumed. By 2008 the average American drank 2.96 gallons per person, up from the 1970 figure of 1.05 gallons.[25] This uptick in consumption helped the Santa Barbara industry expand, but on the downside this growth had sparked a shortage of qualified, trained, and wine-savvy workers to fill all the new industry jobs. In 2015 Alfredo Koch, Cal Poly and UC Davis graduate, responded by starting educational programs at Allan Hancock and Santa Maria Community Colleges. The programs trained workers and undertook local research for the regional industry.²⁶ Even the SBCVA joined the educational surge in 2017 by teaching a class on DIY (Do-It-Yourself) winemaking.²⁷

Winemakers and vineyard owners began to see themselves as an important part of the communities they lived in and championed causes important to themselves and their neighbors. The wine community has always had a reputation of being a generous group, and statewide the industry sponsored numerous philanthropic events for charitable foundations and causes. To this end the SBCVA established the Santa Barbara Vintners Foundation as its charitable umbrella to donate to community organizations. At the semiannual Vintner's Festivals they sponsored silent auctions and donated the proceeds to a number of community organizations, including the Food Bank of Santa Barbara. They also offered scholarships for students in the enology/viticulture department at Allen Hancock College, helped sponsor the Vino de Sueños program, and People Helping People of Santa Ynez Valley.²⁸

The Vintners Foundation also sponsored the biennial Santa Barbara Wine Auction with proceeds going to the organization Direct Relief for ongoing medical assistance to the poor and victims of natural and civil disasters. Between 2000 and 2017 they raised enough money to help Direct Relief leverage more than $90 million for programs in Santa Barbara County, Puerto Rico, Nepal, and throughout the United States.²⁹

ITALIAN WINES SANTA BARBARA STYLE

Some Santa Barbara vintners have always enjoyed trying new and different grapes, wines, and winemaking techniques. In a region that featured French grapes and wine, a small group gravitated toward Italian varietal wine grapes and over time received some recognition. By 2015 Santa Barbara County had over 127 acres of Sangiovese grapes and wineries like Mosby, Silver, Carr, Jonata, Toccata, and Russack utilized the fruit and gained recognition, so much so that Italian wine consultant Alberto Antonini claimed that Ballard Canyon "might as well be Tuscany."³⁰ Alison Thompson, UCSB graduate, studied abroad in Sienna, Italy, and upon returning home entered the UC Davis Enology and Viticulture program. By 2006 she had visited vineyards in Barolo and interned for Sergio Germano in Piedmonte. After completing her enology masters at UC Davis, she worked at Sine Qua Non in Ventura and Palmina in Lompoc. Then in 2013 she started producing three hundred cases per year of her own Lepiane Winery Nebbiolo named after her Calabrian grandfather Luigi Lepiane.³¹

CONTINUED RECOGNITION AND AWARDS

Throughout the 2010s, Santa Barbara wine continued to receive awards. In 2016 the SBCVA awarded Bob and Louisa Lindquest the honor of Winemaker of the Year and the 2017 SBCVA award honored Fred Brander. As an Argentinian native Brander completed a master's degree in food science from UC Davis and then started the Brander Vineyard in Los Olivos. The award cited him for his success with Bordeaux varietals and his work to establish the Los Olivos District AVA.[32] Additional individual vineyard recognition came in 2017 when Bien Nacido Vineyard Pinot Noirs, from numerous vintners, won awards at the Omaha, Nebraska, "Pinot, Pigs, and Poets Competition."[33]

By 2017 Jackson Family wines had become one of the largest beverage companies in the world, with holdings in California, Oregon, France, Italy, Australia, Chile, and South Africa. Much of this success was built upon their successful Santa Barbara and Central Coast Chardonnay brands that had become a valuable part of the global wine community. To increase its premium winery offerings, K-J increased its Santa Barbara holdings in 2017 by purchasing the Lompoc based Brewer-Clifton winery. Under the terms of the deal, Brewer remained as winemaker of the twelve-thousand- to twenty-thousand-case facility.[34]

Wine regions can also be judged by how they integrate new winemakers from the global community. During this period Santa Barbara imported Ernst Storm from a South African wine family. He worked as assistant winemaker at Curtis Winery for many years and in 2006 he struck out on his own and launched his two-thousand-case Storm wine label with Sauvignon Blanc and Pinot Noir wines. In 2014 he also launched Notary Public wines with sommelier Eric Railsback co-owner of Les Marchands restaurant.[35]

BOUTIQUE WINE INDUSTRY:

WINE TOWNS, GHETTOS, URBAN TRAILS, AND GARAGISTE WINE TOWNS

In the 1880s New Yorker Alden March Boyd bought 157 acres of land near Alamo Pintado Creek in the Santa Ynez Valley. Boyd then planted an olive grove and named his new endeavor Rancho De Los Olivos. From this original settlement grew the upscale town of Los Olivos (named after Boyd's olive grove) that gained national recognition in 1986 as the location for the town of "Mayberry" in the made-for-tv movie *Return to Mayberry*. But the town's recent importance began in the 1970s when it became a part of the Santa Ynez Valley wine country with neighbors like Ballard, Buelton, Solvang, and Santa Ynez.

Today the bucolic agricultural setting of Los Olivos is surrounded by vineyards and lies directly in the path of where the wine industry encounters sizable resistance from NIMBY citizens that have gentrified the agricultural setting. As wineries faced resistance for opening tasting rooms and sponsoring events on agricultural lands, the town became a centerpiece for lodging, art galleries, boutique shops, eateries, and wine-tasting rooms. It is almost as if it had become a "Wine Town" as thirty-five tasting rooms opened and by 2015 the town had established a yearly wine festival tradition.[36] Today tourists can taste and purchase wine from Arthur Earl, Bien Nacido, Blair Fox, Ca' Del Grevino, Carhardt, Cinque Stelle, Crawford Family, Draggonette, Andrew Murray, Epiphany Cellars, Evans Ranch Gainey, Larner, Samsara, Saarloos, Stolpman, and Zinke, to name a few.

But as the boutique winery trend expanded, numerous new labels of premium small production wines could not afford vineyard estate tasting rooms or upscale rural retail space for a tasting room. Faced with limited grapes, a lack of crush pad space, expensive tasting room costs, and land-use restrictions, many new vintners creatively established an entry-level business model based on consumer direct sales. They leased spaces in old industrial parks and urban spaces in a move that pleased both urban and rural county supervisors and helped keep local premium grapes in the region.[37] North county residents felt they had protected their agricultural lifestyle, and small vintners got access to customers in high-density urban wine parks.

LOMPOC WINE GHETTO

In 1998 Rick Longoria needed an inexpensive place to house his fledgling winery. His quest for a location included the old agricultural city of Lompoc that in the past had been known for its seed production. Longoria settled on an old industrial park with blocks of empty warehouses, where he rented space and began making wine. In a short time a unique collection of over twenty wineries, tasting rooms, and production facilities followed Longoria to Lompoc giving birth to what became known as the "Lompoc Wine Ghetto." Located off Pacific Coast Highway 1 and 12th Street behind the Home Depot, the low-cost facilities met the needs of bootstrapping boutique winemakers. As a plus the close proximity to the Sta. Rita Hills AVA allowed these low volume producers to source fruit from the area. Wine enthusiasts could still visit a winery and taste some of the best premium wines Santa Barbara County had to offer without offending NIMBY locals by clogging country roads and robbing the region of its agricultural ambience.

While in college Doug Margerum spent three summers in France and quickly embraced the French idea of food and wine terroir. After graduating from UCSB in 1981, his family purchased the Wine Cask in Santa Barbara. While running the shop, he became close friends with Clendenen and Lindquist and together they launched the Vita Nova label. Clendenen bought the label from his two partners in 1998, leaving Margerum in 2001 to start his solo MWC label. At first he sourced local grapes and rented crush and storage space from the Firestone Curtis Winery. As the label grew to over sixteen thousand cases he hired Michael Miroballi as winemaker and in 2009 he moved his entire winemaking operation to the Lompoc Wine Ghetto.[38]

After making a special wine for a sick friend, Kenneth and Sara Gummere launched their Transcendence label in Lompoc. Kenneth had learned the trade from working with Bruce McGuire at Santa Barbara Winery and Brian Babcock at Babcock Winery.[39]

By 2015 tasters flocked to the Wine Ghetto to sample Ampelos, Arcadian, AVE, Bratcher, De Su Propia Cosecha, Fiddlehead, Flying Goat, Holus, Kessler/Haak, Kita, La Montagne, La Vie, Liutum, Montemar, Moretti, Pali, Palmina, Piedrassi, Stolpman, Taste of Sta. Rita Hills, Tyler, and Zotovich Wines. Most importantly, the majority of the forty-three thousand citizens of Lompoc welcomed them and in a short time the Ghetto became the county's second-largest accumulation of tasting rooms. To advertise their location, they developed their own wine trail and advertised with maps, web pages, and eventually sponsored mini-festivals and events.

In the Lompoc city center wine tasters visited wineries like Brewer-Clifton, Longoria, Scott, Transcendence, and Turiya Wineries. For those wishing to actually get out into the vineyards, a quick drive to the Sta. Rita Hills brought them to Alma Rosa, Avant, Babcock, Dierberg, Foley, Huber, Ken Brown, Lafond, Melville, Mosby, and Standing Sun Wineries. In an amazing adaptation to environmental and land-use concerns, the Lompoc wine experience grew to about forty wineries in a concentrated area without destroying the agricultural environment.

THE URBAN WINE TRAIL

As County regulations and land restrictions hampered small wineries, many responded by placing their tasting rooms in the city of Santa Barbara. Within a few blocks of downtown Santa Barbara, on the beach side, wine enthusiasts could now taste some of the finest wines produced in Santa Barbara County. For over forty years Santa Barbara Winery had been the only winery to offer tastings in the downtown area. Then around 2001 many wineries and boutique labels followed the Santa Barbara Winery idea and shifted their tasting rooms to leased space in the city. In a short time these wineries formed the Urban Wine Trail and like the Lompoc Wine Ghetto tasters and tourists could now taste and purchase wine and avoid drinking and driving on country roads. Three locations developed in and around the city—The Presido Neighborhood, The Funk Zone, and Summerland. The common denominator for all the urban wineries was their dependence on the fruit from all six of the Santa Barbara AVAs and their low impact on the agricultural nature of the north county.

Just off State Street in the heart of the city, amidst shopping and eateries, wine visitors frequent eight tasting rooms in the downtown Presidio Neighborhood. The area captured the open-air appeal of coastal California towns built to replicate the European ambiance of walking-neighborhoods with boutique shops, restaurants, and wine shops. Built in Spanish Colonial Revival architecture, the area stretches along Anacapa Street and the El Paseo. Historic preservation and wine met in 2015 when John Wright fashioned a small wine tasting room in the Santa Barbara Presidio's Casa de la Guerra. Wright named the four-hundred-square-foot tasting room the Bodega and poured wines from his Sun Wine labels.[40] Within the confines of the presidio area, tasters can also sample wines from Au Bon Climat, Grassini Family Vineyards, Magerum Wine Company, Jamie Slone Wines, Happy Canyon Vineyard, Silver, and Cebada Vineyard. In a variant of this move downtown, Santa Barbara Winery worked in the opposite manner by opening first in the city in 1962 and later establishing the La Fond Vineyard and Winery in the Sta. Rita Hills. Heading down State Street toward Stearn's Wharf and the Pacific Ocean lies an additional twenty-plus wineries in the Funk Zone.

Over the past few decades, Santa Barbara's Funk Zone, between the Pacific Ocean and Highway 101 and the adjacent Amtrak station, underwent a repurposing of an old industrial district into a gentrified urban center, with artist galleries, restaurants, boutique shops, and over the last decade an Urban Wine Trail. Some of the tasting rooms also serve as retail shops, like the Santa Barbara Wine Collective that features premium wines from Babcock, Brewer-Clifton, Ca' Del Grevino, Fess Parker, and Notary. Older inland wineries, like Riverbench Vineyard (established in 1973) on the bank of the Sisquoc River, opened a second tasting room in the city to reach more customers.

Many of the tasting rooms belong to small labels that do not have vineyards and source grapes from the region. David Potter, Rancho Cucamonga native and UCSB graduate, finished an enology and viticulture degree in Australia and in 2015 launched Municipal Winemakers, dedicated to small-batch premium wines done in various styles. Seth Kunin started Kunin Wines in 1998, focusing on Syrah, Zinfandel, and Viognier and now produces approximately five thousand cases per year, most of which is sold through the tasting room. Others included DV8 Cellars' Rhône selections and the Valley Project that makes wines from all the Santa Barbara AVAs and teaches the terroir of the county with a floor-to-ceiling chalk-art mural depicting Santa Barbara County's wine-growing regions. Just outside the city in Summerland, Nebil "Bilo" Zarif established his Summerland Winery in 2002 and by 2007 Zarif expanded by planting his Theresa-Noelle Vineyard in the Sta. Rita Hills AVA.

GARAGISTE

For start-up winemakers, owning a vineyard and winery seemed impossible and many could not even get the capital to open a boutique Ghetto or Urban Trail operation. Not willing to give up on their wine passions, they reverted to home wine making in their garage and thus became labeled "Garagiste." As the number of the small operations grew, they joined together in 2011 to feature their wines at the Solvang Garagiste Festival. To participate winemakers could make no more than 1,500 cases and most of the producers had no vineyard, no winery, and no tasting room. The festival became their way to promote and sell their wines. In a short time the festival became a semiannual event drawing as many as a hundred producers.[41]

CONTINUED GROWTH OF TRADITIONAL WINERIES

The numbers of new wineries continued to grow as more people decided to enter the wine business. In the 1980s Larry Grassini, Los Angeles trial lawyer, and wife Sharon Grassini bought a 104-acre ranch in Happy Canyon. By the 1990s they got the wine bug and in 2002 with the assistance of Coastal Vineyard Care they planted a Bordeaux style vineyard.[42] Peter Hunken and wife Amy Christine got a thirty-year lease on some land on the Hayes ranch near Sweeny Canyon Road in Lompoc. Pete had attended the Santa Barbara Brooks Institute and worked at Santa Barbara Winery, Stolpman, and Wine Cask, and Amy was a Master of Wine and had worked for Kermit Lynch in Berkeley. Together, they planted a five-acre vineyard and produced their Piedrasassi label.[43]

A key problem for new wineries is the slow return on investment, and many must bring on investors to meet both start-up and operational costs. Delayed profits leave many wineries cash-strapped in their early years, and they have to find creative methods to level out capital requirements. In March of 1999 winemaker and co-owner Brett Escalera partnered with Tom Daughters to create the Consilience label, dedicated to Rhône and Burgundian-style wines sourced from Santa Barbara vineyards. A few years later they added the Tre Anelli label, specializing in Italian and Spanish wines. They quickly found out that the small operation lacked sufficient capital and in 2013 they part-nered with William Sanger, CEO of Colorado-based Envision Healthcare. They used the influx of money to pay off debt, redo labels, and increase their six-thousand-case production.[44]

WOMEN TAKE A LARGER ROLE IN SANTA BARBARA WINEMAKING

During the 2000s the Santa Barbara wine industry moved beyond its male-dominated makeup to include more women in various wine industry positions, including winemakers. Over the past few decades, as American political and civil rights activists pushed women's rights and causes the move-ment benefited women in the wine industry and they loudly proclaimed their "Rosie the Winemaker" belief that women could do any job in the wine industry. As women began to achieve new roles, a 2015 Santa Clara University survey found that 10 percent of the state's 3,400 lead winemakers were women. Hope for further growth grew as 50 percent of the 2015 UC Davis Enology and Viticulture students were women, up from 33 percent in 1999. Santa Barbara met the state average as twenty women served as wine-makers in the region's 199 wineries.

Calls for women in key winery positions increased leading to new internet websites like Women of the Vine (womenofthevine.com) and Women Wine Makers of California (https://webpages.scu.edu/womenwinemakers/index.php) to honor and encourage other women. This influx of women also led to new and reinterpreted tastes of California wine.[45] Adding to the argument for more women in the wine industry was the fact that a recent Yale study revealed that generally women had a better sense of taste than men.[46]

From the 1980s through the 1990s, Santa Barbara women pioneers included Betty Williams (Buttonwood), Alison Green (Firestone), Kathy Joseph (Fiddlehead Cellars), Lane Tanner (Lane Tanner Wines), and Denise Shurtleff (Cambria).[47] This changed in the 2000s as an increasing number of women sought winery jobs and up-and-comers like Angela Solens (Turiza), Rachel Silkowski (Rai and Loring), Kristin Bryden (Zaca Mesa), Tara Gomez (Kitá—Chumash Tribe), Laura Roach (assistant winemaker, Sanford), Sonja Magdevski (Casa Dunetz), and Brit Zotovich (Dreamcôte) made names for themselves. Many like Clarisa Nagy (Riverbench), Angela Soleno (Turiya), Erica Maldonado (Runway

Vineyards), Helen Falcone, Tessa Parker, and Brook Carhartt embraced wine feminism and proudly adopted the title of "Winemakin' Mommas."[48] A true sign that women were on the rise came in 2013 when Barbara Banke, Jackson Family Wines, became the first woman to win the *Wine Enthusiast* Person of the Year award. Banke, after Jess Jackson's death in 2011, had shepherded the company's dramatic expansion into Australia, Carneros, Mendocino, and Oregon.[49]

In 2015, after being inspired by Patricia Arquette's Oscar acceptance speech calling for wage equality, Karen Steinwachs decided to actively engage the issue for the wine industry. Realizing that March was Women's History Month, Steinwachs quickly pulled together a night of wine sharing and drinking among female professionals in the industry. Plus, it's a "good excuse [to get together]," she said. "Wine is a beverage that does exactly this," "It brings people together."[50] Subsequent dinners to celebrate women stipulated that proceeds go to the Women's Fund of Northern Santa Barbara County. The 2017 dinner included women holding winery positions from Cambria, Casa Dumetz, Cebada, Dreamcôte, Fiddlehead, Harrison-Clark, Kitá, La Montagne, Lumen, Nagy, Rideau, Russack, Sanford, Story of Soil, and William James Cellars. Believing, like President Thomas Jefferson, in the power of wine to civilize political rhetoric, Kathy Joseph commented, "During these turbulent political times, we believe people can come together if we simply sit down at a table with wine and a meal."[51]

As interest in the women of the Santa Barbara industry increased, the SBCVA, at their Fall Harvest Festival, sponsored a symposium on Women and Wine. Wine writer Gabe Saglie moderated the session with guests like Barbara Banke, who told the story of past times at wine pairing events where, "People would come up to the table and automatically start talking to him (husband Jess Jackson) about the wine. He would explain that I was the winemaker, that he didn't work at the winery and was helping out with the pouring. No matter what he'd say, these people would still directly question him."[52]

Hispanic Influences

The recognition of and reentrance of Hispanics into the Golden State's wine industry hit a critical mass in 2010 when a small group of Mexican American vintners had gathered in the courtyard of a colonial-era hotel in Morelia, Michoacán, Mexico. The group had been invited by the governor of Michoacán to pour their wines at the state fair. During the meeting they realized the importance of celebrating the rise of Mexicans from the field to ownership and they formed the Mexican-American Vintners Association (MAVA). The Mexican

American community was reinserting itself into California wine industry.

Over the past century the California and Santa Barbara wine industries have been dependent on Hispanic farmworkers to provide the backbreaking field and winery labor. Yet, for years these Hispanic fieldworkers did not achieve positions as management or winemakers, let alone own a vineyard or winery. Despite the Spanish and Mexican roots of the California wine industry, it was mainly the English, French, Germans, and Italians that dominated the industry, while depending on migrant Hispanic workers.

This began to change statewide in the new century as farmworkers began to assume new positions and a few rose to vineyard and winery ownership. In the 1970s Andrés Ibarra left Jalisco, Mexico, to be with his father, who was a mule trainer in Los Olivos. In 1980 he joined the pruning crews at Brander and for the next two decades worked for Brander and the Santa Ynez Winery. In 2005 he became Rideau Vineyard winemaker and Santa Barbara's first field-worker-turned-winemaker.[53] In 1978, Felipe Hernandez left Jalisco, Mexico, as a sixteen-year-old immigrant to work in Santa Ynez agriculture. In a short five years he was given specific parcels of vineyards to oversee and decades later he started his Felíz Noche (Happy Nights) label with local Cabernet, Syrah, Riesling, and Pinot Noir grapes.[54]

Most growers and wineries in Santa Barbara realized how important Hispanic labor was for their business, and in 2007 created an event to celebrate their labor. Longoria, Buttonwood, Alma Rosa, Clos Pepe, Noche, Presidio, and Foxen wineries started a tradition of making a specialty wine labeled Vino de Sueños (Wine of Dreams) to raise money for worker social services. These services assisted vineyard workers with food, housing, and health services from the Santa Ynez Valley People Helping People program. The event turned into a yearly tradition with numerous wineries joining the cause.[55]

Notes

1. Steve Sinovic, "Steve Sinovic, "Profitable strawberry crop lifts county ag value to nearly $1.3 billion," *Santa Barbara News-Press,* 16 April 2013.

2. Mary Ann Worobiec, "Fiji Deal Part of A Wave of Wine Investment," *Wine Spectator,* 15 October 2011.

3. Gabe Saglie, "Local winemaker turns grape growing upside down," *Santa Barbara News-Press,* 2 May 2013.

4. James Laube, "The Chinese Riddle," *Wine Spectator,* 15 December 2011; Matt Kettmann, "Santa

Barbara Wines: Big in Beijing," *Santa Barbara Independent*, 8 June 2012; Matt Kettmann, "Jump-Starting Star Lane Vineyard, *Santa Barbara Independent*, 13 May 2015.

5. Mike Desimone and Jeff Jensen, "Winemaking Between Two World's," *Wine Enthusiast*, 3 May 2012.

6. Gabe Saglie, "Gabe Saglie: In the mood for Merlot," *Santa Barbara News-Press*, 19 January 2017.

7. Charlotte Boechler, "Close to Home: Board the SS Lucas & Lewellen," *Santa Barbara News-Press*, 13 October 2013.

8. Gabe Saglie, "Vintner hopes new Tesla charging station revs up business," *Santa Barbara News-Press*, 29 July 2016.

9. Scott Steepleton, "Wine tasting OK'd at farmers markets," *Santa Barbara News-Press*, 10 July 2014.

10. Marilyn McMahon, "The Alchemist: Santa Ynez Valley resident transforms useless wine into quirky vinegars," *Santa Barbara News-Press*, 20 June 2013.

11. Nora K. Wallace, "Food service considered in Lompoc's Wine Ghetto," *Santa Barbara News-Press*, 27 April 2017.

12. Matt Kettmann, "Vincent Vineyards Aims for Upscale Experience," *Santa Barbara Independent*, 1 September 2015.

13. Chelsey Steinman, "The Power of Palmina," *Santa Barbara Independent*, 14 June 2011.

14. Matt Kettmann, "Solminer Dances on Wine Country's Fringe," *Santa Barbara Independent*, 22 September 2015.

15. "Native Gone Wild," *Santa Barbara Independent*, 20 February 2013; Matt Kettmann, "Longoria Winery's New Home," *Santa Barbara Independent*, 8 October 2014; Matt Kettmann, "New Cult on the Block: Levo Wines," *Santa Barbara Independent*, 9 April 2015.

16. Jordan Mackay, "In Pinched Times, a Frugal Winery Builds," *New York Times*, 1 April 2010.

17. Tim Fish, "Quietly For Sale: West Coast Wineries," *Wine Spectator*, 31 December 2013.

18. Matt Kettmann, "Hall off fame for Richard Sanford," *Santa Barbara Independent*, 22 October 2011.

19. Matt Kettmann, "Richard Sanford Ditches Debt," *Santa Barbara Independent*, 15 January 2014.

20. Matt Kettmann, "Qupé Winery Sold," *Santa Barbara Independent*, 10 October 2013.

21. Matt Kettmann, "Jaffurs Winery Sold," *Santa Barbara Independent*, 15 August 2016.

22. Matt Kettmann, "Elvira the Winemaker," *Santa Barbara Independent*, 14 January 2012.

23. Gabe Saglie, "Ballard is born: Feds recognize canyon as unique wine-growing area," *Santa Barbara News-Press*, 5 October 2013; Steve Heimoff, "The New Rhône Zone," *Wine Enthusiast*, 19 February 2013; "Establishment of Ballard Canyon Viticultural Area (98R-129P)," Department of Treasury Federal Register, 27 CFR Part 9 v. 78 n. 191, 2 October 2013.

24. Gabe Saglie, "Fed's rule distinguishes wine growing in Los Olivos," *Santa Barbara News-Press*, 22 January 2016; "Establishment of Los Olivos District Viticultural Area (98R-129P)," Department of Treasury Federal Register, 27 CFR Part 9 v. 81 n. 13, 21 January 2016.

25. Kenneth Harwood, "Consumers increased demand for wine," *Santa Ynez Valley News*, 17 February 2011.

26. Matt Kettmann, "Want to Work in Wine?" *Santa Barbara News-Press*, 5 November 2015.

27. Dave Mason, "Wine School: Vintners' Association to teach class on DIY winemaking," *Santa Barbara News-Press*, 15 June 2017.

28. "Santa Barbara Vintners' Foundation," *Santa Barbara News-Press*, 19 May 2002; Gabe Saglie, "Santa Barbara vintners hosting vineyard run," *Santa Barbara News-Press*, 29 April 2016.

29. Mitchell White, "Vintners make $1 million donation," *Santa Barbara News-Press*, 25 May 2016.

30. Caroline Helper, "Sangiovese from Santa Barbara," *Santa Barbara Independent*, 22 October 2015.

31. Matt Kettmann, "Lepiane Winery: Beauty of Barbara,Nuance of Nebbiolo," *Santa Barbara Independent*, 17 September 2017.

32. Mary Ann Norbom, "Fred Brander named Vintner of the Year," *Santa Ynez Valley News*, 23 May 2017; Gabe Saglie, "Gabe Saglie: 40th pick: Industry celebrates Fred brander, "*Santa Barbara News-Press*, 6 October 2016.

33. Mary Ann Norbom, "Bien Nacido Pinot Noir Award," *Santa Ynez Valley News,* 27 June 2017.

34. Gabe Saglie, "Revered Santa Barbara wine label acquired by major player," *Santa Barbara News-Press,* 19 May 2017; Mary Ann Norbom, "Acclaimed Winery Sold," *Santa Barbara Independent,* 25 May 2017.

35. Gabe Saglie, "Storm crosses two continents," *Santa Barbara News-Press,* 26 February 2015.

36. Gabe Saglie, "Wine event of record: Los Olivos launches own fiesta," *Santa Barbara News-Press,* 29 January 2015.

37. Brandon Hernandez, "A Wine Lover's Walking Tour of Santa Barbara," *Wine Enthusiast,* 18 March 2010.

38. Mary Ann Norbom, "Doug Margerum builds his wine company into one of the biggest and brightest," *Santa Ynez Valley News,* 31 July 2017; Matt Kettmann, "Industry Veteran Returns to Chardonnay," *Wine Enthusiast,* 8 December 2015.

39. Dennis Schaeffer, "Schaefer on Wine: Transcendence Wines: Bottles that make a difference," *Santa Barbara News-Press,* 7 March 2013.

40. Gabe Saglie, "History served by the glass; local winemaker opens tasting room at Casa de la Guerra," *Santa Barbara News-Press,* 17 September 2015.

41. Gabe Saglie, "Small Wineries, big crowds," *Santa Barbara News-Press,* 31 March 2014; "Garagiste Festival adds new wineries," *Santa Ynez Valley News,* 9 March 2017.

42. Chelsey Steinmann, "New Wines from a New AVA," *Santa Barbara Independent,* 4 August 2010.

43. Matt Kettmann, "Black Sheep Finds Growing Sta. Rita Hills Roots," *Santa Barbara Independent,* 20 April 2006.

44. Gabe Saglie, "Los Olivos-based wineries welcome new owner," *Santa Barbara News-Press,* 11 December 2013

45. Steve Heimoff, "Steve Heimoff Blog, *Women of the Vine and Spirits Foundation,* women-of-the-vine.silkstart.com, 3 May 2013.

46. Matt Kettmann, "The Number of Women Winemakers Is growing, and fast," Wine Enthusiast Magazine, ND/ off internet womenofthevine.com; "Meet some of the Santa Barbara County women winemakers," Napa Valley Register, 13 October 2016.

47. Matt Kettmann, "Quality and Quantity at Cambria Winery: Winemaker Denise Shurtleff Winning on Both Fronts," *Santa Barbara Independent,* 17 September 2017; Matt Kettmann, "Harvesting Grapes and Glee at Fiddlehead Cellars," *Santa Barbara Independent,* 18 September 2013.

48. Matt Kittmann, "Winemakin' Mammas," *Santa Barbara Independent,* 8 May 2013; Kelsey Brugger, "Women Winemakers Thrive in Santa Barbara," *Santa Barbara Independent,* 17 April 2015; Allison Levine, "Tara Gomez, A native American Winemaker," *Napa Valley Register,* 22 October 2015.

49. Steve Heimoff, "2013 Wine person of the Year," *Wine Enthusiast,* 11 December 2013; "Meet some of the Santa Barbara County women winemakers," *Napa Valley Register,* 13 October 2016.

50. Kelsey Brugger, "Women Winemakers Thrive In Santa Barbara," *Santa Barbara Independent,* 17 April 2015.

51. "Female winemakers to celebrate International Women's day," *Santa Ynez Valley News,* 21 February 2017.

52. Mary Ann Norbom, "Women making their mark in winemaking," *Santa Maria Times,* 13 October 2016; "Kristin Bryden Promoted to Winemaker at Zaca Mesa," WineBusiness.com, 6 January 2016.

53. Matt Kettmann, "Their Hands, Your Wine," *Santa Barbara Independent,* 9 November 2011.

54. Jeff Wing, "Happy Days for Fieldhand-Turned-Winemaker," *Santa Barbara Independent,* 30 October 2013.

55. Nora K. Wallace, "Wine event to celebrate agricultural workers," *Santa Barbara News-Press,* 18 October 2014.

Conclusion

Throughout history, grape growers and winemakers have made Herculean efforts to ensure their consumers had ample supplies of wine for their health, religious ceremonies, celebrations, and mealtime needs. For centuries they resolved increased demand pressures by simply planting more vineyards at home and in their New World colonies. As a result, the early American wine industry spent over two centuries attempting to meet consumer demand through a nation-wide quest for grape-friendly regions. This story of *Wine by Design* details how this historic business tenet evolved to create a premium wine industry in California and more specifically the Santa Barbara, California, region.

Wine first rooted in Alta California in the late eighteenth century as Spanish explorers, priests, soldiers, and settlers planted vineyards and made wine for local religious rituals and food consumption. Faced with sixteenth- and seventeenth-century wars that had crippled European trade, consumers faced raising prices and dwindling supplies of their favorite French, Italian, and Spanish wines. In an attempt to alleviate these shortages, all thirteen of the original American colonies had tried and failed to establish a viable wine industry. This left Americans with a drinking pattern that substituted libations like rum and whiskey for wine and resulted in concerns over alcohol moderation— a concern that persists to the present-day. Making matters worse was the fact that the concept of wine as an everyday drink for all Americans suffered even more as yeoman farmers left grape growing and wine production to entrepreneurial gentleman farmers, further deepening the American mystique of wine as a drink for a gentler class.

Yet many, like President Thomas Jefferson, persisted in their attempts to cultivate the European tradition of a wine culture for all Americans. This pro-wine persistence also made economic sense when one considered the fact that rum accounted for one-fifth of the value of all imports from England. Socially, the movement to develop an American wine culture took on a greater urgency as Americans internalized the fact that at the time of the American Revolution all ages and social groups consumed excessive amounts of alcohol, so much so that many foreign travelers reported that America had become a nation addicted to drinking. This led twentieth-century historian William J. Rorabaugh to label the newly established American Republic as the "Alcoholic Republic."

Jefferson and many others worried that this new dependence on distilled spirits would diminish the vitality of the nation's health and pushed to intensify the quest for an American wine industry as a means to moderate drinking habits. These concerns resulted in early nineteenth-century reform measures aimed at moderation through wine consumption and started a national debate on the health and social values of fermented and distilled alcoholic beverages. This is a debate that extends to the present day and affects when, where, and how wine is sold. The important question became whether one considered wine to be an agricultural crop that can be sold at the vineyard or just another form of processed alcohol.

Despite two hundred years of failures, entrepreneurial wine businessmen remained optimistic that they could develop a viable commercial American wine culture. In 1851 Illinois senator Stephen A. Douglas enthusiastically stated that the "United States will, in a very short time, produce good wine, so cheap, and in such abundance, as to render it a common and daily beverage." But, it would be W. J. Flagg in an 1870 *Harper's Monthly* magazine article who best summarized the problem: "The question of wine-drinking in America revolves itself into the question of grape-growing in America." American wine enthusiasts and moderation advocates alike followed the historic pattern to resolve short supplies of their favorite beverage by looking to California as a home for the nation's still undeveloped wine industry.

By the nineteenth century, the era of wine by design had begun in America as California viticultural entrepreneurs developed regional trial-and-error action plans that disseminated information, funded research, formed organizations, vigorously marketed their product, lured investors, sought government support, and relied on university research. Most importantly they drew upon the ideals of Manifest Destiny to spark a new excitement for developing an American wine industry. With California statehood in 1850, wine became an American commercial commodity as zealous wine entrepreneurs, after two centuries of tepid success, brought their viticultural dreams to California and Santa Barbara. These wine businessmen quickly took control of the California industry and ushered in a new wine business era built on the tenets of Gilded

Age agribusiness that by 1890 allowed California to produce over 80 percent of the nation's wine.

This early quest for California wine included the Central Coast region of Santa Barbara, where by the late 1800s the county ranked third in California behind leader Los Angeles and second-place San Francisco. In its third-place position the region produced 5 percent of the state's wine from the county's estimated forty-five vineyards that covered about five thousand acres. By the 1890s the region boasted of successes by winemakers like James McCaffrey, Albert Packard, and Justinian Caire, who produced notable premium wines. But the burgeoning Santa Barbara industry suffered from a geographic disadvantage in that it was relatively inaccessible from national and global markets and its sparse population, under three thousand, could not consume enough wine to justify further expansion. Its only trade routes were through the Stearns Wharf steamer service and the treacherous San Marcos stage road.

For a short time the number one California wine region would be the large commercial plantings in the Los Angeles basin of Southern California. But their initial leadership role deteriorated as Anaheim disease destroyed most of the vines in Los Angeles. The state's southern industry was further hampered by unscrupulous wine growers who either could not afford or refused to spend the money needed to replant their vineyards. These get-rich-quick producers flooded the market with inferior sweeter wines at a time when consumers began to show an interest in better-quality dry wines. By the 1880s the few remaining vineyards of Southern California shifted to table grapes, raisins, and sweet wines.

As a result, the wine industry's entrepreneurial energy gravitated to the northern part of the state where cool climate premium wine grapes flourished. The Bay Area also provided proximity to the ports of the Pacific Ocean, access to the new transcontinental rail system, and San Francisco's status as the banking capital of the western United States. In a short time Bay Area wine entrepreneurs utilized Gilded Age business techniques and created a wine-by-design model of vintibusinesses.

This new era of American corporate wine production and distribution began in earnest in 1894 when seven well-financed San Francisco wine merchants founded the California Wine Association (CWA). Their goal was to vertically integrate the entire wine supply chain from vine to store and produce bulk consistent-quality wines in enough quantity to supply national and international markets. The impetus for the organization came from Percy Morgan, English accountant and financier, who created the monopoly as an entity capable of controlling supplies and stabilizing fluctuating prices. As the direc-tor of CWA, Morgan cared less who drank or why they drank wine as long as members profited. Morgan's leadership of the California industry quickly gave him the status of being called a Gilded Age "Captain of the Wine Industry." Over the next few years, the organization grew to include over fifty wineries that in 1895 produced eighteen million gallons and in 1910 topped forty-five million gallons. In just over a decade CWA grew to control two-thirds of the state's total wine production and small producers in regions like Santa Barbara found it difficult to compete with the wine monopoly.

But this trend toward bigger-is-better and monopolized markets was also the basis for the almost complete collapse of the entire wine industry in the 1920s. The industry had fallen under the control of investors and financiers more interested in profits than in maintaining an American wine culture. Hopes for wine as a moderating force faded as large-scale commercial wine-making obscured wine's essential identity, making it appear to be but another form of alcohol. Dreams of wine as a drink of moderation faltered at a time when concerns about excessive alcohol consumption peaked.

Prohibition slowed down American alcoholic consumption, ended an era of working-class saloons, served as one of the more successful alliances of upper and middle classes to legislate morals and habits, and, in a strange twist, increased wine consumption. Federal laws permitted limited commercial wine production for vinegar, sacramental wine, medicinal wines, industrial alcohol, cream of tartar, and flavorings. More importantly, federal policies permitted Americans to make 200 gallons per year of homemade wine for family use and much of this wine came from California grapes. As a result home wine making skyrocketed and national wine production jumped from an estimated 50 mil-lion gallons per year before Prohibition to 76.5 million gallons per year during Prohibition. In an attempt to stop the consumption of alcohol, Prohibition had become a tool to incentivize the development of an American wine culture.

On the downside, Prohibition destroyed the American commercial wine industry as bonded American wineries fell from 700 in 1919 to below 140 in 1932 and resulted in the complete collapse of the Santa Barbara industry. But the real blow to the wine industry was that the repeal of Prohibition per-mitted each state to establish its own liquor laws and complicated all future growth of a national industry. The wine industry now faced forty-eight (later fifty) different sets of state regulations for the transport, sale, taxation, license fees, and distribution of wine. Also of concern was the resurgence of hard-core

Dry supporters, later labeled neo-Prohibitionists, who continued to wage war against alcohol marketing and distribution. For the California wine industry to gain global and national prominence, many local, state, and federal neo-Prohibitionist roadblocks would have to be overcome. Detractors aside, California's now-legal wine trade became one of the few industries to successfully expand during the Great Depression. In less than one century, America and California had created, lost, and won back a wine culture. The last half of the twentieth century would be spent rebuilding the industry and creating California, including Santa Barbara, as a premium international wine industry.

As World War II cut off Americans from premium European table wines, the industry moved to fill the shortages of imported table wine. Before the war the industry had relied heavily on bulk wine sales (80 percent of all wine produced) and this favored large winemakers and cooperatives. To survive, most smaller wineries had adopted the advice of Dr. Frederic Bioletti, viticulture professor, University of California, to establish their market share by emphasizing the sale of smaller quantities of higher-priced premium wines, a model that would eventually be followed by many winemakers in the Santa Barbara industry. Over time World War II served as the vehicle to help the industry develop national brands, increase acreage of premium wine grapes, establish the practice of at-winery bottling, and brought about a massive influx of capital for modernization. The reversal from bulk and sweet wines to bottled premium dry table wine had begun.

But larger problems loomed on the horizon as marketing for small and large wineries alike faltered under the repeal distribution policies that attacked the concept of "wine farms." These post-Prohibition discussions focused on whether wine was a food or an alcoholic beverage and could wines, grown and produced on family wine farms, be sold at their source like any other agricultural product. In California state policy makers moved to allow small family operated wine farms to promote themselves through tasting rooms and direct retail sales. This worked for the California market but set the stage for a future national confrontation over direct sales across state lines as each state developed its own post-repeal wine marketing policies and regulations.

In the latter half of the twentieth century, the industry came into its own as the Cold War economy gave consumers more disposable incomes and allowed for unbridled economic opportunity. In a move that appeared to consolidate the industry overnight, large liquor companies such as Seagram's, Schenley, and National Distillers, made major investments in California wineries and in the years after World War II they controlled one-half of the nation's commercial wine production. The consolidation resulted in a drop to 271 bonded wineries in 1960, down from a 1936 high of 1,300 wineries. This led UC Davis viticulture and enology professors Maynard Amerine and Vernon Singleton to make a 1965 prediction that: "California winemaking would soon be almost entirely in the hands of a few wineries as their numbers diminished and the survivors grew larger." Corporate industrial wine making again controlled America's wine production.

Fortunately, the liquor companies lacked wine-making knowledge and had little patience to rebuild the industry and gradually winery ownership reverted to resident wine-making entrepreneurs. On the plus side this merger fever had saved the industry with an influx of much-needed capital for expansion and rebuilding of an industry ravaged by Prohibition, depression, and war.

By the 1960s the demand for premium wine-grape vineyards reached a fevered pitch as U.S. wine consumption doubled and dry table wine sales topped 50 percent of all wines consumed. To meet consumer needs marketers had to quadruple foreign wine imports from 14,369,000 gallons in 1964 to a 1971 total of 51,394,000 gallons. There was ample market opportunity for California wineries to expand. These supply pressures drove Northern wineries to look southward to encourage planting of vineyards in the cool climate Central Coast. In response these vintners encouraged grape growers, with guaranteed lucrative contracts to purchase their grapes, to plant regional vineyards to meet production needs. Regretfully, the industry needed more vineyards at a time when agricultural lands were being devoured by suburban development projects.

To overcome the high land prices, driven by the development land boom, many wine corporations, estate wineries, and growers joined forces with environmentalists and anti-growth forces to preserve farmland and landscapes. Together, they lobbied state and local lawmakers to create laws that exclusively zoned land for agriculture and argued that their goal was to preserve a sense of community, secure economic diversity, preserve historic and aesthetic values, and secure open space for recreational and health benefits. Their political determination convinced state legislators to pass the California Land Conservation Act of 1965 (Williamson Act) and the Property Tax Assessment Reform Act of 1966. These laws established a statewide voluntary county participation program, based on property tax incentives, to save valuable farmland.

Initially, these policy measures allowed many investors in Santa Barbara to utilize agricultural acreage as a system of depreciation on full costs of vineyard investment and three years of zero income tax by claiming tax write-offs while waiting for vine production to begin. Thus, vineyard investment became a tax loophole for hedging against the increasing inflation rates faced by large land-holders, cattle ranchers, and agribusiness. For some this tax solution served as a means to transfer agricultural lands from ranchers and farmers to a new generation of gentleman farmers seeking the new version of the good life— the wine industry. The window of opportunity for these advantages only lasted until the 1976 Tax Reform Law that forced many investors to move their money to other more profitable financial schemes. Faced with not being able to sell their land, many farmers, ranchers, and grain growers then converted some of their own land to the new agricultural "hot crop"—wine grapes.

Between 1964 and 1978 farmland preservation and tax legislation coupled with projected grape profits gave rise to a new era of California wine industry expansion. During this period Santa Barbara County became part of the new solution to American wine shortages and began the process of replanting its wine industry. The new viticultural pioneers that undertook the rebuilding were mainly nonindustry investors that gambled their personal resources and skills as architects, retired business executives, ranchers, real estate developers, doctors, and dentists. In a relatively short time, their gamble produced 5,836 acres of wine grapes—the equivalent size of the industry before it was decimated by Prohibition.

By the mid-1970s, many Santa Barbara County growers began to lament that their premium wine grapes were blended into lesser quality Central Valley and northern wines. It had become painfully apparent that wineries, not grape growers, profited most from the expanding industry. Operating profit margins for wineries jumped over 40 percent while grape costs declined and the cost of materials as a percent of sales decreased from 62 percent to less than 50 percent. Santa Barbara growers also feared a settling out of the marketplace as Napa acreage and wine-grape tonnage nearly tripled. The pressing question for the fledgling Santa Barbara grape growers was how to get the highest possible price for their grapes. Most began to realize that a local wine industry would help establish the region's reputation and in the long run secure the best prices for local fruit.

To meet their profitability concerns, many Santa Barbara County grape growers built smaller vertically integrated farms and wineries, called estate wineries, to take advantage of the 1930s idea of the family wine farm with sales directly to consumers. But the fledgling local wine industry confronted a disorderly market that was controlled by boom-and-bust cycles, shifts in consumer tastes, and both domestic and foreign trade struggles. Overcoming these problems required continuous efforts stretching from technology, to marketing, to vertical integration, political lobbying, consumer education, and new scientific approaches to pests and diseases. Branding became a major concern for the region, and local growers addressed the problem by getting approval of AVAs (American Viticultural Areas) and created the Santa Barbara Vintners Association. Their efforts paid off as Santa Barbara County rapidly developed a reputation for high-quality premium wines and garnered awards and recognition from national press articles for their Chardonnay, Pinot Noir, and Rhône wines.

Despite two decades of expansion that resulted in Napa growing from 31,623 acres to 40,186 acres, Sonoma from 32,036 acres to 48,967 acres, and Santa Barbara County from 9,407 acres to 14,626 acres, the industry still could not meet consumer demands. As a result of these domestic wine shortages, the prices of premium wines increased 10 percent. Large commercial wineries celebrated the growth and increased prices, while growers on the other hand lamented that the prices of grapes had stagnated. Since fruit only accounts for about 15 to 20 percent of the total cost of retail wine, growers were not sharing equally in the booming industry.

By the end of the twentieth century premium wine-grape shortages sent corporate wineries on a second raid of the Santa Barbara industry. This time they bought estate wineries and vineyards instead of just grapes. The county had become the target for "Napazation" by large wine corporations seeking stable supplies of premium wine grapes. In a short time Mondavi, Kendall-Jackson, and Wine World purchased over $36 million worth of Central Coast vineyards and wineries. By 1996 California's fifteen largest wine-grape growers created a "vineyard royalty" that increased their statewide vineyard ownership by 75 percent. For Santa Barbara County this meant that Wine World, Robert Mondavi Winery, and Kendall-Jackson assumed ownership of over 6,300 acres of the county's 14,626 acres of premium wine grapes.

While many believed that expansion of the Santa Barbara region could be an answer to the domestic wine shortages, the honor fell elsewhere. Market forces had pushed commercial wine growth to Monterey, San Luis Obispo, and the Central Valley, where cheap land, water, and cheap labor still existed.

But more problems were on the horizon for Santa Barbara growers and wineries as they faced a new set of challenges that affected both large vinti-businesses, estate wineries, and small boutique wineries. New environmental concerns, anti-growth factions, lack of availability of cheap vineyard land, and anti-alcohol forces placed pressure on large and small wineries alike. In Santa Barbara these problems created a new model of winery business, where small winemakers purchased grapes from estate wineries and vineyards and made and sold their wines in urban industrial areas.

Early in his tenure as CEO of the Wine Institute, John De Luca identified the tension between the wine industry and environmentalists. In his words; "I have said on a number of occasions, people and grapes have one thing in common: they love to live in beautiful places." By 2000 Napa had grown to 45,401 acres, Sonoma supported 57,149 acres, Monterey County grew to 42,259 acres, Santa Barbara had reached 17,566 acres, and the entire state now had over 425,695 acres of wine grapes. Wine businesses were running out of places to build estate operations that were tourist friendly. This time they met the legal wrath of past supporters as environmentalists and land-use NIMBY proponents, which Santa Barbara vintners labeled "ranchette vigilantes," became their adversaries.

This concerned estate and small Santa Barbara wineries and growers, who had become dependent upon winery tourism to market and sell their premium wines directly to consumers. Many county citizens feared that their home would become another tourist trap like Napa and Sonoma. Less than three hours from Los Angeles, the small towns of Santa Ynez, Los Olivos, Buelton, and Solvang became crowded with over 3.5 million tourists yearly and locals began to complain that Highway 246 had become impassable. By the mid-1990s wine industry expansion had slowed as environmentalists and no-growth citizen groups fought what they saw as the invasion of "Grapescape" upon their rural landscape. In the long run, some of the stress of Santa Barbara expansion declined as communities developed restrictive land-use policies that inflated prices of Santa Barbara agricultural land and forced wine-grape developers to look to Monterey and San Luis Obispo for cheaper vineyard land with fewer restrictions.

As Santa Barbara County developed its premium wine industry, competitive small wineries sought ways to expand their market share. Over 75 percent of the county's premium wineries (over two hundred today) are small family owned businesses producing fewer than fifteen thousand cases annually. Most of these artisan wineries rely on agritourism, local retail, and direct wine shipments to customers for up to 75 percent of their sales. The rural destination allure of wineries, when coupled with a strong economy that provided ample disposable income for consumers, made artisan wineries very successful.

To overcome new industry roadblocks, the Santa Barbara wine industry evolved into a viable wine region by retaining established commercial wineries, who controlled the majority of the grapes, restricted the growth of estate wineries, and incentivized a growing number of boutique non-vineyard operations to consolidate their wine tourist operations into urban areas. Decades of struggles between farmers, ranchers, winemakers, environmentalists, and citizens had slowly shifted the development of wineries and vineyards in the region to more sustainable agricultural practices, more regulated winery growth, regulated events, and development of concentrated urban tasting rooms that took some of the pressure off the rural landscape.

The new wine industry design promoted the ideals of wine farms and facilitated new premium, small-production operations previously unable to afford an estate vineyard tasting room or upscale rural retail space for a tasting room. They could now enter the industry by renting old industrial spaces in the towns of Lompoc, Los Olivos, or in downtown Santa Barbara. New vintners had creatively established an entry-level business model based on consumer direct sales. They leased spaces in old industrial parks and urban areas, in a move that pleased both urban and rural county supervisors, and kept local premium grapes in the region. North county residents felt they had protected their agricultural lifestyle, and small vintners got access to customers in high-density urban wine parks like the Lompoc Wine Ghetto, the town of Los Olivos, the Urban Wine Trail, the Funk Zone in downtown Santa Barbara, and garagiste home production.

Santa Barbara had created a mixed wine industry that contained industrial operations, estate wineries, and small boutique labels that evolved from problems presented by environmentalism, land-use restrictions, and neo-Prohibition. This Santa Barbara model, along with the larger industrial California model, utilized a wine-by-design philosophy that promoted good science, sustainability, mixed corporate and independent winery ownership, and nurtured the concept of an American wine culture.

Acknowledgments

This book is the end result of a three decade labor of love born from life experiences, research, wine industry work, teaching, oral histories, and tastings that produced a dissertation, monograph, numerous articles, oral histories, and finally this book.

Although central to my life, wine and grapes were not always my passion. As a young boy I remember working at my Father's side in San Diego County vineyards. In our family the tradition of father-son in the vineyard and home-winemaking spanned multiple generations from Sicily to America. I reluctantly paid my dues during winter, spring, and summer breaks from school and grumbled as I performed the routine vineyard tasks of pruning, hoeing, and picking grapes. Harvest-time visits to the produce markets in San Diego and weekends working the family roadside grape-stand tended to bore this citified teenage boy. My Dad easily convinced me that sharecropping vineyards was not the career path I should take. So over a three decade span I completed a BA and MA in History from San Diego State University and a PhD in History from the University of California Santa Barbara all funded through a twenty-five year career as a K–University educator.

After a few decades of settling into life and raising three sons I began a life journey back to my agricultural and wine roots. During this time my good friend and teaching colleague Patrick Shaw taught me all the wonders and nuisances of store-bought wine. For years we enticed our spouses and children to spend their spring breaks camping at the Napa Bothe campground so that their oenophile fathers could dance with Bacchus in Napa, Sonoma, and Mendocino counties. As a middle school social studies teacher I pacified my new passion by pursuing a Master's Degree in History and writing a thesis on the raisin industry of El Cajon, California where my grandfather Michelangelo Geraci had immigrated in the early 1900s. By now I was hooked on both wine and history and jumped at the opportunity to complete my doctoral program at the University of California Santa Barbara where my research focused on the wine industry of the Central Coast of California.

This circuitous walk through the vineyards—both literal and figurative—led to this book and my heartfelt thanks to those who helped me reap this intellectual harvest. The first major acknowledgments emanate from the many people involved in my graduate studies. At San Diego State University Professor Raymond Star mentored my master's program and introduced me to the history world of research and writing. In 1992 I entered my UCSB doctoral program just as the Santa Barbara County Vintners Association (SBCVA) contracted the University of California Santa Barbara Public History program to write a short tabletop history of the county's wine region. Graduate students Sarah Harper Case, Susan Goldstein, Richard P. Ryba, Beverly J. Schwartzberg, and myself undertook the project as a client sponsored seminar course. Under the guidance of Professor Otis L. Graham the team researched, conducted oral interviews, wrote, and published *Aged In Oak: The Story of the Santa Barbara County Wine Industry*. My involvement in the project proved to be an invaluable beginning for my dissertation *Grape Growing To Vintibusiness: A History of the Santa Barbara, California, Regional Wine Industry, 1965-1995* that morphed into my first monograph *Salud: The Story the Santa Barbara Wine Industry*. This book utilizes all these sources plus new oral histories and decades of new research that moved the story along an additional twenty-five years and helped contextualize the fifty year history of the modern Santa Barbara wine industry.

Many within the local wine industry supported my research. The past executive director of the SBCVA, Pam Maines Ostendorf, opened the doors and always asked what more she could do. Within the industry I thank Rick Longoria, Jeff Newton, and Barry Johnson for their patience in answering my continual barrage of winemaking and grape-growing questions. While completing my graduate studies Dan Gainey, Gainey Vineyards, provided me with a job as a Tasting Room manager that gave me firsthand access to many of the principals in the story. Years later my positions as the Food and Wine Historian and Associate Director of the Center for Oral History at the UC Berkeley Bancroft Library gave me access to John De Luca, past President of the Wine Institute, who provided much wise council and opened many doors in the wine industry.

Academic support for a research project is an invaluable asset for any scholar. The late Otis Graham, as chair of my dissertation committee, pushed and pulled me through the initial phases of all the research and writing. A special thanks to R. Douglas Hurt, past editor of *Agricultural History*, for his encouragement that I had an agricultural story worth telling and friend and colleague the late Gordon Bakken, Professor of History at California State University Fullerton, who always provided mentorship.

Most important to this process are those I love the most. First to my parents and grandparents who provided the multigenerational ethnic and viticultural heritage that underscores this work. My hope is that through my story my sons Matthew, Gregory, and Damien, my stepdaughter Nichole, and my grandchildren Jordan, Victor, Karime, Sophia, Hailey, and Ethan will someday come to understand why they had to share me with grapes and wine. To Danelle, "Salud é Saluti." You shared the spirit and the pains of life, the dissertation, the research, the numerous publications and books, and our version of the wine life-style.

Victor W. Geraci
Murrieta, California

Selected Bibliography

NEWSPAPERS
Chicago Tribune
Escondido Daily Times Advocate
Los Angeles Herald Examiner
Los Angeles Times
Los Padres Sun
Modesto Bee
Napa Valley Register
New York Times
Sacramento Bee
St. Helena Star
San Francisco Chronicle
Santa Barbara Independent
Santa Barbara News-Press
Santa Rosa Press Democrat
Santa Ynez Valley News
The Guardian
Washington Post

MAGAZINES
Advertising Age
American Heritage
Business Week
California Farmer
California Law Business
California Wine Tasting Monthly
Condé Nast Traveler
Decanter Magazine
Elle
Forbes
Pacific Wine and Vines
Relax: The Travel Magazine for Practicing Physicians
Santa Barbara Magazine
The New Yorker
The Wine News

Time Magazine
U.S. News and World Report
Wine Business Monthly
Wine Enthusiast
Wine Spectator
Wines and Vines

JOURNAL ARTICLES

Alley, Lynn, and Golino, Deborah A. "The Origins of the Grape Program at Foundation Plant Materials Service," *American Journal of Enology and Viticulture*, 51:5, 2000.

Amerine, Maynard A. "An Introduction to the Pre-Repeal History of Wine." *Agricultural History* 63 (April 1969): 259–68.

———. "The Napa Valley Grape and Wine Industry." *Agricultural History* 49 (Spring 1975): 289–91.

Best, Michael R. "The Mystery of Vintners." *Agricultural History* 50 (April 1976): 362–76.

Breimyer, Harold F. "The Economic Returns of Agricultural Education." *Agricultural History* 60 (Spring 1986): 65–72.

Bunce, Richard. "From California Grapes to California Wine: The Transformation of an Industry, 1963-1979." *Contemporary Drug Problems* (Spring 1981): 55–74.

Caire, Helen. "A Brief History of Santa Cruz Island from 1869 to 1937." *Ventura County Historical Society Quarterly* 27 (Summer 1982): 3–33.

———. "Santa Cruz Vintage," *Noticias Quarterly Magazine of the Santa Barbara Historical Society* 35 (Spring/Summer 1989): 142–51.

Cipolla, Carlo. "European Connoisseurs and California Wines," *Agricultural History* 49 (Spring 1975): 294–310.

Folwell, Raymond J., and Mark A. Castaldi. "Economies of Size in Wineries and Impacts of Pricing and Product Mix." *Agribusiness: An International Journal* 3 (Fall 1987): 281–92.

Fusonie, Alan E. "John H. Davis: His Contributions to Agricultural Education and Productivity." *Agricultural History* 60 (Spring 1986): 97–110.

Geraci, Victor W. "El Cajon, California, 1900." *Journal of San Diego History* 36 (Fall 1990): 221–33.

———. "The El Cajon, California, Raisin Industry: An Exercise in Gilded Age Capitalism." *Southern California Quarterly* 74 (Winter 1992): 329–54.

———. "The Family Wine-Farm: Vintibusiness Style." *Agricultural History* 74, no. 2 (Spring 2000): 419–32.

Luckett, Liz."Carey Cellars Fit for Future." *Grape Grower* 23 (August 1991): 4–5.

McGee, Irving. "The Beginnings of California Winegrowing." *Historical Society of Southern California Quarterly* 29 (March 1947): 59–71.

———. "Early California Winegrowers." *California Magazine of the Pacific* 37 (September 1947): 34–37.

———. "Jean Paul Vignes, California's First Professional Winegrower." *Agricultural History* 22 (July 1948): 176–81.

Olmstead, Alan L. "Induced Innovation in American Agriculture." *Journal of Political Economy* 101 (February 1993): 100–118.

Peele, Stanton. "The Conflict between Public Health Goals and the Temperance Mentality." *American Journal of Public Health* 83 (June 1993): 805–10.

Peters, Gary L. "Trends in California Viticulture." *Geographical Review* 74 (October 1984): 463 (455–76).

Pickleman, Jack. "A Glass a Day Keeps the Doctor . . ." *American Surgeon*. 56 (July 1990): 395–97.

Renaud, E. B. "Wine, Alcohol, Platelets, and the French Paradox for Coronary Heart Disease." *Lancet* 339 (8808) (20 June 1992): 1523–26.

Samsel, Lynn, Diane I. Hambley, and Raymond A. Marquardt. "Agribusiness' Competitiveness for Venture Capital." *Agribusiness* 7 (July 1991): 401–413.

Spitze, R. G. F. "A Continuing Evolution in U.S. Agricultural Policy." *Agricultural Economics* 77 (1990); 126–39.

Winkler, A. J. "The Effect of Climatic Regions." *Wine Review* 6 (1938): 14–16.

———. "Better Grapes for Wine." *American Journal of Enology* 9 (1958): 202–3.

———. "Varietal Grapes in the Central Coast." *American Journal of Enology and Viticulture* 15 (1964): 204–5.

Winters, Donald L. "The Agricultural Ladder in Southern Agriculture." *Agricultural History* 61 (Fall 1987): 36–52.

Books

Adams, Leon D. *The Wines of America*. San Francisco: McGraw-Hill, 1990.

Adlum, John. *A Memoir on the Cultivation of the Vine in America, and the Best Mode of Making Wine*. Washington, D.C.: Davis & Force, 1823.

Amerine, Maynard A., and Maynard A. Joslyn. *Commercial Production of Table Wines*. Berkeley: California Agricultural Experimental Station, College of Agriculture, University of California, 1940.

———. *Table Wines: The Technology of Their Production*. Berkeley: University of California Press, 1951.

Amerine, Maynard A., and H. Phaff. *A Bibliography of Publications by the Faculty, Staff, and Students of the University of California, 1876–1980, on Grapes, Wines, and Related Subjects*. Berkeley: University of California Press, 1986.

Amerine, Maynard A., and Vernon L. Singleton. *Wine: An Introduction*. 2nd ed. Berkeley: University of California Press, 1972.

Asher, Gerald. *A Vineyard in My Glass*. Berkeley: University of California Press, 2011.

Ausmus, William A. *Wines and Wineries of California's Central Coast*. Berkeley: University of California Press, 2008.

Balzer, Robert L. *California's Best Wines*. Los Angeles: Ward Ritchie Press, 1948.

Bancroft, Hubert Howe. *California Pastoral 1769–1848*. San Francisco: History Company, 1888.

Bogue, Allan G. *From Prairie to Corn Belt: Farming on the Illinois and Iowa Prairies in the Nineteenth Century*. Chicago: University of Chicago Press, 1963.

Braconi, Frank, Morton Research Corporation. *The U.S. Wine Market: An Economic Marketing and Financial Investigation*. Merrick, NY: Morton Research Corporation, April 1977.

Brenner, Deborah. *Women of the Vine: Inside the World of Women Who Make, Taste, and Enjoy Wine*. Hoboken, NJ: John Wiley & Sons, 2007.

Burnham, John C. *Bad Habits: Drinking, Smoking, Taking Drugs, Gambling, Sexual Misbehavior, and Swearing in American History*. New York: New York University Press, 1993.

Byles, Stuart Douglass. *Los Angeles Wine: A History from the Mission Era to the Present*. Charleston, SC: American Palate, 2014.

Campbell, Christy. *The Botanist and the Vintner: How Wine Was Saved for the World*. Chapel Hill, NC: Algonquin Books, 2004.

Carlson, Vada F. *This Is Our Valley*. Santa Maria, CA: Santa Maria Historical Society, 1959.

Carosso, Vincent P. *The California Wine Industry: A Study of the Formative Years*. Berkeley: University of California Press, 1951.

Chiacos, Elias, ed., *Mountain Drive: Santa Barbara's Pioneer Bohemian Community*. Santa Barbara, CA: Shoreline Press, 1994.

Colman, Tyler. *Wine Politics: How Governments, Environmentalists, Mobsters, and Critics Influence the Wines We Drink*. Berkeley: University of California Press, 2008.

Comiskey, Patrick J. *American Rhône: How Maverick Winemakers Changed the Way Americans Drink*. Berkeley: University of California Press, 2016.

Conaway, James. *Napa*. Boston: Houghton Mifflin, 1990.

Coombs, Gary B., ed. *Those Were the Days: Landmarks of Old Goleta*. Goleta, CA: Institute for American Research, 1986.

Cowan, Robert G. *Ranchos of California: A List of Spanish Concessions, 1775–1822, and Mexican Land Grants, 1822–1846*. Fresno, CA: Academy Library Guild, 1956.

Dercierdo, Margarita Arce. *Mediating Conflict in California Fields, 1975–1977*. Oakland, CA: Center for Third World Organizing, 1980.

Fay, James S., senior editor. *California Almanac: 5th Edition*. Santa Barbara, CA: Pacific Data Resources (ABC-Clio), 1991.

Fisher, M. F. K. *The Story of Wine in California*. Berkeley: University of California Press, 1962.

Gallo, Ernest and Julio, with Bruce Henderson, *Ernest and Julio Gallo: Our Story*. New York: Random House, 1994.

Gates, Paul W. *California Ranchos and Farms 1846–1862; Including the Letters of John Quincy Adams Warren of 1861, Being Largely devoted to Livestock, Wheat Farming, Fruit Raising, and the Wine Industry*. Madison, WI: The State Historical Society of Wisconsin, 1967.

Geraci, Victor W. *Santa Barbara New House: The First Forty Years, 1955–1995*. Santa Barbara, CA: Santa Barbara New House, Incorporated, 1995.

——. "Vintibusiness: The History of the California Wine Industry 1769 to the Present." In *California History: A Topical Approach*, edited by Gordon Morris Bakken. Wheeling, IL: Harlan Davidson, 2002.

——. "Wine, Women, and Song." In *Encyclopedia of Women in the American West*, edited by Gordon Morris Bakken and Brenda Farrington. Thousand Oaks, CA: Sage Publications, 2003.

——. *Salud! The Rise of Santa Barbara's Wine Industry*. Reno, NV: University of Nevada Press, 2004.

——. *Making Slow Food Fast In California Cuisine*. Cham, Switzerland: Palgrave MacMillan, 2017.

Geraci, Victor W., and Elizabeth S. Demers, eds, 2011. *Icons of American Cooking*. Santa Barbara, CA: Greenwood, 2011.

Gidney, Charles M. *History of Santa Barbara, San Luis Obispo, and Ventura Counties*. Chicago: The Lewis Publishing Co., 1917.

Graham, Otis L., Jr, Robert Bauman, Douglas W. Dodd, Victor W. Geraci, and Fermina Brel Murray. *Stearns Wharf: Surviving Change on the California Coast*. Santa Barbara, CA: Graduate Program in Public Historical Studies University of California, Santa Barbara, 1994.

Graham, Otis L., Jr., Sarah Harper Case, Victor W. Geraci, Susan Goldstein, Richard P. Ryba, and Beverly Schwartzberg. *Aged in Oak: The Story of the Santa Barbara County Wine Industry*. Santa Barbara, CA, Cachuma Press, 1998.

Haeger, John Winthrop. *North American Pinot Noir*. Berkeley: University of California Press, 2004.

Hannickel, Erica. *Empire of Vines: Wine Culture in America*. Philadelphia: University of Pennsylvania Press, 2013.

Heimoff, Steve. *New Classic Winemakers of California; Conversations with Steve Heimoff*. Berkeley: University of California Press, 2008.

Hilgard, Eugene W. *University of California—College of Agriculture Report of the Viticultural Work during the Seasons 1887–1893 with Data Regarding the Crush of 1894–95*. Sacramento, CA: Superintendent State Printing, 1896.

——. *Report of the Professor of Agriculture to the President of the University*. Sacramento, CA: State Printing Office, 1879.

Hurt, R. Douglas. *American Agriculture: A Brief History*. Iowa City, IA: University of Iowa Press, 1994.

Hussmann, George. *Grape Culture and Wine Making in California: A Practical Manual for the Grape Grower and Wine Maker*. San Francisco: Payot, Upham, 1888.

Hyatt, Thomas H. *Hyatt's Handbook of Grape Culture; or, Why, Where, When, and How to Plant a Vineyard, Manufacture Wines, etc*. San Francisco: H. H. Bancroft and Company, 1867.

Johnson, Hugh. *Vintage: The Story of California Wine*. New York: Simon and Schuster, 1989.

Jones, Frank. *The Save Your Heart Wine Guide*. New York: St. Martin's Press, 1996.

Jones, Idwal. *Vines in the Sun: A Journey through the California Vineyards*. New York: Ballantine Books, 1949.

Kladstrup, Don, and Petie Kladstrup, with J. Kim Munholland. *Wine and War: The French, the Nazis, and the Battle for France's Greatest Treasure*. New York: Broadway Books, 2001.

Kolpan, Steven. *A Sense of Place: An Intimate Portrait of the Niebaum-Copola Winery and the Napa Valley*. New York: Routledge, 1999.

Kramer, Matt. *Making Sense of California Wine*. New York: William Morrow and Company, 1992.

———. *Making Sense of Napa Valley, Sonoma, Central Coast, and Beyond*. Philadelphia, PA: Running Press, 2004.

Lampard, Eric E. *The Rise of the Dairy Industry in Wisconsin 1820–1920*. Madison, WI: The State Historical Society of Wisconsin, 1963.

Lapsley, James T. *Bottled Poetry: Napa Winemaking from Prohibition to the Modern Era*. Berkeley, CA: University of California Press, 1996.

Lapsley, James, and Kirby Moulton. *Successful; Wine Marketing*. Frederick, MD, 2001.

Larsen, John W. *Vineyard Development Financing in California*. San Francisco: Wells Fargo Bank, 1972.

Lukacs, Paul. *American Vintage: The Rise of American Wine*. New York: Houghton Mifflin Company, 2000.

Mason, Jesse D. *History of Santa Barbara County, California*. Oakland, CA: Thompson and West, 1883.

Matasar, Ann B. *Women of Wine: The Rise of Women in the Global Wine Industry*. Berkeley: University of California Press, 2006.

McGinty, Brian. *Strong Wine: The Life and Legend of Agoston Haraszthy*. Stanford, CA: Stanford University Press, 1998.

McPhee, John. *Assembling California*. New York: Farrar, Straus and Giroux, 1993.

McWilliams, Carey. 1946. *California Country*. New York: Duell, Sloan and Pearce, 1946.

———. *Factories in the Field: The Story of Migratory Farm Labor in California*. Berkeley: University of California Press, 2000.

Melville, John. *Guide to California Wines*. Garden City, NY: Doubleday, 1955.

McCoy, Elin. *The Empire of Wine: The Rise of Robert Parker, Jr. and the Reign of American Taste*. New York: Ecco, 2005.

McNutt, Joni G. *In Praise of Wine: An Offering of Hearty Toasts, Quotations, Witticisms, Proverbs, and Poetry Throughout History*. Santa Barbara, CA: Capra Press, 1993.

Mendelson, Richard. *Wine in America: Law and Policy*. New York: Wolters Kluwer Law & Business, 2011.

Millner, Cork, *Vintage Valley: The Wineries of Santa Barbara County*. Santa Barbara, CA: McNally and Loftin, 1983.

Mondavi, Robert, with Paul Chutkow. *Harvests of Joy: My Passion for Excellence*. New York: Harcourt Brace & Company, 1998.

Muscadine, Doris, Maynard A. Amerine, and Bob Thompson, eds. *The University of California/Sotheby Book of California Wine*. Berkeley: University of California Press, 1984.

Peninou, Ernest P., and Sidney S. Greenleaf. *A Directory of California Wine Growers and Winemakers in 1860*. Berkeley: Tamalpais Press, 1967.

Perkins, Edwin J. *The Economy of Colonial America*. New York: Columbia University Press, 1980.

Phillips, Rod. *A Short History of Wine*. New York: Harper Collins, 2000.

Pinney, Thomas. *The City of Vines: A History of Wine In Los Angeles*. Berkeley: Heyday, 2017.

———. *A History of Wine in America: From the Beginnings to Prohibition*. Berkeley: University of California Press, 1989.

———. *A History of Wine in America: From Prohibition to the Present*. Berkeley: University of California Press, 2005.

Prial, Frank. *Decantations: Reflections on Wine by* The New York Times *Wine Critic Frank J. Prial*. New York: St. Martin's Press, 2001.

Robertson, Carol. *The Little Red Book of Wine Law: A Case of Legal Issues*. Chicago: ABA Publishing, 2008.

Rorabaugh, William J. *The Alcoholic Republic: An American Tradition*. New York: Oxford University Press, 1979.

Schaefer, Dennis. *Vintage Talk: Conversations with California's New Winemakers*. Santa Barbara, CA: Capra Press, 1994.

Schama, Simon. *Landscape and Memory*. New York: Random House, 1995.

Schoonmaker, Frank. *Frank Schoonmaker's Encyclopedia of Wine*. New York: Hastings House, 1964.

Schoonmaker, Frank, and Tom Marvel. *The Complete Book of Wine*. New York: Duell, Sloan & Pearce, 1941.

Smith, Sydney D. *Grapes of Conflict*. Pasadena, CA: Hope House Publishing, 1987.

Sommers, Brian. *The Geography of Wine: How Landscapes, Cultures, Terroir, and the Weather Makes a Good Drop*. New York: Plume Book, 2008.

Stuller, Jay, and Glen Martin. *Through the Grapevine: The Real Story behind America's $8 Billion Wine Industry*. New York: Harper-Collins West, 1994.

Sullivan, Charles L. *A Companion to California Wine: An Encyclopedia of Wine and Winemaking from the Mission Period to the Present*. Berkeley: University of California Press, 1998.

———. *Like Modern Edens: Winegrowing in Santa Clara Valley and Santa Cruz Mountains, 1798–1891*. Cupertino, CA: California History Center, 1982.

———. *Napa Wine: A History from Mission Days to Present*. San Francisco: Wine Appreciation Guild, 1994.

Taber, George M. *Judgement of Paris: California VS. France and the Historic 1976 Paris tasting. That Revolutionized Wine*. New York: Scribner, 2005.

———. *To Cork Or Not to Cork: Tradition, Romance, Science, and the Battle for the Wine Bottle*. New York: Scribner, 2007.

Teiser, Ruth, and Catherine Harroun. *Winemaking in California*. New York: McGraw-Hill, 1983.

Terlato, Anthony. *Taste: A Life In Wine*. New York: Surrey Books, 2008.

Thompson, Bob, ed. *California Wine: Where & How It's Made, The Winemakers . . . Past & Present, A Sunset Pictoral*. Menlo Park, CA: Lane Magazine & Book Company, 1973.

Tompkins, Walker A. *Santa Barbara History Makers*. Santa Barbara, CA: McNally & Loftin, Publishers, 1983.

Trubek, Amy B. *The Taste of Place: A Cultural Journey into Terroir*. Berkeley: University of California Press, 2008.

Tyrrell, Ian R. *Sobering Up: From Temperance to Prohibition in Antebellum America, 1800–1860*. Westport, CT: Greenwood Press, 1979.

Unwin, Tim. *Wine and The Vine: An Historical Geography of Viticulture and the Wine Trade*. New York: Routledge, 1991.

Wait, Frona Eunice. *Wines and Vines of California, or A Treatise on the Ethics of Wine Drinking.* San Francisco: Bancroft Company, 1889. Reprint. Berkeley: Howell-North Books, 1973.

Walker, George M. and John Peragine. *Cucamonga Valley Wine: The Lost Empire of American Winemaking.* Charleston: SC: American Palate, 2017.

Wetmore, Charles A. *Ampelography of California. A Discussion of Vines Now Known in the State, Together with Comments on Their Adaptability to Certain Locations and Uses.* San Francisco: Merchant Publishing Company, 1884.

Winkler, A.J. et al., *General Viticulture.* Rev. ed. Berkeley, CA: University of California Press, 1974.

GOVERNMENT PUBLICATIONS

Agricultural Extension Service, *The Climate of Santa Barbara County: Plantclimate Map & Climatological Data.* Santa Barbara, CA: University of California Agricultural Extension Service, 1965.

Amerine, M. A., and A. J. Winkler, *Grape Varieties for Wine Production*, Division of Agricultural Sciences, University of California (March 1963); pamphlet number 154.

Blout, Jesse S. *A Brief Economic History of the California Wine-Growing Industry.* San Francisco: Bureau of Markets, California Department of Agriculture, 1943.

Bioletti, Frederic T. *A New Method of Making Dry Red Wine.* Berkeley: Agricultural Experiment Station, 1906.

———. Agricultural Experiment Station, Berkeley, California, "Grape Culture in California; Its Difficulties; Phylloxera and Resistant Vines; and Other Vine Diseases," Sacramento: Superintendent of State Printing, 1908.

———. Agricultural Experiment Station, Berkeley, California, "Grape Culture in California; Improved Methods of Wine Making," Sacramento: Superintendent of State Printing, 1908.

———. Agricultural Experiment Station, Berkeley, California, "Grape Culture in California; Yeasts From California Grapes," Sacramento: Superintendent of State Printing, 1908.

California Agricultural Statistics Service, *California Grape Acreage, 1970–2017.* Sacramento, CA: California Agricultural Statistics Service.

———. *California Agriculture: Statistical Review 1986 and 1987.* Sacramento, CA: California Department of Food and Agriculture; California Agricultural Statistics Service.

California Agricultural Experiment Station. State Board of Public Health. Bureau of Food and Drug Inspection. *Regulations Establishing Standards of Identity, Quality, Purity and Sanitation, and Governing the Labeling and Advertising of Wine in the State of California.* Sacramento: California State Printing Office, 1942.

Federal Register. Department of the Treasury, Bureau of Alcohol, Tobacco and Firearms/Rules and Regulations, "Santa Maria Viticultural Area," 46:150 (5 August 1981): 39811–39812.

———. Department of the Treasury, Bureau of Alcohol, Tobacco and Firearms/ Rules and Regulations, "Santa Ynez Valley Viticultural Area," 48:74 (15 April 1983): 16250–16251.

Hoch, Irving, and Nickolas Tryphonopoulos. *A Study of the Economy of Napa County, California.* University of California; California Agricultural Experiment Station Giannini Foundation of Agricultural Economics Research Report Number 303, August 1969.

Mouton, Kirby S., ed. *The Economics of Small Wineries: The Proceedings of Two Seminars at University of California, Davis, May 1979 and May 1980.* Berkeley: Cooperative Extension, University of California, 1981.

Quayle, H. J. Agricultural Experiment Station Berkeley, California, "The Grape Leaf-Hopper," Sacramento: Superintendent of State Printing, 1908.

Winkler's, A. J. "Grape Growing in California," California Agricultural Extension Service Circular 116, November 1950.

ORAL HISTORIES

Adams, Leon. *California Wine Industry Affairs: Recollections and Opinions.* An oral history interview conducted by Ruth Teiser in 1986, Oral History Center, The Bancroft Library, University of California, Berkeley, 1990.

Addis, Craig. Interview by Beverly Schwartzberg, 28 January 1994, Santa Barbara. Tape Recording. Special Collections, University of California, Santa Barbara.

Amerine, Maynard A. "The University of California and the State's Wine Industry." An oral history interview conducted by Ruth Teiser in 1969–1971, Oral History Center, The Bancroft Library, University of California, Berkeley, 1972.

Babcock, Bryan. Interview by Susan Goldstein, 2 February 1994, Santa Ynez. Tape Recording. Special Collections, University of California, Santa Barbara.

Banke, Barbara. Interview by Richard P. Ryba, 11 February 1994, Santa Maria. Tape Recording. Special Collections, University of California, Santa Barbara.

Bedford, Stephan. Interview by Victor W. Geraci, 24 February 1994, Santa Ynez. Tape Recording. Special Collections, University of California, Santa Barbara.

Beko, Norman. Interview by Sarah Harper Case, 28 January 1994, Santa Maria. Tape Recording. Special Collections, University of California, Santa Barbara.

Bettencourt, Boyd. Interview by Beverly Schwartzberg, 8 April 1994, Santa Ynez. Tape Recording. Special Collections, University of California, Santa Barbara.

Blewis, Sharon. Interview by Sarah Harper Case, 9 February 1994, Santa Ynez. Tape Recording. Special Collections, University of California, Santa Barbara.

Block, David. Interview by Richard P. Ryba, 28 January 1994, Santa Ynez. Tape Recording. Special Collections, University of California, Santa Barbara.

Brander, C. Frederick. Interview by Beverly Schwartzberg, 16 February 1994, Santa Ynez. Tape Recording. Special Collections, University of California, Santa Barbara.

Brown, Byron Kent. Interview by Richard P. Ryba, 14 September 1994, Santa Maria. Tape Recording. Special Collections, University of California, Santa Barbara.

Brown, Dean. Interview by Victor W. Geraci and Jeff Maiken, 25 October 1995, Santa Ynez. Tape Recording. Special Collections, University of California, Santa Barbara.

Brown, Michael. Interview by Victor W. Geraci, 22 November 1996, Santa Barbara. Tape Recording. Special Collections, University of California, Santa Barbara.

Clendenen, Jim. Interview by Richard P. Ryba, 10 February 1994, Santa Maria Tape Recording. Special Collections, University of California Santa Barbara.

Critchfield, Burke H.; Wente, Carl F., and Frericks. Andrew G. "The California Wine Industry during the Depression," an oral history interview conducted by Ruth Teiser in 1972, Oral History Center, The Bancroft Library, University of California, Berkeley, 1972.

Cruess, William V. 1967. "A Half Century in Food and Wine Technology." An oral history conducted by Ruth Teiser, Oral History Center, The Bancroft Library, University of California, Berkeley.

De Luca, John. 2007. President and CEO of the Wine Institute, 1975–2003. An oral history conducted by Victor W. Geraci, Ruth Teiser, and Carole Hicke in 1986–2007, Oral History Center, The Bancroft Library, University of California, Berkeley.

Di Giorgio, Robert, and Joseph A. Di Giorgio, "The Di Giorgios: From Fruit Merchants to Corporate Innovators." An oral history conducted in 1983 by Ruth Teiser, Oral History Center, The Bancroft Library, University of California, Berkeley, 1986.

Duggan, Sheryl. Interview by Sarah Harper Case and Victor W. Geraci, 27 January 1994, Santa Ynez. Tape Recording. Special Collections, University of California, Santa Barbara.

Firestone, A. Brooks. "Firestone Vineyard: A Santa Ynez Valley Pioneer," an oral history conducted in 1995 by Carole Hicke, Oral History Center, The Bancroft Library, University of California, Berkeley, 1996.

———. Interview by Richard P. Ryba, 18 February 1995, Santa Barbara. Tape Recording. Special Collections, University of California, Santa Barbara.

Firestone, Catherine Boulton. Interview by Victor W. Geraci, 3 February 1994, Santa Ynez. Tape Recording. Special Collections, University of California, Santa Barbara.

Gomberg, Louis, "Analytical Perspectives on the California Wine Industry, 1935–1990," an oral history conducted in 1990 by Ruth Teiser, Oral History Center, The Bancroft Library, University of California, Berkeley, 1990.

Haley, Brian. Interview by Susan Goldstein, 1994, Santa Barbara. Tape Recording. Special Collections University of California, Santa Barbara.

Hampton, Dale. Interview by Victor W. Geraci and Susan Goldstein, 10 February 1994, Santa Maria. Tape Recording. Special Collections, University of California, Santa Barbara.

Hayer, T. Interview by Richard P. Ryba, 29 June 1994, Santa Ynez. Tape Recording. Special Collections ,University of California, Santa Barbara.

Hill, Stanley. Interview by Teddy Gasser, 10 January 1987, Santa Barbara. Collection of the Santa Barbara Historical Society.

Holt, Ed. Interview by Richard P. Ryba, 21 April 1995, Santa Ynez. Tape Recording. Special Collections, University of California, Santa Barbara.

Houtz, David. Interview by Sarah Harper Case, 28 January 1994, Santa Ynez. Tape Recording. Special Collections, University of California, Santa Barbara.

Houtz, Margy. Interview by Sarah Harper Case, 28 January 1994, Santa Ynez. Tape Recording. Special Collections, University of California, Santa Barbara.

Jackson, Jess. Interview by Richard P. Ryba, 11 February 1994, Santa Maria. Tape Recording. Special Collections, University of California, Santa Barbara.

Jessup, Hayley Firestone. Interview by Victor W. Geraci, 3 February 1994, Santa Ynez. Tape Recording. Special Collections, University of California, Santa Barbara.

Johnson, Barry. Interview by Susan Goldstein, 28 January 1994, Santa Ynez. Tape Recording. Special Collections, University of California, Santa Barbara.

Kerr, John. Interview by Sarah Case, 9 February 1994, Santa Ynez. Tape Recording. Special Collections, University of California, Santa Barbara.

Knox, Mel. Interview by Richard P. Ryba, 1 July 1994, Santa Ynez. Tape Recording. Special Collections, University of California, Santa Barbara.

Lafond, Pierre. Interview by Beverly Schwartzberg, 28 January 1994, Santa Barbara. Tape Recording. Special Collections, University of California, Santa Barbara.

Lanza, Horace O. "California Grape Products and Other Wine Enterprises." An oral history interview conducted by Ruth Teiser in 1969, Oral History Center, The Bancroft Library, University of California, Berkeley, 1971.

Longoria, Rick. Interview by Victor W. Geraci, 14 August 1996, Santa Ynez. Tape Recording. Special Collections, University of California, Santa Barbara.

Lucas, Louis. Interview by Richard P. Ryba, 29 June 1994, Santa Maria. Tape Recording. Special Collections University of California, Santa Barbara.

Maiken, Jeff. Interview by Sarah Case and Victor W. Geraci, 27 January 1994, Santa Ynez. Tape Recording. Special Collections, University of California, Santa Barbara.

Marks, Donna. Interview by Beverly Schwartzberg, 8 March 1994, Santa Ynez. Tape Recording. Special Collections, University of California, Santa Barbara.

McGuire, Bruce. Interview by Beverly Schwartzberg, 28 January 1994, Santa Barbara. Tape Recording. Special Collections, University of California, Santa Barbara.

Meyer, Otto E., "California Premium Wines and Brandy." An oral history interview conducted by Ruith Teiser in 1971, Oral History Center, The Bancroft Library, University of California, Berkeley, 1973.

Miller, Bob. Interview by Richard P. Ryba, 15 September 1994, Santa Barbara. Tape Recording. Special Collections, University of California, Santa Barbara.

Moone, Michael. "Management and Marketing at Beringer Vineyards and Wine World.," an oral history conducted by Lisa Jacobson in 1989, Oral History Center, The Bancroft Library, University of California, Berkeley, 1990.

Mosby, Gary. Interview by Sarah Case on 24 March 1994, Santa Ynez. Tape Recording. Special Collections, University of California, Santa Barbara.

Mosby, Geraldine. Interview by Susan Goldstein, 28 January 1994, Santa Ynez. Tape Recording. Special Collections, University of California, Santa Barbara.

Murray, Fran. Interview by Susan Goldstein, 16 February 1994, Santa Ynez. Tape Recording. Special Collections, University of California ,Santa Barbara.

Murray, Jim. Interview by Susan Goldstein, 16 February 1994, Santa Ynez. Tape Recording. Special Collections, University of California, Santa Barbara.

Muscatine, Doris. Food and Wine Writer. An oral history conducted by Victor W. Geraci in 2004, Oral History Center, The Bancroft Library, University of California, Berkeley, 2006.

Newton, Jeff. Interview by Victor W. Geraci, 15 June 1994, author's notes.

Olmo, Harold P. "Plant Genetics and New Grape Varieties." An oral history interview conducted by Ruth Teiser in 1972–1973, Oral History Center, The Bancroft Library, University of California, Berkeley, 1976.

Ostendorf, Pam Maines, "Director Of The Santa Barbara Vintner's Association." An oral history conducted in 1994 by Vic Geraci, PhD, Oral History Center, The Bancroft Library, University of California, Berkeley, 2007.

Ough, Cornelius. "Researches of An Enologist University of California Davis, 1950–1990." An Oral History conducted by Ruth Teiser in 1989, Oral History Center, The Bancroft Library, University of California, Berkeley, 1990.

Parker, Fess. Interview by Victor W. Geraci, 17 April 1995, Santa Ynez. Tape Recording. Special Collections, University of California, Santa Barbara.

Perelli-Minetti, Antonio. "A Life in Wine Making." An oral history interview conducted by Ruth Teiser in 1969, Oral History Center, The Bancroft Library, University of California, Berkeley, 1975.

Pfeiffer, Harold. Interview by Richard P. Ryba, 21 April 1995, Santa Ynez. Tape Recording. Special Collections, University of California, Santa Barbara.

Rice, Fred. Interview by Richard P. Ryba, 28 January 1994, Santa Ynez. Tape Recording. Special Collections, University of California, Santa Barbara.

Rossi, Edmund A. "Swiss Colony and the Wine Industry." An oral history interview conducted by Ruth Teiser in 1969, Oral History Center, The Bancroft Library, University of California, Berkeley, 1971.

Sanford, Richard. Interview by Victor W. Geraci and Otis L. Graham Jr., 7 March 1995, Santa Barbara. Tape Recording. Special Collections, University of California, Santa Barbara.

Scott, Doug. Interview by Beverly Schwartzberg, 10 February 1994, Santa Ynez. Tape Recording. Special Collections, University of California, Santa Barbara.

Tanner, Lane. Interview by Susan Goldstein, 3 February 1994, Santa Maria. Tape Recording. Special Collections University of California Santa Barbara, Santa Barbara, California.

Tchelistcheff, André. "Grapes, Wine, and Ecology." An oral history conducted in 1979 by Ruth Teiser and Catherine Harroun, Oral History Center, The Bancroft Library, University of California. 1983.

Whitcraft, Chris. Interview by Beverly Schwartzberg, 3 February 1994, Santa Ynez. Tape Recording. Special Collections University of California Santa Barbara, Santa Barbara, California.

Wilkes, Jeff. Interview by Susan Goldstein, 3 March 1994, Santa Maria. Tape Recording. Special Collections University of California Santa Barbara, Santa Barbara, California.

Woods, Bob. Interview by Richard P. Ryba, 12 April 1995, Santa Ynez. Tape Recording. Special Collections University of California Santa Barbara, Santa Barbara, California.

Woods, Jeanne. Interview by Richard P. Ryba, 12 April 1995, Santa Ynez. Tape Recording. Special Collections University of California Santa Barbara, Santa Barbara, California.

Yager, David. Interview by Sarah Harper Case and Otis L. Graham Jr., 18 January 1995, Santa Barbara. Tape Recording. Special Collections University of California Santa Barbara, Santa Barbara, California.

UNPUBLISHED MANUSCRIPTS, THESES, DISSERTATIONS

Conard, Rebecca Ann. *The Conservation of Local Autonomy: California's Agricultural Land Policies, 1900–1966*. Ph.D. dissertation, University of California, Santa Barbara, 1984.

Curry, James Harold, III. *Agriculture Under Late Capitalism: The Structure and Operation of the California Wine Industry*. Ph.D. dissertation Cornell University, 1994.

de la Peña, Donald Joseph. *Vineyards in a Regional System of Open Space in the San Francisco Bay Area: Methods of Preserving Selected Areas*. Master's thesis in City Planning in the College of Environmental Design, University of California, Santa Clara, 1962.

Della Valle, Andrea Laura. *The Taste of Globalization: The Wine Industry of Ontario (Canada)*. Master's thesis University of Windsor (Canada), 1996.

Fauntleroy, Phylicia Ann. *An Economic Analysis of the United States' Demand for Distilled Spirits, Wine, and Beer Incorporating Taste Changes through Demographic Factors, 1960–1981 (Beverage Alcohol)*. Ph.D. dissertation, The American University, 1984.

Geraci, Victor W. *Grape Growing to Vintibusiness: A History of the Santa Barbara, California, Regional Wine Industry, 1965–1995*. Ph.D. dissertation, University of California, Santa Barbara, 1997

——. *The Rise & Fall of the El Cajon, California Raisin Industry: 1873–1920*, Master's thesis, San Diego State University, 1990.

Haley, Brian D. *Aspects and Social Impacts of Size and Organization in the Recently Developed Wine Industry of Santa Barbara County, California*, Working paper. Santa Barbara, California: University of California, Santa Barbara Center for Chicano Studies, 1989.

Heien, Dale M. *The Impact of the Alcohol Tax Act of 1990 on California Agriculture*. A position paper sponsored by the United Agribusiness League, Irvine, California, July 1990.

Heintz, William F. *The Role of Chinese Labor in Viticulture and Winemaking in Nineteenth-Century California*. Master's thesis, California State University, Sonoma, 1977.

Hofer, James D. *Cucamonga Wines and Vines: A History of the Cucamonga Pioneer Vineyard Association*. Master's thesis, Claremont University, 1983.

Knox, Trevor McTaggart. *The Economic Organization of Winemaking: French Cooperatives and California Corporations in Historical Context*. Ph.D. dissertation, University of Connecticut, 2000.

Levi, Anette Ellery. *Domestic and Foreign Wine Demand in Major Wine Producing and Consuming nations (Domestic Wine Demand, Wine Demand, Demand Analysis)*. Ph.D. dissertation, Washington State University, 1990.

Mink, James V. *The Santa Ynez Valley: A Regional Study in the History of Rural California*. Master's thesis, University of California, Los Angeles, 1949.

Poletti, Peter Joseph, Jr. *An Interdisciplinary Study of the Missouri Grape and Wine Industry, 1650 to 1989*. PhD dissertation, Saint Louis University, 1989.

Schnier, Robert F. *A Study of the Will to Survive of the Family-Owned Wineries of California*. Master's thesis, Pepperdine University, 1982.

Shaw, David Scott. *Firm Export Strategies and Firm Export Performance in the United States Wine Industry: A Longitudinal Study*. Ph.D. dissertation, Purdue University, 1996.

Sims, Eric N. *A Study of the California Wine Industry and an Analysis of the Effects of the Canadian-United States Free Trade Agreement on the Wine Sector, with a Note on the Impact of the North American Free Trade Agreement on California Wine Exports*. Ph.D. dissertation, University of Arkansas, 1995.

Solana Rosillo, Juan B. *Firm Strategies in International Markets: The Case of International Entry into the United States Wine Industry (Market Entry, International Trade)*. Purdue University, 1997.

Waters, Alejandro. *Rebuilding Technologically Competitive Industries: Lessons from Chile's and Argentina's Wine Industry Restructuring*. PhD Dissertation Massachusetts Institute of Technology, 1999.

White, Anthony Gene. *State Policy and Public Administration Impacts on an Emerging Industry: The Wine Industry in Oregon and Washington*. PhD Dissertation Portland State University, 1993.

REPORTS

Bank of America. *California Wine Outlook: An Economic Study Prepared by Bank of America*. San Francisco: Bank of America, 1973.

Bank of America National Trust and Savings Association. *Outlook for the California Wine Industry*. San Francisco: Bank of America, 1970.

Braconi, Frank, Morton Research Corporation. *The U.S. Wine Market: An Economic Marketing & Financial Investigation*. Merrick, NY: A Morton Report, April 1977.

Gomberg, Fredrikson & Associates. *The Wine Industry's Economic Contribution to Santa Barbara County: Based on the Santa Barbara County Vintners Association 1992 Economic Survey*. San Francisco: Gomberg, Fredrikson & Associates, 1994.

———. *The Wine Industry's Economic Contribution to Santa Barbara County: Based on the Santa Barbara County Vintners Association 1996 Economic Survey*. San Francisco: Gomberg, Fredrikson & Associates, 1997.

Lee, Wendell, C.M. *U.S. Viticultural Areas*. San Francisco: The Wine Institute Legal Department, 1992.

Pacific Gas and Electric. "Finest Dry Wine Grapes: New Tepusquet Vineyard Blessed with Ideal Climate."

Stetson Engineers. Santa Ynez River Water Conservation District Water Resources Management Planning Process, Phase 1, August 31, 1992.

Index

About the Author

After twenty years teaching history at the secondary level, Victor W. Geraci completed his master's degree in public history from San Diego State University in 1992 and in 1997 completed his doctorate in American history from the University of California, Santa Barbara. Between 1997 and 2003 Geraci held positions as Assistant and later Associate Professor of History at Central Connecticut State University. While at CCSU, Geraci served as the History Department's Director of the Secondary History/Social Science Teacher Education program, taught upper-division American history courses, and helped establish a Master's Degree program in Public History, where he taught the Introductory and Oral History courses. In 2003, Geraci came to the Oral History Center at the University of California, Berkeley's Bancroft Library, as a Food and Wine Historian/Specialist, where he utilized oral and public history methodologies honed through projects involving Sicilian immigration, alcoholic centers, local history, environmental organizations, viticulture, vintner associations, forestry, and over forty years of secondary and university teaching and curriculum development. His main areas of research include American Agriculture (Post–Civil War to Present) with a specific focus on California food and wine. In 2013, Geraci retired from his position as Associate Director of the Oral History Center. He has written journal articles and reviews in *Gastronomica*, *the Southern California Quarterly*, *Journal of Agricultural History*, *The Public Historian*, *JIWA*, *Connecticut History*, and the *Journal of San Diego History*. Geraci's book publications include *Making Slow Food Fast In California Cuisine*, *Salud: The Story of the Santa Barbara Wine Industry*, *The Lure of the Forest: Oral Histories from the National Forests in California*, *The Unmarked Trail: Managing National Forests in a Turbulent Era*, and coauthored books *Aged in Oak* and *Icons of American Cooking*.